*"If you're a man wishing to understand himself better, or a woman who loves a man, this book has the power to change your life. It's time for men to break out of the prison of traditional masculinity. **The True Heart of a Man can** help."*

Terrence Real, Ph.D.
Bestselling Author of *"I Don't Want to Talk About It: Overcoming the Secret Legacy of Male Depression"*

The
TRUE HEART
of a MAN

HOW HEALTHY MASCULINITY WILL TRANSFORM YOUR LIFE, YOUR RELATIONSHIPS, AND THE WORLD

Hanalei Vierra, Ph.D.

BALBOA.
PRESS
A DIVISION OF HAY HOUSE

Balboa Press books may be ordered through booksellers or by contacting:

Balboa Press
A Division of Hay House
1663 Liberty Drive
Bloomington, IN 47403
www.balboapress.com
1 (877) 407-4847

Print information available on the last page.

ISBN: 978-1-5043-4651-1 (sc)
ISBN: 978-1-5043-4653-5 (hc)
ISBN: 978-1-5043-4652-8 (e)

Library of Congress Control Number: 2015920223

Balboa Press rev. date: 10/03/2016

This book is dedicated to my wife,
M'Lissa, and my daughter, Kekoa,
whose wholehearted love and support inspire
me every day to do the one thing myself that I
challenge the men in my private practice to do –
walk my talk.

"Know Thyself"

(Inscription above the portico at the Temple of Apollo in Delphi, Greece; c. 600 BC)

Table of Contents

Preface

For the past 27 years, I have been a psychotherapist in private practice working with adult men of all ages who are confused and frustrated in their relationships with women. Quite honestly, most of these men come into my office initially because they have been given some sort of ultimatum from the woman they love. They have been told that their relationship is on the brink of ruin unless they "get help."

I find, however, that most of these men believe all they need to do is learn a few things from me to calm her down so she will stop complaining. More often than not, by the time a guy arrives in my office, he has tried everything he can think of but is still not getting results. From the woman's perspective, she has usually seen and heard everything he has to offer and is still looking for something much different from him. This means that his customary attempt at placating her is the one thing she can no longer tolerate.

Here is his challenge: In order to learn a new approach to his relationship, he must open himself up to a different, deeper kind of change that is both unfamiliar and uncomfortable. It is at this point in the first therapy session that I let him know that he cannot continue in therapy if he is only in my office to learn how to pacify her. I explain that unless he can see the value of self-examination – which means exploring and understanding himself at a deeper level – therapy will be ineffective and a waste of his time and money.

This phenomenon has repeated itself enough in my office for me to recognize a consistent, unhealthy, belief system and pattern of behavior that men continue to choose – even though it makes them miserable, and they feel powerless to change it. The patterns and stories that have shaped and influenced the masculine identities of these men from their early boyhood experiences have painted an almost predictable panorama in my mind of the journey of the male species. I relate deeply and personally to this panorama, and my therapeutic experiences with these men have led me to believe it is time for men to develop their own emotional awareness and strength, *despite being trained in so many ways to avoid that very thing.* This book is an examination of this panorama as a way of offering men a *choice* out of this pattern – a pattern that I believe has become a mental and emotional prison for men.

Here is *my* challenge: My worst fear as an author would be to send a message to men that they are somehow "not enough" because they have emotional blind spots. This book is my best attempt to help men see how they create their own feelings of inadequacy and "not being enough" by disregarding what is in their True Heart. Until we as men finally see the *high personal price we pay* for wearing the "Mask of Masculinity" that distances us from our emotional world, we will forever be haunted by a false inferiority that we constantly seek to overcome by "doing more". This book offers men a way to finally believe more in *who they already are beneath that mask,* and that they no longer need to measure their self-worth by some un-attainable ideal that traditional masculinity beats them up with.

I have also had the privilege of working with my wife, who is a licensed psychologist with her own long-standing private practice, working individually with women. For more than 20 years, she and I have worked together as relationship counselors for couples who are struggling with how to create and recreate emotional intimacy with one another. The conjoint couples counseling I have done with her has given me the opportunity to apply the clinical insights I have gained through my work with individual male clients, many of whom are also in couples counseling with us. This work has also given me the opportunity to learn about women's struggles with the men in their lives and what they need on their side of the relationship equation.

This book is also the result of my ongoing cause-and-effect observations in working with hundreds of male clients in my private practice as a licensed marriage and family therapist for over two and a half decades. My hope is that you will gain a broader insight as to how you have been trained to "be a man" in some ways that are very self-defeating. This larger perspective of yourself can help you better understand whatever destructive behavior you are bringing into your relationship. This is not to say that women are squeaky clean in how they approach relationships! They have their own problems to figure out in the toxic dance that weighs a relationship down. I am writing here only about the male side of that dance.

By the way, while over the course of time I have had any number of gay men in my individual practice seeking help for many of the same issues that my heterosexual clients have, I do not claim this book to represent a guide or standard for gay men's personal and inter-personal issues. I will say that very few if any of the issues presented by my gay clients were very different than those of my straight clients. However, my expertise lies in my experience with the predominance of my male client base, which by and large has been heterosexual.

I have been able to compare my own lifelong search for healthy masculinity with my objective scrutiny of the guys I work with. The questions and uncertainties I have wrestled with in my own life are rarely different from those of my clients. While I may have the benefit of many years of professional training, education, and experience, it is the journey of seeking a deeper experience of my own True Heart that has motivated me to help other men gain a deeper understanding of theirs.

I so appreciate and respect the level of courage it takes for men to ask for help in making better sense of their lives. It is an honor and a privilege for me whenever a guy has the guts to come into my office and finally get around to asking the question, *"Who am I?"* to this stranger sitting across from him. *There is no question more important than this!* My commitment has been and continues to be how to help men find their own answers to that question.

Therefore, ultimately, this book is the culmination of my own personal and professional journey that I hope will help men break out of the prison they are held captive in by a culture that challenges them to be masculine by "living up" to a very low bar of authenticity, personal integrity, and self-respect. It is a huge irony to me that traditional masculinity's guideline for "how to be a man" trains men to stay locked up and functioning in their adult lives as emotionally immature, wounded little boys. This book will challenge men to grow up by learning to trust and reveal what is in their hearts to their loved ones. It is a call for us as men to stop hiding behind the lame excuse that we don't know how to figure out our emotional world because "we're just guys" and, therefore, incapable of handling feelings "the way women do."

Men do not have to handle their feelings the way women do!

We need to grow up and take charge of our feelings in a way that *makes sense to us as men.* It may look, sound, walk, and talk differently than the way women do it, but what really matters is that we find the courage, i.e., *the balls,* to do it because it opens us up to becoming bigger and better versions of *ourselves.* We cannot be trying to "prove" to the woman we love that doing this personal growth work on ourselves is how we demonstrate that we are *worthy of her love,* and, therefore, she should never leave us. We must learn that knowing and sharing our emotional world gives us the gift of our authenticity, personal integrity, and self-respect – *whether she loves us or not.* Only then can we create closeness and intimacy with the woman we love.

My hope is that this book will help you chart a course toward your unique, *authentic self* – a course that will take you straight to your True Heart without fear that doing so will make you less of a man.

Acknowledgments

For all the years that have passed since I began writing this book, the one person who has been by my side urging me on has been my wife, M'Lissa. No way I would have finished this without her encouragement. Her understanding and support were tested many times as I would "disappear" for chunks of time in order to discipline myself enough to sit and write. Her belief in me has never wavered, even when I was less than available to her and our daughter Kekoa. They have both shown extraordinary patience with me, and their love has fueled me to find the focus I needed to finish writing this book.

I would also like to thank my parents Julie and Alfred Vierra, as well as my two brothers Don and Allan Vierra, for setting the stage of how I developed my personality. Their love and concern were all instrumental in how the foundation of my character became what it is. I am also very grateful to my extended family in Hawai'i who have always deeply influenced my knowledge and appreciation of my identity as a *kanaka maoli* (native Hawaiian). Intricately a part of that process were Candace Lienhart and Abraham Kawai'i, both of whom were excellent teachers for me about my own light side and dark side. As my life journey traversed a path that at one point felt direction-less and random, other role models appeared in my life who helped me heal my personal wounds as well as help me shape my professional identity: Brenda Scott-Mead, David Cornsweet, Virginia Wink-Hilton, Jan Berlin, Gayle Welch, Judy Abell, and Ellae Elinwood.

Leading and participating in men's groups over the past thirty years has been a huge part of my personal and professional development. These have included the annual California Men's Gathering in Los Angeles, as well as the therapist's men's group that came from the CMG in 1985 that included Larry Graber and Ken Simpson. The first men's group I organized and ran in 1988 in Del Mar, CA that started out for six weeks and ended up lasting for six years helped me cut my teeth on working with men in groups and the whole process of how to balance the jagged edge of testosterone with the vulnerability of a man's True Heart. The group of men that I interviewed for my doctoral dissertation in 1990 helped me reality-check whatever messed up stereotypes I myself grew up believing about masculine identity. My years of working with the Turning Point and Oz programs of the YMCA in San Diego under the direction of Kim Morgan gave me an enormous amount of experience working effectively with dysfunctional families. The Mankind Project of San Diego and the men of the associated Encinitas I-Group gave me a straightforward, no-nonsense, supportive environment to learn how to be emotionally vulnerable with other men. This in turn taught me a tremendous amount about who I am as a man, and I am truly grateful to the men of that group for how they influenced me to lead a courageous life. The Del Dios Men's Group gives me the ongoing opportunity to bask in the glow of deep love and trust of men that I have had the privilege of knowing for many years. I so appreciate their unconditional acceptance of my human-ness, especially on those days when I struggle with that very thing.

I am also very grateful to the expertise of my wife M'Lissa Trent, William Sieber, John Ciullo, Melanie Votaw, Stephen

Daugherty, Mark Byrne, Laura Carroll, Michael Marx, David Welborn, and everyone at Balboa Press for helping me make this book readable enough to get it into print.

Finally, nothing would be written on these pages without the daily willingness of the men in my private practice who have trusted me enough to show me the depth of their true selves. It has been nothing short of an honor and privilege for me to witness each of their journeys and to help them remember who they are. Their courage to learn how to be emotionally vulnerable inspires me to do the same – every moment of my life.

Introduction

Try as you may, when you struggle as a man to better connect emotionally with the woman you love, *you probably feel caught between a rock and a hard place*. Unwittingly, you have been trained your whole life to disregard and even snub the one resource you have inside you, which I call your *True Heart*, that would help you so much in your relationship struggles. Without knowing it, your *inability* to create and sustain emotional intimacy in a relationship *has been your reward* for conforming to an image of masculinity that you have been brainwashed to believe is healthy. Worse than this, however, is the fact that you have also paid a high personal price for conforming to an outdated ideal of *what is manly*, an ideal that has unnecessarily kept you locked in a cage of ignorance and fear.

If you are a guy reading this book on your own, you've probably already gotten some kind of smack-upside-the-head, Wake-Up Call moment in your life that compelled you to push the "buy" button online. It is totally humbling to realize that, despite your wish that you knew what the heck it meant to *step up* and participate more in the emotional connection of your intimate relationship, there is still something about that process that you *just don't get*. Maybe you are a guy who is starting to feel a lack of satisfaction with the life you busted your butt for umpteen years to create. Maybe you now feel the blue funk of midlife-melancholy. Maybe the woman in your life handed you this book because she got tired of being the only one in the relationship to care about the quality of your emotional connection with her. Maybe you're still recovering from the last time some woman drove a truck through your heart, and you're feeling snake-bit about "doing the relationship thing" again. Whatever your reason for reading this right now, I have yet to meet a man, myself included, who has not struggled with why it is so difficult to *create and sustain a deep emotional connection with a woman.*

Here is the good news: This book will begin to teach you the steps necessary to achieve and sustain emotional closeness with the woman you love. But the even bigger reward is that it will offer you a way to *take better care of yourself* by helping you define a clearer picture of *who you really are* and how to get what you really want and need in your life.

Here are just a few things you will learn from this book:

- How the one thing that you are probably really good at is also the one thing that is totally messing up your relationships.
- How your survival instinct is intricately intertwined with your decision-making about relationships and your self-concept as a man.
- How the unexplored dark side of your masculinity not only subtly crushes your spirit, but also puts others at risk.
- How you have been lied to as a man about how unimportant your emotional world is to your own peace of mind.

- How your struggle with creating emotional intimacy with your wife or girlfriend is actually a sign of your lack of self-worth.
- How the world can become a better place to live in when men like you (and me) do the work necessary to live life from our True Hearts.
- How to launch onto this journey toward Healthy Masculinity using a 7-step roadmap (Chapter 8) that will put all the previous points into perspective.

If you are a woman reading this book, you might be looking for new information about men because you're tired of feeling confused, scared, hurt, angry, or even discouraged about what is possible in your intimate relationships with them. Maybe you're looking for another book of relationship advice to give to the guy in your life so that he can finally get his "relationship act" together. Whatever it is, my hope is that you will find value in the personal and clinical experiences presented here. I hope you will see that there *is* a way for men to become full emotional partners in an intimate relationship.

Finally, I admit to having an ulterior motive in writing this book beyond wanting to help men. It is this: There are an awful lot of messed up things going on in the world right now that I think are a direct result of the toxic mindset that has "ruled the world" since humans first started to beat each other up in order to feel powerful. The patriarchal ideology that is present all over the planet that contaminates our perceptions of each other as men and women is unfortunately alive and well today in many ways that I outline in Chapter 7. My belief and hope in writing this book is to give men a very basic way of "doing their part" to help deconstruct this very destructive element of human social interaction. *It starts with men healing their own personal wounds that can often deteriorate into a need to dominate and oppress others, which is the underpinning of patriarchal ideology.*

Since it is still very much alive and well in most nations around the planet, I feel it is men's responsibility to take up the effort alongside women to eradicate patriarchy in order to create a more egalitarian world. The premise of this book is not driven by any feminist agenda against men. It is driven by the urgent need for men to wake up out of their denial and take a stand against the prevalence of patriarchal oppression of both women AND men around the world.

There are many men who demonize feminism as somehow victimizing men and masculinity. *Feminism battles against patriarchy – not men – because patriarchy seeks to destroy feminine self-worth and self-respect. As an equal opportunity oppressor, however, patriarchy also seeks to destroy masculine self-worth and self-respect.* As men, until and unless we join forces with women to combat this cynical ideology, we remain flunkies of the patriarchy. This book's agenda is motivated by a desire to equip men with the ability to see themselves at a deeper level, where they can embrace their authenticity, personal integrity, and self-respect as a crucial piece of their masculine identities. *Traditional masculinity does not teach this to men!* By acquiring empathy and compassion, men will be less inclined to feel the need to disenfranchise or marginalize others in order to feel powerful.

As men heal themselves more and more, they will be less and less tolerant of how this harsh and ruthless social system degrades human life. I challenge everyone who reads this book to take up this gauntlet and ***do something*** to combat the misogyny, sexism, racism, and homophobia that exist at every social level no matter where you live – in whatever way you can, large or small. If you have ever wondered what you could do to help make this world a better place, please consider the challenge this book puts forward. We are all capable of doing so much more.

Chapter 1

PRISONERS of a PARADOX

"The tragedy of life is what dies inside a man while he lives."
– Albert Schweitzer

Let's face it, most guys are still trying to figure out what the world expects of them these days in terms of what it means to "be a man". For the past 50 years we have been caught between two different worlds of expectation that previous generations of men never had to struggle with. Our fathers and grandfathers never had to think about whether or not they had choices in how to express their masculinity. And they certainly had no question in their minds about what they would teach their sons about manly behavior.

We have yet to create and even celebrate a healthier version of masculinity to teach our sons that is relevant to a 21st century planet. Our struggle thus far seems to be less about *what to teach them* and more about figuring out *who and what we are becoming ourselves*. Once we take care of this second piece we'll be able to address the first one. All of this is because we are finally waking up and seeing the unhealthy consequences that *traditional masculinity* has had on our people and our planet for thousands of years. Like it or not, the "story" of traditional masculinity is in the throes of being re-written, and it is in all of our best interests to pay attention and have the courage to evolve with it.

Without getting too cheesy by coining some phrase like *men's liberation*, I believe that there *is* a need for men to set themselves free from the story they have inherited from their fathers and grandfathers about who and what a "real man" is. That traditional image of an emotionally stoic and insensitive "manly man" has devolved into a stereotype that, unfortunately, most men have successfully lived up to, and the world is no longer a better place because of it. The high personal price I believe men have paid for carrying out this malignant legacy is this: *By ignoring and dismissing the truth men feel in their hearts, they ignore and dismiss their true happiness and calling in life.* As men continue to carry out this limited version of masculinity, they sacrifice feeling a more authentic experience of themselves that they also keep from sharing with their loved ones.

> *Whenever a man chooses to disregard and/ or misrepresent what he feels in his True Heart, he in essence gives up his personal integrity and becomes a lesser version of himself.*

If there is one consistent observation I have made over the course of my 27 years of working with male clients in private practice as a marriage and family therapist, it is this: *the universal definition of "masculinity" that men have identified with for millennia has become so unconsciously synonymous with their survival instinct that the two have become indistinguishable.* A man's instinctive urge to protect, provide, and procreate has evolved into a nearly equivalent expression of his "manliness." In and of itself, this may not be a psychologically significant insight, but the ramifications appear in very specific ways when men are challenged to step beyond their survival "roles" as protectors/providers/procreators.

This challenge is particularly evident in how my male clients, almost without exception, report their ignorance of *how to create emotional intimacy with a woman*. There is a recurring glazed-over look of cluelessness in their eyes when I ask them to describe, in even the most general terms, the "emotional connection" they have with their wife or girlfriend. I understand that I can't generalize my anecdotal observations to describe the population of men at large, but it cannot merely be a coincidence only among the men who find their way into my office. As a clinician, I'm more interested in motivating changes in behavior rather than collecting empirical data. Still, I'm struck by the utterly consistent feedback I have seen across a wide range of men regardless of age, race, religion, and socioeconomic status. Nearly all of them seem to be confused about how to participate in their intimate relationships beyond fulfilling the protector/provider/procreator roles that they identify with coming from their survival instincts.

This observation has helped me understand that naturally and unconsciously equating masculine identity with survival has an effect on men's "access" to or understanding of their own emotional world. There is a paradox here that is subliminal, yet unavoidable, and is a direct result of this interchangeability between masculinity and survival. As a result of this phenomenon, here is what I consider to be the epic dilemma for my male brethren and me: The *one thing* that defines a man's sense of masculinity in so many ways and which men are so highly skilled at and so proud of, i.e., *survival*, also happens to be the *one thing* that severely limits their depth of self-actualization and personal happiness. I call this the *Survival Paradox*. This, in turn, keeps them clueless about emotional intimacy: what it is, how to create it, and how to sustain it with a woman. As crucial and prevalent as it is in his awareness, a man's instinct for survival – that primitive, fundamental, fight-or-flight urge to keep himself and his loved ones physically alive – actually *constricts his ability to truly know and love himself,* which then constricts his ability to truly know and love another person.

> ***Men struggle with how to create authentic, emotionally connected relationships with women because they are prisoners of the Survival Paradox.***

The irony here is how the men I observe almost always report feeling anxious at times about their feelings of inadequacy in their role as protector/provider/ procreators and how that inadequacy affects their desirability as relationship partners. Men assume that their competence at being adequate protector/provider/procreators is *the thing* a woman looks for in a potential mate, despite whether or not the woman can protect and provide for herself. This is a fundamental piece of the survival instinct of all human beings in order to successfully propagate the species. However, it is also important for men to understand that this is not the only thing that women look for in a mate. The challenge for men is to *construct a definition of masculinity that goes beyond this survival imperative.* Otherwise, they will remain limited in their happiness as well as their

4

ability to participate in and create a significant emotional connection with their loved ones.

The INADEQUACY MYTH

It's pretty normal for us humans to "wear a mask" as we engage the world on a day-to-day basis. This mask or persona, which we also call "ego", is a way for us to protect a more authentic and vulnerable part of ourselves from the random irritants and toxicities of everyday life. This ego mask version of ourselves is a way for us to *give an impression* of being a certain way that may fit whatever occasion we feel is needed. A problem arises, however, if we rarely take this mask off in order to allow ourselves to show a deeper, more authentic version of who we are to others. Most of my clients have become so accustomed to living their lives wearing this mask that they have assumed the mask now represents who they really are. Not true! The genuine "true self" version of who we really are behind the mask is not shaped by our need to appear in a certain way to others. This authentic inner part of us is simply the unaltered, unedited expression of both the good news and the bad news of our personality. It is both amazing and imperfect all at the same time. However, it is this imperfect piece of our masculine-ness that we hide from others because we fear that our flaws will not only be seen, but that we will then be judged as being undesirable, unmanly, and "not good enough" *because we have these flaws.* While this fear is understandable, it is also a myth that we as men cripple ourselves by because our imperfections are a part of the definition of being human that every person on the planet has to deal with. I call this our "Inadequacy

Myth" because the myth of it is that we think we are lovable only when we are un-flawed and perfect, *which is an impossible standard for any human being to achieve.* This social standard of perfection holds us hostage to our shortcomings. Another example of this is how women are constantly being judged for their outward appearance by a so-called "Beauty Myth" that is shallow and unrealistic. As a result, *women struggle to not judge themselves* by this relentless expectation of physical beauty that is unrealistic and oppressive.

When men judge themselves as being "not man enough" or "not good enough" or "not lovable enough", this gives the Inadequacy Myth rattling around in their heads a lot of power and influence over the choices they make in their lives. This has become a tangible obstacle to a man's self-worth and happiness that is in deep need of a reality-check. Quite often this Inadequacy Myth comes from the home environment that he was raised in as a boy. Based on his interaction with parents and siblings, a boy's belief system about his self-worth comes from the milieu that gives him "feedback" about who he is. If that feedback is nurturing and supportive, he will grow up with a sense of self-esteem that will give him confidence about himself and his abilities. If that feedback is judgmental and criticizing, he will grow up believing the lie that he is "not enough", and this lie will become the story that the "critical voice" rattling around in his head will remind him of whenever he feels his very human limitations.

Another huge contributor to this Inadequacy Myth is a boy's social environment outside the home. One of the rites of passage for boys is the mockery and derision that is inherent in the way boys "relate" to each other. The ideal of being emotionally bulletproof and physically superior to the next kid is where toxic masculinity gets its start. Young boys inherit this unhealthy version of masculinity from a culture that trains them to point out the imperfections of others as a way of feeling better about themselves. It is also very similar to the mockery and derision that occurs in his head about himself whenever he screws up. While much of this back and forth sarcasm among boys may not have contempt as its intention, this type of peer ridicule can validate whatever negative story a boy may already have running in his head about himself that comes from his home environment.

As a man grows into his adulthood, this story of insecurity then plays an important role in how he looks for love and approval from others. Like a software program that always runs in the background on a computer, his Inadequacy Myth "rents space" in the back of his mind, and it cannot help but influence his approach to feeling "good enough" in a job or in a relationship. For example, a client I will call Albert felt very unappreciated by his wife. He explained that his way of showing love was to "do things" for her, like chores around the house, helping with grocery shopping, and chauffeuring the kids. While she appreciated his efforts to get things done, she still needed more from him emotionally that he totally avoided, like talking to her about the things they disagreed about, sharing his life experiences with her, and being interested in what she was experiencing emotionally in her own life. As she expressed her need for these things, Albert felt criticized and unappreciated for all the things he *did* do. He also felt that no matter what he did, it was "not enough" for her. By the time he came in to therapy with me, his Inadequacy Myth was loud in his head and wreaking havoc on his self-worth. He grew up believing that his efforts to "do things" for his wife should be enough to get her love and approval. Instead, his Inadequacy Myth of "not being enough" was inundating him with shame.

It's not a bad thing to want to "do things" for the woman you love, but for Albert it became his operational definition of love: *"She gives me approval and love when I do things for her, so my way of loving her is to continue to do things that make her happy with me"*. This is the opposite of being authentic. This is more about "performing" to earn praise and acceptance rather than being emotionally vulnerable in order to be real and connect with her. This may have been enough for Albert's wife at the beginning of the relationship, but inevitably it felt like he was hiding his *real self* behind all his efforts to please her by performing tasks.

As he and I worked together, he started to remember how painful it was for him at a young age to feel both his parents' anger and disappointment when he got bad grades in school. Despite his best efforts, he could not focus his attention on whatever he studied. They accused him of not trying hard enough and would discipline him for "being lazy". What little praise he got from them centered on him doing chores around the house. By the time he reached adolescence, however, he grew tired of their complaints that made him feel so inadequate and bad about himself. So he rebelled in high school by drinking alcohol and getting high, which also helped him dull the emotional pain he felt his whole childhood. By the time he met his wife and got married at age 29, his life was very much a product of his Inadequacy Myth. Because no one ever showed him a healthier version of love, he grew up believing that love was all about performing tasks to get another person's approval and to keep her from being disappointed in his shortcomings. By the time he and his wife had been married for 6 years, all he could feel from her was her disappointment that he was not "doing enough" for her and the relationship.

This is the power that a man's
Inadequacy Myth has over him.

In getting Albert to see how this "story of his inadequacy" had been following him around his whole life inside his head, he was able to reality-check whether or not it was really true. He was also ready and willing to learn a healthier version of love that could actually help him feel better about himself, as well as how to hear his wife's needs, without continuing the legacy of his parents' judgments.

A Man's TRUE HEART

As long as a man is at the whim of his Inadequacy Myth, he will be caught in the undertow of his survival instinct that keeps him emotionally cut-off from his wife or girlfriend. More importantly, *he will not have access to his own authentic and true feelings.* It is this suppression of his emotional world that cuts a man off from understanding and appreciating the *true, authentic self* that lives inside him.

This genuine, impeccable part of a man, what
I call his "True Heart", is locked inside the
prison of a man's Survival Paradox.

A man's True Heart is that place inside his *heart*, not in his *head*, where:

- He connects to his authenticity, personal integrity, and self-respect.
- The whole range of his emotional world lives, both the light and dark sides.
- The dignity, self-worth, creativity, intuition, and imagination that define his uniqueness resides.

To find and set his True Heart free from the psychological prison of the Survival Paradox, a man must get out of his head and courageously dive into the real experience that lives in his heart. This usually puts him in contact with an unfamiliar experience of himself. It is the deeper, authentic version of himself that does not wear a mask or hide from an open and genuine exchange with the people he loves. This brings him face to face with parts of himself that he may have little awareness of or that he himself may have purposely judged as being unimportant, inadequate, and therefore unlovable.

Understandably, trudging through this unexplored territory inevitably puts him in contact with the pain of his life that is otherwise known as his *dark side*. Because a man is trained to avoid his feelings, especially his fear, pain, anger, sadness, and shame, it is very confusing and unknown terrain for him. Of course, talking about doing all of this is easier said than done. If it were a simple thing to do, men would already be participating emotionally in their intimate relationships in healthier ways.

As a man accesses the courage to explore the authentic aspects of his personal history, cultural training, and generational legacy that have shaped his identity over the course of his lifetime, he will discover the buried treasure of his *true self*. He will see that no one ever taught him to value that true self as the sacred work of art that it is. As a clinician, the challenge for me is this: *How do I guide a man out of an emotional jail cell that has not only become his comfort zone, but which is also the accepted cultural belief regarding how a man defines himself as a man?*

To be clear, the "prison" that men are held captive in is *not* the instinct to survive; all humans need that instinct no matter what gender they are. Rather, the cage around a man's heart is how his fight-or-flight survival wiring has become deeply associated with *who he believes himself to be as a man*. Unfortunately, men are taught in so many ways that they need not focus their attention and energy on anything beyond survival, because for thousands of years, the default traits of masculinity have become synonymous with a survival mentality. As I have said, though, this limits men from opening to the *emotional vulnerability* that allows for an exploration of their emotional world, as well as creating emotional maturity and maintaining emotional closeness with a woman.

A survival mentality unwittingly trains men to avoid participating in the emotional connection of an intimate relationship. This means that if a man really doesn't want to end up alone in his life, he must risk doing the one thing he struggles with the most, which is to open up and reveal his emotional world to his partner.

The question becomes, in order to attain happiness in the 21st century with himself and with the person he loves, how does a man free himself from this prison without ignoring his instincts to protect and provide for his loved ones? What is being suggested here is *not* some intellectual exercise. Men need a legitimate experience and appreciation of what feels *real* in their hearts, guts, and balls – even in the face of disagreement, judgment, and possible rejection from others. Each man needs to make an effort to be open, transparent, and accepting of whatever personal Truth is his and his alone. This is the only way that he will then be capable of courageously approaching the woman he loves in an open, transparent, accepting, and vulnerable way.

The Hole in a Man's Heart and Soul

I have rarely met a man who as a boy was taught by an adult male to recognize the difference between the thoughts generated in his head and the feelings generated in his heart, let alone the important role each plays in the quest for personal happiness. I have asked many men if they knew the difference, and every one of them has given me the same *"Are you crazy?"* look. They guffawed at the idea of some male role model in their young lives guiding them to notice or appreciate the feelings buzzing around inside of them. That was definitely *not* what most men, including myself, were taught as boys. The fatherly life-lessons offered to most men during childhood was much more practical: Depend on your logic and reason to succeed in life? *Absolutely.* Be the problem-solving-guy-with-all-the-answers in a relationship? *Bring it on!* But figure out if you're feeling scared or hurt or angry or sad or ashamed and then talk about that to someone else? *Why would I need to do that?*

The men of the Great Depression/World War II generation delivered a survival-based model of masculinity to the boys of the Baby Boomer generation. That model taught the same fight-or-flight values that every generation of men before them had harnessed and identified with since humans first learned to wield a club to keep from being eaten. Capitalizing on the success of a survival imperative that was based on equal parts physical strength, resourceful intelligence, and a drive to "sow their seed", it was a natural evolution for the physically powerful to enforce its will and influence on those who were not as physically strong.

We will go into more depth about this in Chapter 3, but suffice it to say that the fathers of Baby Boomer boys have been the ultimate, archetypal, survival-of-the-fittest warriors given their involvement in World War II and the Great Depression. They taught us well the lessons of a survival approach to social, economic, and political power. Unfortunately, over the course of thousands of years, this lack of vulnerability combined with a "might is right" attitude has also morphed into a "tradition" of oppression and dominance over the less-advantaged that is based on race, class, gender, and heterosexuality. While the main purpose of this book is to focus on the lingering adverse effects that survival instinct has had on men's self-concept, it is my hope that it will also serve as a vehicle for men to educate themselves about and stop the culturally instilled misogyny, sexism, racism, and homophobia that victimizes women, children, and men all over the world.

Men have always played the role of physical protectors of nations, communities, and families from predators of all sorts. This has brought with it the social, political, and economic power that has shaped patriarchal cultures all over the world. Women have played the role of bearing and nurturing the next generation of children and keeping the fires lit at home, which traditionally put them on a lower rung in a hierarchy that deferred all decision-making to the male point of view. Once women refused to no longer accept the hypocrisy of being treated like second-class citizens in a "free and democratic society", men were automatically challenged to re-define the social expectation that they were somehow more capable, powerful, and valuable than women. What remains is that men have yet to define themselves beyond their traditional survival-role identities the way that women have. It has been challenging for men to get beyond this limited view of manhood because questioning their identity also indirectly challenges their core instinct to survive.

Looking beyond a man's survival-role identity would require him to ask himself deeper questions beyond a task-oriented approach to life, such as: *"Who am I?" "Does my life have meaning beyond my intellect and ability to accomplish tasks?" "Do I feel fulfilled as a person?" "How can I make my relationships better, not just by "doing" more things to please the people around me, but by becoming a more fully aware and actualized person myself?"* These are existential questions that examine a man's emotional and spiritual self-awareness. They certainly challenge him to explore his identity through the little known filter of non-logic.

I would be remiss if I did not point out that there is a light side to this traditional model of masculinity. College professors Mark Kiselica (College of New Jersey) and Matt Englar-Carlson (California State University, Fullerton) studied the positive traits associated with "strengths" of masculinity that are mentioned below. They are:

1. **Male relational styles**: Forming relationships through shared instrumental activities.
2. **Male ways of caring**: Protecting others and action-empathy.
3. **Generative fathering**: Engaging and responding to a child's needs while attending to larger developments.
4. **Male self-reliance**: Using resources to overcome adversity and "be your own man."
5. **Worker/provider tradition**: Having meaningful work that provides for others.
6. **Group orientation**: Tending to collaborate and associate in larger networks.
7. **Male courage**: Achieving great things through daring and risk-taking.
8. **Humanitarian service**: Joining fraternal organizations that have a strong history of service for others.
9. **Men's use of humor**: Using humor to connect to others and cope with stress.
10. **Male heroism**: Engaging in heroic acts, which have a long tradition as part of manhood. (Kiselica and Englar-Carlson, 2010).

Once again, however, there is an obvious lack of inclusion of any type of emotional maturity as a desirable characteristic or trait to be associated with masculinity.

While men have definitely made progress over the past 40 years by participating more in such tasks as childcare and housekeeping duties, knowing and revealing the qualities of an inner life are far down on the priority list. My observation is that asking a man to describe his feelings about himself beyond his problem-solving and task-performance abilities is consistently met with an *"I've never thought about that"* remark that is now very predictable. When a man doesn't know the internal world of his emotions, he lacks in having a deeper understanding of who he really is. Without an awareness of his emotional world, his ability to know what motivates him to make the choices he makes is severely limited. A man's feelings give him important information about the framework of his True Heart. Much like the wooden frame of a house serves as the skeleton for its inevitable appearance, *a man's feelings serve as the infrastructure of his personal identity.*

When it comes to understanding masculine identity from the inside out, there is very little cultural input into a man's life that teaches him to know *who he is*, while there is an enormous amount of cultural input toward him to create and measure *what he does*. This orients his self-concept toward performance of tasks. During moments of stress and anxiety, this also orients him toward the survivor/warrior prototype of traditional masculinity that shows up as either a "victor" or "vanquished" approach towards other people. It is another way of describing a fight-or-flight perspective to social interaction that is either dominant and controlling toward others or placating and passive toward them. I have observed this all-or-nothing behavior to be very consistent in male clients who have little awareness of their emotional world.

Of course, just because men may not consciously track their emotions doesn't mean that men are emotion-*less*. It just means that they operate in their lives being largely oblivious to the part of themselves that offers valuable information about their experiential truth. My hope is that more men will start to consider the possibility that *emotional maturity* is an aspect of personality that is just as important as their rational intellect. This book will hopefully give them an understanding of how emotional maturity can profoundly serve men to create a more relevant and responsible expression of masculinity that can also serve humanity.

Due to the shift in social consciousness of the 1960s, women demonstrated their intelligence and ability to be equally capable breadwinners beyond the traditional caretaker roles that were expected of them. Unfortunately, men did not similarly examine the limitations of their own deeply ingrained, centuries-old, survival-role identities. Instead, they reacted to this new zeitgeist with a very predictable fight-or-flight stance. Men have adopted either the a) *"hell no we won't go down without a fight"* type of backlash, or the b) *"walk on eggshells and don't make waves so women aren't offended"* type of passivity. As a result, men continue to pass up the opportunity to learn some important lessons about themselves beyond their traditional survival-role identities. Because such an idea challenges his core instinct to survive, a man usually reacts with defensiveness rather than a receptivity to explore an updated version of masculinity that more closely reflects the changing cultural landscape... which brings us back to The Paradox.

As I stated in the Introduction, it is my belief that men are prisoners of a paradox that starts at a young age in most every boy's life. There is a pervasive cultural training that humiliates boys if they show any kind of "weakness" to be evidence that they are less than "manly". As a result of this social conditioning, the bottom line question becomes: *Is emotional vulnerability in men a sign of strength or a sign of weakness?* Boys who are raised to "be a man" from the perspective of traditional masculinity can be summed up in this way:

> *If you show vulnerability, you are weak.*
> *If you are weak, you are inadequate as a man.*
> *Therefore, if you show vulnerability,*
> *you are inadequate as a man.*

This belief comes from centuries of cultural indoctrination that a "real man" has very few, if any, perceived or real weaknesses – which has translated into a need for few, if any, vulnerabilities. The resulting cascade effect causes men to believe that "being emotional" is a sign of weakness and therefore, is unmanly. This, in turn, activates feelings of shame and inadequacy for even the *possibility* of being perceived as unmanly, which activates the survival instinct to put on a "mask" of confidence to hide any trace of weakness. Therefore, in men's eyes, wearing this mask is what makes them worthy of the attention of a woman.

What traditional masculinity fails to teach men is the important role emotional maturity plays in creating emotional intimacy with a woman. This creates the battle inside a man between his need for emotional and physical intimacy versus his need for emotional and physical survival. The challenge is that there are many more ways that men have been taught to physically survive than they've been taught to emotionally connect with a woman. Under stress, a man's default move is to self-preserve and survive, even if the so-called "threat" comes in the form of an emotional challenge from the woman he loves. The learning curve for men is to trust that in an intimate relationship, *staying open and creating an emotional connection when there is turmoil* rather than shutting down and becoming defensive will serve the overall purpose of making the relationship better. Learning how to create an emotional connection is a skill set that he can add along side the survival skills he will continue to need in the appropriate moments.

As a result of all of this, men don't understand how to "heal the hole in his heart and soul" so to speak. If he can think of the "hole" as his lack of self-knowledge and lack of self-worth, then improving or strengthening his self-concept would seem to be the best prescription. This would require an emotional awareness, however, of how his life experiences construct his belief system and shape his personal values. This inside-out approach to self-knowledge is limited to whatever degree a man has explored and charted his own emotional terrain.

Many men derive their self-worth from an intellectual ability to solve problems and perform tasks efficiently. Because this creates a reliance on getting positive feedback from his environment for "performing" well, a man learns to "feel good" about himself based on this outside-in feedback. While the pride derived from this feedback is a valuable source of esteem toward his personal identity, it can train him to believe that his ability to perform tasks and solve problems represents his full worth as a man. This problem-solving ability can also become the best and only way that a man shows his care and affection for others. While "doing things" for loved ones is a powerful and legitimate way to show love for them, it also disregards the need for him to share his knowledge of *who he is beyond his performance abilities* as a way to create emotional intimacy with another person. Until a man can trust that the positive regard he receives from others is an acknowledgment of his personal character and ethos along with his behavior, his self-worth will ebb and flow with that outside-in feedback.

Once a man learns how to divulge a vulnerable piece of truth that "comes from his heart" as a more effective way to show his care and affection for others, he also takes the risk of exposing his authentic self to feel either understood and appreciated or to feel rejected and judged by them. He must decide whether or not it is worth it for him to take such a risk. However, the best way for a man's self-esteem to truly grow is to trust that his whole authentic self is appreciated and loved, both light side and dark side. As he becomes more familiar with his emotional world, he will have a more authentic experience and understanding of who he is *beyond what he does* that he can always access because it lives in and comes from his True Heart.

The Role of Shame in Men's Lives

One observation I have made in my clinical practice, which has been validated consistently by other clinicians I have interviewed, is the impact of shame on male clients. These other clinicians almost without exception acknowledged: 1) consistent reports from male clients in psychotherapy of feeling ashamed and inadequate whenever any element of their masculinity was brought into question, and 2) upon contact with these feelings of shame, another level of shame was evoked, such that the clients reported experiencing shame about feeling or experiencing their original shame. Both of these clinical observations are documented characteristics in the study of shame phenomena. (Harper & Hoopes, 1990; Meth & Pasick, 1990; Kaufman, 1989)

So, the *experience of inadequacy* quite naturally predisposes a man to feel shame whenever a complaint from someone is expressed regarding almost any aspect of his personal or professional life that is somehow judged as "not enough." For example, a man can feel both proud and defensive about how hard he works in order to provide for his family. He can be proud to contribute to the lives of his loved ones this way. Where this goes off the rails in a relationship is when a man believes that this somehow relieves him of any responsibility to "contribute" to the emotional sustenance of the family. It becomes difficult for him to not hear such a request from a woman as a complaint and a judgment of his lack of character. This then creates resentment in him for not feeling appreciated for what he is already doing for his family, which then leads to him feeling "not enough".

Another important source of feedback a man gets is from his family-of-origin that helped shape the version of masculinity he integrated into his personality as a boy. If he received positive and affirming comments about who he was as a person, he was likely to grow up with a strong sense of self-respect. If he heard criticism and personal attacks, the resulting feelings of shame and humiliation no doubt torpedoed his self-respect and set him up to see himself as inadequate and incompetent. In his book, *No Place to Hide*, Michael Nichols defines shame in a way that I think succinctly explains the challenge for men regarding their emotional maturity. He explains that shame

"...wells up in us from sudden and unexpected exposure to the critical eyes of another person. In that moment, we stand revealed and painfully diminished. This experience then leads us to feel insecure and avoid any situation that might then lead to humiliation, which becomes a fear of that painful exposure." (Nichols 1991, 28).

This drive-to-survive filter was utilized by my parents and the culture I grew up in as a way to teach me about my personal sense of masculinity and thus, to a large degree about who I was supposed to be as a person. Like an innocent babe in the woods, the picture they painted for me about how life would be was all I could imagine. But there was also a dissonant voice in my head that questioned their input and wondered if there could be more to life than just the "getting by" life lessons of survival that they taught me to expect. They both came from blue collar, lower middle class working families that had very little knowledge of the world other than what existed on the most isolated piece of terrain on the planet – the Hawaiian Islands.

There was also the clash in my head of how risky it was for me to have any opinions at all – much less express them in an alcoholic household. If my survival instincts taught me anything as a young boy, it was that revealing my opinions, beliefs, or truths was a threat to my emotional and physical safety. At a practical level, this "flight" approach to life became my survival template for what masculinity meant.

Today, I am able to see that my naïve approach to life felt threatening to my alcoholic father's survival-minded worldview. Though I truly believe that my dad did the best he could with what he knew as a result of being raised by an alcoholic and abusive father himself, he nonetheless foisted the unhealed pain of his life onto his wife and three sons because he had such a deep hole in his own heart and soul. Along with this came his expectation that his sons would adopt his life perspective as their moral compass by which to guide their own life decisions. This included his sense of what masculinity meant at both a personal and collective level. I can see now that my dad's "fight" approach to life was definitely his survival template for what it meant to "be a man".

In his study of how childhood experiences of shame influence adult masculine identity, psychoanalyst Gary Thrane defined shame as a feeling about our failure to live up to the value system developed in accordance with our deepest held morals and personal sense of identity. His research went on to show that there were specific injunctions handed down to participants from their father figures as to what constituted "manhood." (Thrane, 1979)

In the research conducted for my doctoral dissertation, I reported that – in order to avoid feeling shamed or abused – my research subjects, who were all male, reacted with any number of opposing impulses to: (a) avoid the appearance of weakness by not crying or by not showing feelings; (b) appear to have no limit for enduring pain; (c) appear competent and capable by manipulating rules to gain an advantage; (d) appear dominant and powerful by expressing anger as rage (Vierra, 1994). These are similar findings to David & Brannon, whose research described four types of norms that define the male role: (1) *"no sissy stuff"* describes the denunciation and disapproval against anything vaguely feminine; (2) *"sturdy oak"* suggests a manly air of toughness, confidence, and self-reliance; (3) *"the big wheel"* describes achieving status, success, and the need to be looked up to; and (4) *"give 'em hell"* conforms to an aura of aggression, violence, and daring. (David & Brannon, 1976, p.18). What is obvious (read: sad) to me is that none of these types include *emotional maturity* as a desirable characteristic, nor is there an alternative to the previous four types that expresses emotion in a mature way.

The Price Men Pay

The influence of thousands of years of a survival filter on the collective psyche of men can best be seen in the picture of men's mental health. Despite any man's determination to create the impression that "everything is fine," there are, in fact, a number of mental health issues for men in every country of the world that challenge the quality of their lives. One example is how symptoms of depression are still very much a reality of life for men in the 21st century. The National Institute of Mental Health lists on its website that an estimated six million men in the United States suffer from one or more types of depression. (NIMH, 2012).

It is often a combination of factors that cause depression. The Mayo Clinic (2013) has shown that depression tends to express itself differently in men than in women. While both sexes exhibit the usual symptoms of depression such as isolation, melancholy, fatigue, difficulty sleeping, and lack of pleasure from activities they once enjoyed, men also exhibit behaviors that are not typically recognized as depression. These include escapist behavior, such as spending a lot of time at work or at sports; alcohol or substance abuse; controlling, violent, or abusive behavior; irritability or inappropriate anger;

and risky behavior, such as reckless driving. What is even more concerning is the fact that these symptoms very often go unnoticed because men don't reveal or talk about their depressed condition to anyone.

The best book I have read about men's depression was written by Terrence Real and is called *I Don't Want to Talk About It: Overcoming the Secret Legacy of Male Depression.* He calls depression the "silent epidemic" in men due to the stigma men feel about being perceived as weak and unmanly if others know they struggle with any of these symptoms. His research shows that in an attempt to escape depression, men typically turn to substance abuse, domestic violence, suicide, and workaholism (Real, 1998).

Berger *et al* (2012) found that because so few men seek help for their problems, they are four times more vulnerable to suicide and substance abuse than females. Although women attempt suicide more than men, males are more likely to complete suicide because men: 1) use methods that are more likely to be lethal, such as guns; 2) act more quickly on suicidal thoughts; and 3) show fewer warning signs, such as talking about suicide. Men account for nearly eight in ten suicides in the U.S. today, even though women are diagnosed more often with depression and make far more suicide attempts (CDC, 2007).

Such numbers are hardly exclusive to U.S. males. All over the world, distraught men are dying by their own hand in ever-greater numbers. Nowhere, in fact, do female suicides appear to outnumber those of males. Researchers everywhere have struggled to explain why. Many believe that socialization, not biology, lies at the root of this lethal disparity. University of New South Wales associate professor Judy Proudfoot conducted research on men who had survived suicide attempts in each state and territory in Australia. She found that almost all of the men in her study reported that their masculine beliefs taught them to avoid managing their emotions, especially when it came to enduring the anxiety of being perceived as having weaknesses or failures. She found that their tendency was to ignore or misinterpret their own depression or anger as warning signs for suicide, which then led them to further avoid their feelings through use of unhealthy drugs, alcohol, gambling, or excessive work strategies. These inevitably led them to attempt suicide. (Player, Proudfoot, *et al.*, 2015)

In 2012, sociologist Anne Cleary published a study in the journal *Social Science & Medicine* that found in a sample of 52 young Irish men who survived suicide attempts that they all were reluctant to disclose to anyone the emotional pain that overwhelmed them. She concluded that, "They all opted for suicide rather than disclose distress or seek help." (Cleary, 2012). In 2003, psychology professors Michael Addis (Clark University) and James Mahalik (Boston College) conducted research exploring the reasons men are reluctant to seek help for themselves from health professionals. Their findings suggest that available physical and mental health services do not "match up" with the ways traditional masculinity has influenced men's needs to emphasize self-reliance, emotional control, and power (Addis & Mahalik, 2003). Their findings suggest that mental health services have not yet figured out how to help men overcome the cultural training that brainwashes them to believe that they "should" be able to overcome their problems without asking for help.

This is a deep-rooted dilemma that is culturally present around the globe and gets in the way of a man's sense of self-worth: *He would suffer in silence and consider ending his life rather than risk being seen stewing in his agony of inadequacy.* Just the act of showing vulnerability, which can range from simply asking for street directions to admitting having made some social *faux pas* to revealing to someone that he feels scared, hurt, angry, sad, or ashamed, puts him into the dicey territory of exposing his lack of competence and "enough-ness". The irony of this is how well-trained a man is to take care of others, yet the idea of taking better care of himself, especially emotionally, is a foreign concept. The term "self-care" is, unfortunately, still an obscure option for men. It is, however, the road-less-traveled to a man's True Heart.

So, the price that a man pays for perpetuating a survival-focused version of masculinity that does not encourage him to share his emotional world:

1) Keeps him unaware of making choices that increase self-respect and self-esteem.
2) Keeps him ignorant of his dark side and the unconscious influence it has on his decision-making.
3) Keeps him living a life of pain and fear due to his avoidance of healing his childhood wounds.
4) Keeps him in the dark about how to empathize with the emotional experiences of others.
5) Precludes him from being aware of his own depression or anxiety as a result of his denial of fear, pain, anger, sadness, or shame that unconsciously influences his behavior with himself and with others.

6) Prolongs his mistrust of his own emotional world that would give him a deeper access to his authenticity and personal integrity.

I can look back at my childhood and see that I clearly learned the above lesson at a young age that continued into my adulthood. One of my more powerful memories occurred when I was five years old. I was walking my usual mile and a half route home from kindergarten after school one day, and I had been feeling physical pain in my stomach for about two weeks. I vividly remember making a conscious decision to not let my parents know how much pain I was in. Despite my hope that the pain would dissipate (it just got worse), what I distinctly remember to this day is how afraid I was of anyone thinking I was a wimp because I was complaining. My two brothers and I were – as were all the boys around us – always under the scrutiny of parents and peers to live up to that "John Wayne" standard of "suck it up, be a man, don't complain." Finally, after a week of enduring this ever-increasing knife-in-my-gut feeling, I was staggering that endless trek home after school one day to the point of literally dragging myself via the back way home so that no one would see me struggling. I collapsed through my front door onto the living room floor, delirious and screaming in pain. Thank God my mother took one look at me, threw me in the car, and raced me to the emergency room, where I immediately had my nearly ruptured appendix cut out of me. In that following week of recovery in the hospital and all the "you're-really-lucky-to-be-here-kid" glances that I got from the hospital staff, all I can remember is how pissed off my parents were at me for not telling them sooner about my pain. I certainly don't remember a whole lot of compassion coming my way. Though I wasn't mature enough to get it at the time, I know now that the mixed message of "suck-it-up-and-don't-complain" versus "why-didn't-you-tell-us-you-were-hurting?" was pervasive and confusing throughout my young life. Looking back, I can see how totally ill equipped I was to share anything even remotely vulnerable. I was doing exactly what every other male around me – age notwithstanding – was doing. How could I have done it any other way? Even if I had wanted to (and I didn't), I had absolutely no idea of what the upside to revealing this type of information could possibly be. Over five decades later, I still wrestle with this original wiring in my system to open up and reveal myself to others. I'm much better at it now than I've ever been, but the critical voice in my head that hollers at me to "suck it up" and not risk being too vulnerable can still be loud at times.

The hole in a man's heart and soul comes from this insincere and outdated cultural "myth of masculinity" that a man need not know or trust what he feels in his heart and guts. Because a man is trained from his childhood to ignore his emotional make-up, he functions in his adult relationships with women as an emotionally immature adult male, i.e., a little boy inside a grown-up man's body. Not only is he unfamiliar with how and what he feels inside, but even the idea of getting a negative reaction from someone else can provoke a level of anxiety that a) automatically activates his fight-or-flight, red-alert warning system, which then b) triggers a reflex action that shuts him down emotionally in order to "survive" and, thus, ward off the perceived threat. This emotional lockdown prevents him from staying in contact with how he feels, let alone opening up and talking about those feelings to someone else. *The challenge a man faces is how to not automatically react with a survival approach to a situation that might actually benefit from an emotionally vulnerable approach.* But learning about the specific terrain of his emotional landscape and attempting to communicate it requires an openness that can be uncomfortable and very confusing for men.

Luckily for me, sports not only became my way to explore my competitive, masculine side, but it also offered me a daily escape from my dysfunctional, alcoholic household. Despite my promise to myself that I would not "become like him" (my father), I had plenty of opportunity as a young boy to inherit the survival mentality my father demonstrated on a daily basis. It became the filter through which my manhood was constantly measured: Could I fight to defend myself, or was I a sissy? Could I win at sports, or was I a loser? Was I strong and tough, or was I weak and wimpy? Could I endure pain, or would I "cry like a girl"? These were the benchmarks that my masculinity was constantly measured by.

As I grew older, the challenge to my developing sense of masculinity was that, unlike the generations before me, the opportunities to "prove my manliness" were different from what my father experienced. It was the 1960s, and between the Civil Rights Movement, the Women's Movement, and the undeclared war in Vietnam, a very different attitude toward authority and the "establishment" had taken hold among the younger generation that questioned everything our parents' generation blindly accepted, especially about gender roles. There was no way to avoid getting caught up in this zeitgeist, and it really started the ball rolling against my father's teaching of what it meant to be a man.

Masculinity 2.0

As a man unwittingly equates his survival skills with his masculinity, it makes sense that when he experiences stress and anxiety, survival is the only filter through which he can see himself and the world around him. While on the one hand it may make sense to use a fight-or-flight filter to deal with stressful life circumstances, the price a man pays for doing that is disconnecting from his own emotional and psychological needs in order to live life in a "fix-it" mode. He doesn't realize how he sacrifices his self-respect by seeing himself through such a narrow filter as "survivor".

He abandons living from his True Heart and wears a mask that allows him to appear capable, adequate, and that he "has his act together." This type of survival approach is *the opposite of self-care.* Understandably, it is second nature for him to address his ongoing physical and intellectual health. The problem is that he has very little understanding of what self-care means when it comes to his *emotional health.* The price he pays for neglecting his emotional world is that he also neglects creating a life of quality for himself from the inside out. In other words, he may very well acquire a lot of "stuff" that is a reflection of his material success, but the whole quest for a life of happiness and high quality requires more of a grasp of inner strength and self-knowledge. *This is not possible if a man has no appreciation of his emotional world.*

If instead he learns to honor what is in his True Heart, he can prioritize self-care to at least a similar level as survival, but this can only come from his willingness and courage to be more open about his need to be vulnerable towards others with the truth of his feelings. *The progress I observe in my male clients toward their own self-actualization begins with their ability to recognize and differentiate their survival skills from the personality traits that express their "larger" sense of masculinity.* Unless and until they become aware of the need to separate these two aspects of their personality, their ability to create emotional intimacy with another person remains severely limited.

The bottom line is that it is definitely time for men to update their perception of masculinity to reflect a deeper, more authentic experience of themselves. If we as men want to engage in healthier relationships, we must take the risk of embracing our emotional world and *becoming more emotionally mature.* Every man owes it to himself and to his loved ones to let go of an outdated masculine stereotype and embrace his True Heart, bringing a more mature version of "being manly" to his everyday life. We must wake up and create a more relevant standard of masculinity that will serve us as men, our relationships, and the world in the 21st century and beyond. We must open up and aspire to "Masculinity 2.0".

Chapter 2

The WAKE-UP CALL

"If you want to waken all of humanity, then awaken all of yourself. Truly the greatest gift you have to give is that of your own self-transformation."

- Lao Tzu

There comes a moment of truth in every man's life when despite all attempts at convincing himself and others that he has his act together, he is humbled by some chink in the armor of his "got-it-all-together" masculine façade. This moment – this *Wake-Up Call*, if you will – is a sobering flash of insight. A man suddenly sees that his choices for managing his life are not providing him with freedom or happiness. Even though he may not know what other choices he could make to lead him to his own *happy place*, the Wake-Up Call is at least a moment when he realizes he has to do something different.

The Wake-Up Call is quite often precipitated by a traumatic event, such as the death of a loved one, the loss of a job, or some other life-threatening circumstance. *The loss or potential loss of an intimate relationship* seems to be especially motivating for a man to wake up from the denial he has used to keep himself emotionally distant from the woman he loves. The Wake-Up Call is a kick-in-the-ass reminder for him to dive deep and resuscitate the authentic version of himself that he abandoned long ago. The initial reaction to this, however, is rarely to ask for help by getting into therapy. Most of the men who come to see me for therapy are there because their wife or girlfriend pushed them to come in for their depression/anxiety or gave them an ultimatum to either "get help" to save their relationship or she will walk away. Just because a man seeks therapy does not necessarily mean that he has already gotten his Wake-Up Call, however. It means that he may simply be trying to "up the ante". He figures if he goes to therapy, he can show her that he cares enough about the relationship to actually follow through on her ultimatum.

One of my very first clients many years ago – I will call him John – arrived in my office resistant to making any kind of change and admitted that the only reason he was there was because his girlfriend had threatened to leave him if he did not "work on himself." The attitude he expressed was, *"Hey, Doc, if it ain't broke, what is there to fix?"* In other words, the relationship was just fine from his point of view and did not need any type of "fixing" as his girlfriend had claimed. It became obvious that John came into therapy only as a way to placate his girlfriend so that she would stop complaining to him. I asked him about his plan, and he admitted that he thought he could just come to a few sessions, learn a couple of things from me to say to her to calm her down, and then wait for her tension to go away. As a therapist, it is crucial for me in the first session to reality-check a client's motivation to be seeking help in the first place. Left to their own devices, most guys come in with some amount of willingness to at least learn how to communicate better with their partner. This also, however, can become a teachable moment for a guy to learn how to change for the right reasons. It is an opportunity for him to see the personal benefit of increasing his self-awareness, but too often, like John, he's just trying to learn how to placate the woman he loves to get her to quit complaining.

A Man's Moment of Truth

Mid-life brings adversity to men, providing a humbling reality check to any "high and mighty" or "this-is-just-me-being-me" stance they have taken. It is important for men to understand the difference between how to live life from their True Heart versus how to live life from behind the mask they show to the world.

Treat adversity as a Wake-Up Call to grow and mature into a stronger and healthier life condition.

When a woman threatens to leave a relationship, it is usually borne from the hopelessness of a stockpile of grievances. Here are a few of the complaints that I have consistently heard over the years from women in couples therapy:

- It's crazy making for her to be in a relationship with someone and still feel alone.
- She feels exhausted to be the only one who keeps the emotional connection alive.
- She feels disrespected when he walks on eggshells around her because he's too afraid to speak honestly to her.
- She feels depressed and lonely as he lives his married life more like a "me" rather than as a "we."

- She's sad and angry that it takes her threatening to leave the relationship to finally jolt him out of his complacency and see the need for change.

This is when the Wake-Up Call arrives.

Sooner or later, every guy gets a Wake-Up Call. And another. And another. Until he finally pays attention to and chooses to figure out the idiosyncrasies of his personality that drive him to keep a loved one at arm's length. Either this, or he continues to languish in a prison of loneliness and personal mediocrity. As unfamiliar and challenging as it may feel, this is also an opportunity for him to identify the life-shaping events in his past that have pushed him to build a wall around his heart for protection. It is an opportunity to heal the wounds from the fear, pain, anger, sadness, and shame of his life that clearly influence his behavior toward other people. This can become the moment that it finally sinks into his brain that his manly pride can no longer keep him from feeling the very personal and private pain of his shortcomings as a human being.

John came to a couple of therapy sessions, but despite my urging him to do therapy for himself and not to placate his girlfriend, he disappeared back into his life. Four months later he called me wanting to come back into therapy. Doing my best not to sound smug over the phone, I asked him what would be different about him doing therapy this time around. He let me know that his girlfriend threatened to end the relationship unless he "figured out his bullshit". He admitted that this finally compelled him to get in touch with the fact that did not want to lose his relationship with her. As we began therapy again, it became apparent to me that John had indeed gotten his Wake-Up Call because he gave himself permission to become vulnerable with me as I helped him explore and identify his emotional blind spots.

SIGNS You Are Getting a WAKE-UP CALL

- When you finally realize that you suck at making relationships work;
- *When you finally realize that the fear you have of ending up alone on the planet forever keeps you involved in unhealthy relationships;*
- When you finally realize that the Mask of Masculinity you hide behind is a façade that undermines your personal integrity and self-respect;
- *When you finally get tired of living your life at half speed because you feel lost, inadequate, and confused about who you are and why you are here;*
- When you finally start to see that there is a difference between living a life of fear (from ego) versus living a life of courage (from authentic self);
- *When you realize you can no longer blame anybody else for the emptiness you feel in your gut.*

One by one, as any of these scenarios start to collide and converge inside a man's head, a slow-burning fuse gets lit that winds its way down from his head to his heart and ignites the realization that the one thing he *really* wants, i.e., to share his life with somebody, seems to be the one thing that he keeps messing up. It is the nagging doubt in his head that says maybe, just maybe, there is something he does that keeps women at a distance and causes them to leave. Maybe there really *is* some part of his personality that shows up and makes them run for the hills or that keeps him feeling unsatisfied with whatever woman he chooses.

While it may appeal to him to fleetingly think, "Screw it! It's much easier for me to be by myself!", there is also the sobering thought of what it would be like to never again breathe in the scent of a woman, and this scares the hell out of him. When a man is in his twenties, he has time to be cavalier about relationships enough to deflect any urgency to "wake up." But once he enters the battle-worn years of middle age, his fear of ending up alone forever is the reminder note that gets push-pinned onto his forehead and flushes him out of his cave back out into the world. It is about finally acknowledging the soul-ache a man carries from holding on to an outdated code of manliness that keeps him unfeeling and insensitive to his own wants and needs.

This is also what the Wake-Up Call is about.

While the mask he wears may not show this to be a problem, the authentic part of him feels the pain of low self-worth and limited emotional availability to other people. Because physical and emotional vulnerability activates a man's survival instinct, it also makes sense that masculine identity has evolved to measure itself by that same lack of vulnerability. John Wayne was the poster-boy for this *strong and silent* guy in his movies

for a 20th century American culture that believed *might is right.*
No fight was ever so scary that his character would walk away
because both his survival and his manhood were always on
the line. Even if he got hurt or scared in battle, it was never
acceptable for him or his audience to let that be seen. His mask
was fixed and unfailing, which also always won him the girl.

Whether he knows it or not and whether he likes it or
not, every guy inherits a cultural legacy about being a man
that wires him up to be emotionally ignorant throughout
his boyhood. This then sets him up to remain emotionally
immature and childlike once he moves on to his adult intimate
relationships. Because of this cultural training, a man enters
into a relationship thinking he knows how to handle its ups
and downs, but soon learns that he has a limited ability to
articulate what he knows to be true for himself in his heart.

Recognizing the Wake-Up Call

As I have said, the Wake-Up Call experience is usually a
result of some distress or upheaval in a man's life. There is the
eye-popping whack-over-the-head variety, such as the death
of a loved one; the loss of a job; a debilitating illness or car
accident; or getting dumped from a relationship out of the blue.
Then, there is the less ominous but equally effective "AHA!"
epiphany-type Wake-Up Call that spontaneously erupts in a
man's brain as a result of having what I call an attention-getting
Close Call. There is a big difference between a Close Call and a
Wake-Up Call. The Close Call gets a guy's attention to the fact
that – before the relationship gets any worse – he needs to do
some things differently before it is too late. The problem occurs

if he makes a half-ass effort in following through with changes that merely attempt to placate the woman he loves.

The common element is usually some very humbling experience where a man's emotionally dysfunctional behavior causes enough heartache that he feels desperate for relief, but it's still not the harsh chokehold that the Wake Up Call usually is. This usually happens when the woman in his life lets him know that she needs more from him emotionally and *strongly* suggests that they either get into couples counseling or attend a couples workshop or read a relationship book together. If he is paying attention to his own feelings and can relate to what she is saying about feeling the lack of emotional connection, then he will usually seize this moment as the Close Call that leads him to his Wake Up Call that saves his relationship. This is what happened for my client John. The thing about a Close Call is that if a guy doesn't use it as a way to pay attention to the quality of his relationship, it will take him longer to get the Wake Up Call he needs to see the reality of his relationship falling apart. However, there actually is a "point of no return" where the Close Call that leads to the Wake Up Call comes too late.

My wife is an astute psychologist and a very smart woman who has helped educate my male mind to the fact that a woman will tenaciously reach out in an attempt to deepen the emotional connection with the man she loves. But when she makes a substantial effort over and over again with no response or good faith effort coming back toward her, she will slowly detach. Quite often by the time her man finally quits blowing her off and gets the Wake-Up Call, it will be too late because she will have completely closed her heart to him. Because a man may not understand how important it is for a woman to feel emotionally connected because of his emotional ignorance, he will not be able to take her tenacious attempts seriously. Without his own emotional awareness, he will have no context of how to recognize her efforts.

The Wake-Up Call is about the deeper level of change that is needed when a man starts to clearly see that aspects of his personality are not only getting in the way of his connection with his wife or girlfriend, but more importantly, that those characteristics are clear indications of his lack of self-respect and self-worth. Whichever way it happens, he needs the clarity to understand two things: 1) the high personal price he pays by not knowing how to speak the truth from his heart to his partner and to himself when it matters most, and 2) the high price his relationship pays as a result of his lack of emotional awareness and maturity. Every man gets to decide whether or not it's worth it to move out of his comfort zone and do the internal exploration necessary to help his relationship. It would, in fact, increase his overall quality of life to a degree if he could even *consider* the possibility that familiarizing himself with his emotional world could serve him both personally and interpersonally.

Making the Most of a Wake-Up Call

The challenge for a man is to keep from justifying his way back into denial and apathy when the Wake-Up Call hits him between the eyes. To "stay awake," however, means he has to question a fundamental piece of his masculine identity about what makes him feel manly. This is a very confusing course of action for most men to wrap their heads around.

As I mentioned before, waking up and actually dealing with the part of ourselves that wreaks emotional havoc in our relationships is certainly *not* what we've been taught in terms of how to "be a man". It's a natural instinct for men to downplay the importance of this awakening. Otherwise, we would have to give up our comfort zone inside our cave, which is both a sanctuary *and* a prison.

Since our cultural training fails to support men to become emotionally vulnerable, which is the one thing necessary in order to create true intimacy, we try to "fix" relationship problems in concrete, rational, and emotionally non-vulnerable ways that are way off the mark of intimate interaction. Due to that same cultural training, we also don't learn the psychological skillset required to identify and work on whatever emotional wounds we have endured in our own lives. Our fight-or-flight default-mode survival approach makes sure that does not happen.

When a man takes a *fight* approach to his life, he becomes the angry, controlling, and blaming hard-ass who tries to convince his partner that all of their relationship problems are her fault. When he takes the *flight* approach, he becomes the angry-on-the-inside, doormat-on-the-outside guy who bails out on the relationship either by taking all the blame or passively withdrawing. This, of course, can lead to the infamous midlife crisis that drives some men to leave a long-term relationship for another (usually younger) woman. For other men, it means finding a mountaintop for meditation/isolation or a new sports car for distraction – anything but dealing with the emotional pain that threatens to rise to the surface. For others, it means wallowing in confusion and self-doubt about how "women are just too difficult to figure out."

Like most guys I've known or worked with, I had pretty much approached life with a similar attitude of, "If I think it ain't broke, what's there to fix?" Until I got some humbling proof that what I was doing with my life was not working, I assumed – and would tell anyone who cared to listen, that I was doing just fine, thank you! I was a carefree guy, living a life that I also wanted others to see as being carefree, even if in reality it wasn't. I was also adept at bobbing and weaving around any evidence that I might need to reevaluate any aspect of how I lived my life. No need to wake up or fix anything because I was the "positive" guy, and nothing about my life was "broken."

This level of denial ruled my life up to about the age of 35 when I ended up alone again after another failed relationship with a woman. Throughout my twenties, I was a typical, immature, commitment-phobic guy. I had very little understanding of what it took to make and keep a deep connection in a relationship. So, I assumed that one day, I guess I would just figure out how to do the "forever thing" with a woman – as if there was some magical moment waiting for me in my future to enlighten my brain about how to create a healthy, long term relationship.

I was in a committed relationship with someone at the time, and I thought she had the potential of being "The One." I remember wondering if I had it in me to develop this into a "forever" relationship. I knew that sooner or later, I needed to expect more from myself than just being a good boyfriend. I really wanted to be the kind of guy who could get married and settle down to raise a family. I just wasn't sure how, other than to be a good person and try to "do the right thing." But like most guys my age, I was very emotionally immature, which also meant I really didn't know who I was.

Looking back now to that time of my life, I can see that my lack of maturity also predisposed me to live most of my life doing what I thought others expected of me. In other words, I had no idea how to make decisions for the "right" reasons, i.e., based on the Truth that lived in my heart and soul. Instead, I was constantly wondering whether other people approved of me or liked me. So, I had no way of living my life other than from behind a mask, afraid that others would judge me as being unlikable and unworthy of their approval. The mask helped me ignore and forget the shame of "not being enough." It was a façade that kept me busy by making sure others never got a chance to see my dark side of fear, pain, anger, sadness, and shame.

During the four years in my committed relationship at that time in my life, I didn't have the maturity or the courage to be honest and talk about my dark side. Instead, I ignored my gut and tried to do what my mind thought was the "right thing". So I asked her to marry me. I very naïvely thought that the proposal would jumpstart something inside me that would help me figure out how to do the whole "forever" thing with her.

The good news about a Wake-Up Call is that it is Mother Nature's way of telling a man that he has a blind spot that is severely limiting his ability to be happy. The bad news about a Wake-Up Call is that a man often doesn't recognize what it is really about until after the blind spot has actually done irreparable damage to his life.

So, there I was, engaged to be married, and proud of myself for having gone boldly where I had never gone before. But because my choice came more from my head (the practicality of "doing the right thing") rather than from my heart (an expression of my personal Truth), I had no way of knowing what to do or where to go from that point. There was no personal conviction behind my choice. There was no essential Truth that I was taking a stand for. Did I love her? Well, I loved her the way any emotionally immature guy in his early thirties is capable of loving.

To call my experience in matters of the heart sophisticated or profound would be like calling paper plates and plastic forks dinnerware. Hell, I still had blind spots about the blind spots I had yet to identify. I assumed that once I asked someone to marry me, all of my questions about how to be with that person "happily ever after" would automatically be answered. But not only did I not get any of those answers, I became more and more confused about why I was getting married in the first place. I had caved-in to the self-imposed pressure of "what others would think" if I couldn't take the relationship to the next level after four years.

Being the carefree guy that I was, I also grew up believing that the best way for me to handle my problems was by myself without asking for any help. I was actually too embarrassed to tell anyone how deeply confused I felt. This, along with the fact that I had never learned how to identify and express any feeling in my emotional world, isolated me at the worst possible time.

Another important thing for a man to know about a Wake-Up Call is that it comes in two parts that are crucial to distinguish. Part #1 is when a Wake-Up Call smacks him upside the head in an effort to stop him from doing whatever takes him further away from his Personal Truth. The initial challenge is recognizing when a painful or embarrassing life event is actually an opportunity to learn something about a blind spot that is sabotaging a man's happiness.

A year after I proposed, it became obvious that I was flaking out on the whole marriage deal. I couldn't bring myself to talk about arranging a date or any other aspect of the wedding. The proposal had reinvigorated the relationship, but that momentum slowed to an inauspicious trickle of excuses and avoidant behavior on my part. Even through the thick haze of my own denial, I could see the pain in her eyes, and there was no way for me to carefree-guy my way out of the situation. Confused as I had been up that point, one salient fact managed to claw its way up from the knowing part of my heart into the sensible clarity of my juvenile brain: I was in way over my head. I could no longer deny the rumblings in my heart and soul that seriously challenged the status quo of my predictable little world. Like a gradual awakening from a deep slumber, some dim cognition took hold in my mind and began to mess with my limited self-concept.

That bleak brainwave slowly amplified into a commotion of guilt and embarrassment. I realized that I had absolutely no idea how to help make a marriage last past the "I do's," let alone for even a fraction of forever. As newer and deeper layers of truth exploded inside my thick head, I could no longer deny that my real reason for proposing to her was not because I wanted her to be my life-partner, but because I was terrified of "how it would look" for me to fail at yet another relationship. How would it look if I ended up alone again – this time, maybe forever? It was unfortunate that I didn't have the balls to admit this to myself or to her until a year after the proposal. Needless to say, she was devastated when I was finally honest with her. She was a wonderful person who deserved much more than my immaturity and lack of awareness.

Part #2 of the Wake-Up Call is the awareness of what the man is actually being awakened *to*. The challenge here is that it might first appear to be something on the surface that eventually reveals something deeper about his betrayal of some core Personal Truth he has long neglected. Finding this bit of treasure takes a good deal of soul-searching, but it's crucial to identify in order to change the pattern that led to the Wake-Up Call in the first place.

At first, the big revelation I thought I had to wake up to was that my fiancé must not be The One. That might have even been a correct assessment at the time. However, I had met plenty of Wrong Ones before, so this was nothing new for me to realize. When I finally looked at my situation, not from the perspective of whether or not she was The One, but from the angle of what was actually going on inside me, I came upon some more humbling discoveries. As I watched this other person take the hit for my immaturity and selfishness, a deeper level of awareness about myself emerged out of the fog and settled into my consciousness quietly and calmly. It was so nakedly obvious and real that I was both stirred at how deeply it resonated inside me and awed by its simple pronouncement: **I had absolutely no idea how to create emotional intimacy in a relationship because I had absolutely no idea of who I really was as a person.** *And I didn't know who I was because until then, I hadn't been aware that my carefree guy act was just a mask.*

How was I supposed to know? I was living a life as what I thought was the "Real Me" without understanding that I had to determine if my life was truly coming from a Real Me place. Like most guys, I had assumed that the image of myself that I showed to the world was an authentic expression of who I was. I did not know that there was a deeper version of my identity that had yet to be explored, understood, and lived.

The Taste of Authenticity

Naturally, the Wake-Up Call generates questions in a man's mind as he begins his journey of opening up to himself and others in a new way. My responsibility as a clinician has been to guide male clients through their transition from being emotionally cut-off from themselves and others to becoming emotionally aware, mature, adult men who can appreciate, access, and express the different feelings inside them.

Most men assume that if they aren't aware of a feeling, it must not exist. Since behavior is usually a result of some underlying emotional state, men can begin to use their behaviors as clues as to what's going on in their own hearts. This is a pivotal teachable moment for a man to finally claim what he feels without judgment, regardless of what the feeling is.

Over the course of many years, I have found that the best way to "normalize" this experience for men is to re-orient or re-label what a man feels in his heart as something that is simply part of his Personal Truth. This bypasses all of the voices in his head that come from a macho culture that warns him to not appear feminine or weak by being "too emotional." Once he does this shift in his own head and gives himself permission to not only explore but to assert his feelings as his Personal Truth, *he now has a way to express his integrity and authenticity.* This depth of honesty can be a very powerful entry point into personal fulfillment and peace.

The majority of men in my practice who have been given an ultimatum by a girlfriend or wife also report to me that they are equally as unhappy in their relationships, but they wouldn't have sought help without the woman's prodding. Despite her complaints about wanting/needing more emotional feedback from him about himself, it is confusing for him to understand how it's possible to provide that feedback or even why it's valuable. The main question that clients ask as we begin therapy is: *Why is it so difficult for me to even know how to give my wife or girlfriend the emotional closeness that she is asking for?* The blind spot he is on the verge of discovering is that, despite whatever physical, financial, or intellectual competence a man may achieve throughout his life, it is his lack of emotional maturity that will consistently and predictably sabotage his intimate relationships. Because a man is trained by the culture-at-large to identify himself more with his mind than his heart, many of my male clients whose marriages are falling apart protest, *"I'm not a feelings kind of guy, Doc. I can't do that. It's just not me."*

In the face of this narrow perception of himself, I offer this example: "It would be like you telling me that if you were stranded on an island where coconuts were the only available food source, you wouldn't cut into a coconut and eat it just because you've never considered yourself to be a 'coconuts kind of guy.'" I know that sooner or later, he would bust open that big seed to chow down on what would probably become his favorite food. It's the same thing with *talking about feelings.* Every guy on the planet has plenty of emotional experiences rattling around inside of him every day of his life. If he has never learned how to pick one up and *do* something with it, like describe or share it with someone else, he's going to assume that he should avoid it. After all, it's unfamiliar and foreign to his personality "taste buds." *What he doesn't realize is that this overall lack of regard for his emotional world actually creates a lack of personal integrity that weighs a grown man down with the emotional maturity of an adolescent boy.* This, in turn, torpedoes any attempt at creating a healthy, authentic, compassionate relationship with another adult person.

A number of important themes have emerged over the years from the self-reports that I hear from my male clients. Here are five of the most consistent and noteworthy:

Theme #1 – They reported feeling both censured and humiliated by others throughout their lifetimes for any display of emotional vulnerability – in particular, crying – that was a result of an authentic emotional experience of fear, pain, anger, sadness, or shame.

Theme #2 – They learned not to acknowledge the emotional experiences that came as a result of their personal experiences with Theme #1.

Theme #3 – They learned at a young age to create a *public persona* to the people around them that adhered to the cultural expectations that they thought defined "masculinity."

Theme #4 – They rarely, if ever, questioned or examined the true nature of the internal, authentic personality that exists "underneath" their public persona.

Theme #5 – They admitted to feeling the inner conflict of both a discomfort with and a desire for others to know and appreciate the true nature of their authentic personality.

There is a direct negative correlation between emotional immaturity and a survival mentality. The "training" men receive from childhood regarding the importance of survival to their masculine identity is what prevents emotional development. It is in a man's primitive, innate wiring to want to survive and compete because it's part of the embedded self-preservation code in his DNA. His primal need to *stay alive*, however, is very different from his equally as important need to *not feel alone*. This is what compels him to seek social and intimate relationships. Besides procreation, it's what gives a man a sense of "tribe" – another powerful reason to stay alive. Unfortunately, his survival sense of competition and his desire for quality relationships collide with each another as long as he is emotionally immature.

It's no wonder that men can have a deer-in-the-headlights look when a woman asks him how he feels. In the world of survival, many men think that the best way they can demonstrate their love is to protect, provide, and fix problems for the person they love most. Those three things come from a sense of being good at "doing his job," which is to survive and make sure those around him survive as well. That's what we've all been taught "being a man" means. Again, this creates a conflict between the masculine paradigm and a man's ability to make a deep connection with a woman. The infuriating stereotype for me is how men are painted as being emotionally inept. What is worse than that stereotype is how men have learned to tolerate and even hide behind that portrait of masculinity. Therefore, from my perspective, an important objective for men in the 21st century is to discover what *healthy masculinity* would look like and walk like and talk like in order to pass that knowledge on to future generations of boys.

But a reminder: The highest priority for a man and the most important reward for discovering healthy masculinity is not to improve his relationships, but to become a bigger and better version of himself. In order for a man to achieve this authenticity, he must become more honest with himself, more humble, more committed to a life of personal integrity, and willing to understand the effects his emotional wounds have had on his heart and his personality.

Finding My Missing Peace

Once the Wake-Up Call got through my thick head, I started to consider the possibility that I didn't know as much about life as I had thought. I got into therapy and started to become conscious of how my personality as a man was shaped to a large degree by the painful family experiences I had as a boy. I learned that there really was a difference between the man I was on the inside versus the mask I showed others on the outside. I learned that I had yet to make room for a deeper expression of myself in my life because I was unaware of the value of living from the authenticity of my heart. I had never been able to value "real-ness" because I had rarely witnessed other people living their lives from that "real" perspective. I had always lived my life in survival mode, showing others the mask that I thought they would accept and love.

I had probably gotten this opportunity to "wake up" before, but it took the experience with my fiancé for it to finally pierce its way through the 35 years of denial that protected my heart. After many years of personal growth, I came to understand that as a boy, I had been judged and criticized so much that I learned to survive by hiding and wearing my carefree guy mask. This false persona created many years of loneliness, confusion, anger, and shame. It was definitely not the ideal foundation for building a happy and meaningful life for myself.

After all these years of exploration and discovery on my travels inward, I feel privileged to be able to offer other men the benefit of my personal experiences, combined with my training, education, and professional experiences as a marriage and family therapist who has specialized in working with men of all ages. What I ultimately learned was that my missing peace had less to do with trying to be positive and more with finally healing the pain and heartache of my life. In order for me to do that, I had to journey into the very pain and angst that I had so skillfully avoided up until that point. If there is one crucial piece of awareness that I woke up to, it was this: Trying to always be the upbeat, positive, fun guy that everyone loved had trained me to disregard the experiences that created fear, pain, anger, sadness, and shame in my life. There was a lot of it growing up in my alcoholic childhood home. In making the decision to not become like my angry, inebriated father, I also cut myself off from my "negative" feelings to such a degree that I was cut off from my true self. In becoming the carefree guy, I set myself up to avoid dealing with fully half of the reality that shaped my personality and character. This form of denial, while a brilliant survival strategy for a child, no longer served me as an adult in a useful or healthy way. In fact, it was officially getting in the way of my knowing who I was and learning how to heal all those wounds from my past; wounds that kept me emotionally stagnant and immature.

As I got into therapy and started to read books that expanded my view of life, I especially appreciated the works of Dr. Carl Jung (1875 – 1961), a Swiss psychiatrist and psychotherapist who is known for his theory on archetypes and what he called the *collective unconscious* of the human psyche. He believed the collective unconscious was a reservoir of all the experience and knowledge of the whole human species, and he referred to the unexplored pain and anger of a person's life as the "dark side" or "shadow." (Jung, 1959)

Writer Joseph Campbell, best known for his work in comparative mythology and comparative religion, writes of Carl Jung that he: "...*believed that the controlling psychological force in our lives is the knowledge and understanding of all the 'pairs-of-opposites' that exist in our lives. So that anybody fixing his eyes on but one is left open at the back to the other; whereas the art is to learn of both, to recognize and come to a knowledge of both light and dark.*" (Campbell, 1976). American Jungian analyst and author Robert Johnson also talks about how it is in the nature of our cultural life to "...*focus on the good possibilities as opposed to the bad ones. In doing this, he says that we banish the bad ones so thoroughly that we lose track of its existence. These banished elements make up our shadow, but they do not stay in exile forever, and about mid-life is the time that they come back to haunt us for not attending to them.*" (Johnson, 1993)

The paradigm these men teach makes sense to me, as my experiences personally and professionally have taught me that our lives have both a light side and a dark side that are important to integrate. Every experience has both good news and bad news to learn from. Unfortunately, men are taught to focus on what they judge to be "positive" and to ignore and even avoid what they judge to be "negative." This directs their attention away from the part of their emotional world that is scared or hurt or angry or sad or ashamed. While this may be convenient for any man in the short term, he pays a high personal price in the long run for not being familiar with his dark side, which empowers those lifelong neglected feelings to influence his life without knowing it.

What I observe on a daily basis in my clinical practice is how an attitude of staying "positive and optimistic" has become a sort of mantra to avoid feeling fear, pain, anger, sadness, and shame, all of which are very much a part of the very imperfect and flawed life that all humans experience. This attitude blurs a man's ability to deal with adversity in an honest way and keeps him ignorant of a very real part of his personality that he labels as "negative." He fails to see the opportunity these feelings offer to him to live his life without a mask and become an improved and freer version of himself by knowing his dark side.

Chapter 3

A MAN'S WORLD of SURVIVAL

"When the fight begins within himself,
a man's worth something."

-Robert Browning

Even though Robert Browning was an English poet from the 19th century, his words ring true today. A man's internal fight begins when he desires to know his authentic self and *how to relate to others in an authentic way.* To create an intimate connection with a woman, self-worth and self-respect cannot be some minor afterthoughts. They are the foundational pieces of a man's character that demonstrate his trustworthiness and integrity to others. Yet, our culture does not teach boys and men the importance of this very basic piece of personal identity. If a person is not clear about the difference between his/her *self-worth* and his/her *self-absorption*, achieving healthy intimacy with another person will be a difficult task.

What human culture has always taught males both young and old throughout history has been the importance of learning how to survive because survival skills are crucial to the continuing existence of our species. As a default piece of our human wiring, it's a tribute to our amazing resilience as humans to witness our abilities to survive the harshest and most challenging of living conditions on this planet. Back when our cave-dwelling ancestors were hunting and gathering food to eat, every moment of their lives was preoccupied with averting the threat of serious bodily harm and danger from any number of other competitors on the food chain. This kept them in a perpetual, hyper-alert state as either the hunter or the hunted, which left little opportunity to develop an experience of life "beyond survival." Their success at staying at the top of the evolutionary food chain depended on their ability to respond to any physical threat by either fighting for their lives or running away to get out of danger. This has come to be known as the "fight-or-flight" response.

When a man brings this fight-or-flight mentality to deal with his intimate relationships, he not only compromises those relationships, but more importantly, he sacrifices his authenticity, personal integrity, and self-respect. A blind-spot in his self-awareness develops from holding onto a version of masculinity that is primarily based on that fight-or-flight mentality.

The biggest challenge for any man who wants to figure out his authentic self is for him to start by distinguishing the traits of his masculine identity from the traits of his survival instinct.

What I mean by this is that the primitive, human urge I have in me to survive at all costs naturally compels me to protect, provide, and procreate with my wife to keep myself, my family, and my tribe alive. However, upon deeper inspection, I also notice that the main character traits that define my personality of what it means to "be a man" are equivalent to those same survival drives to protect, provide, and procreate. In other words, I have always run my life as if these two crucial pieces of my identity were essentially the same, because I never received any input from my family, culture, or social environment that told me they could be different. This observation of myself prompted me in my therapeutic work with male clients over the years to ask them – in as non-leading a way as possible – to define both of these aspects of their personalities for me. The consistent report I have gotten from them describes a similarly high correlation between these two parts of their identities to the point that one is automatically assumed to represent the other.

The significance of this observed parallel between my survival instinct and my masculine identity came down to the fact that as long as I was in that protect, provide, procreate "mode" in my day-to-day life, I was oblivious to feeling any kind of vulnerability – either physical or emotional. As regards my need to survive, this for me was good news. The bad news, however, was that as soon as I would come home from work after a day of slaying dragons, I would bring this fight-or-flight attitude to my family assuming this was the way for me to "be the man" of the house. Doing this got in the way of me being the caring and compassionate guy that my family needed from me whenever I walked through the door.

I think it is noteworthy to point out that there has also been research done to suggest that fight-or-flight is more of a "male response" to stress than for females. Shelley Taylor, a psychology professor at UCLA, first offered a different paradigm of survival for women in 2000. She and five of her colleagues did research to develop a model called "tend-and-befriend" to describe the stress response for women that challenges the notion that the individualistic, aggressive "fight or flight" model applies to all humans, observing that *"the human response to stress is characterized at least as much by tending to and befriending others, a pattern that is especially true of women."* (Taylor *et al*, 2000) While I believe this piece of research is fascinating and helps to paint a picture of the female response to stress that deserves further exploration by the reader, I also maintain that women have their own version of a fight-or-flight survival instinct that is common to all humans.

The Post-WWII American Zeitgeist

I believe the successive occurrence of five events that were crammed into a 40-year period in mid-20th century America combined to cause social change of epic proportions. These were: the creation of the atomic bomb, the Civil Rights Movement, the Vietnam War, the Women's Liberation Movement, and the Gay Liberation Movement. I believe that the convergence of these five events disrupted and disoriented the psyche of heterosexual, Caucasian men in America in ways that had never happened before, especially regarding their beliefs as to what constituted masculine identity. Each of these historical events took issue with an established expression of masculinity that had never been questioned before.

While using the atomic bomb gave America the "win" in World War II, it also introduced another giant leap in weapons technology that provided a reality check for the warrior archetype of our military forces. Dropping "the bomb" on Hiroshima and Nagasaki did not remove our need of a national military for protection. However, how could it not impact the "profile" of what is expected of a warrior if there is less and less need of hand-to-hand combat as we have evolved from our origins of using sticks and stones to establish dominance over each other. The irony I think it created in the male psyche was this: while state-of-the-art weaponry may represent a way to win a conflict utilizing a different level of involvement of traditional combat for our fighting forces, atomic weaponry also symbolizes the mass destruction of humanity. This very sobering possibility for the first time in human existence introduced the notion that the warrior prototype of the male psyche is no longer the ultimate determining factor of survival-of-the-fittest. I believe this was the first monkey wrench thrown at traditional masculine identity.

In 1955, despite almost 100 years having passed since Abraham Lincoln abolished slavery in this country, African Americans finally took up the cause of ending racial segregation in order to assert their right to equal treatment under the law. The Civil Rights Movement that gained momentum in the 1960s and 1970s demanded the deconstruction of institutionalized racism in American society. This also called into question the long-established status quo of white male political, social, and economic power that up to this point felt entitled to dominate and define the ideas and beliefs of the time. This was another reality check to the status quo of male power and privilege that defined masculine identity.

By the mid-1960s, another challenge to the "establishment" came in the form of a movement against U.S. involvement in the Vietnam War. The decision to send U.S. soldiers into an undeclared war on foreign soil resulted in an appalling number of them returning home in body bags or being physically and psychologically wounded beyond repair. This was enough for people from all walks of life, including for the first time in American history many young men who were opposed to becoming those soldiers, to demonstrate their opposition to the prevailing military warmongers. American involvement in World War II "made sense" because we were attacked and drawn into it, which compelled men to sign up for military service. The Vietnam War, however, became a symbol of an anti-establishment mentality that bucked the status quo assumptions of masculine identity for men in America because it was another nation's civil war.

For every generation of men before my own, some type of experience as a warrior-soldier had been a required component of being a man both in his own judgment and in the judgment of others. As a boy, I learned that any guy who considered himself to be "manly" would serve in some branch of the military. Participation in combat forces was a badge of honor that reflected courage in a man's character.

My high school and college years were plagued by the onus of whether or not I would be drafted into the military and sent to Vietnam. It hovered over me like a dark cloud. In my mind, there were many valid reasons to not want to participate in that war. At the end of the 1960s, there was no choice to serve in the military that would not require some involvement with that undeclared armed conflict.

My generation was the first ever to question whether or not it made sense to join the American military in order to fight someone else's war. This is probably because the 1960s and 70s were exploding with social consciousness. American involvement in Vietnam was fast on the heels of the Civil Rights Movement and at the same time as the Women's Liberation Movement. Like many of my peers, we questioned thousands of years of survival masculinity that expected us to "follow orders" and be sent into harm's way. However, because it was an undeclared war, there was no possible way for me to feel like it would fulfill some patriotic duty to put my life at risk. Because it was another country's civil war, it also was a military conflict that posed no real threat to American freedom. Just from a survival standpoint, the war in Vietnam simply became a threat to my life, and I was determined to use the "flight" side of my fight-or-flight instinct to survive.

Though I knew that my father had concerns about sending his sons into a war that was sending many other sons home in body bags, he also could not understand how I could question signing up for the draft, much less refuse to go to war as he did. My own brand of patriotism in those days did not look like my father's version, but it felt patriotic nonetheless to protect the American way of life in a very different way than he could have ever imagined, i.e. by questioning authority. Luckily, I was able to avoid going to Vietnam by qualifying for a student deferment as long as I was a full-time college student making satisfactory progress toward a degree. Nonetheless, I still had to battle with my father's expectation of me to become the man he thought I should be.

All of this served as a natural lead-in to the changing zeitgeist of American women who had pushed for women's right to vote with the passage in 1920 of the 19th Amendment. By 1967, the spirit and mood of the country lit the next social fuse that became the Women's Liberation Movement. Now a new generation of women would carry on the work of the suffragettes to call for equality under the law. This social movement helped continue the theme of the Civil Rights Movement, fighting for women to have a say in their government, to receive a job and earn wages equal to men, and to be able to put an end to the hypocrisy that male privilege and power imposed onto a so-called "free society". The status quo of masculine identity started to crack wide open into a full-on identity crisis as women let men know that they would no longer conform to a patriarchal hierarchy that viewed them as being inferior to men.

It was only a matter of time before another group that felt discriminated against would raise their voices for social equality. The Gay Liberation Movement starting in 1969 urged gay men and lesbians to demonstrate "gay pride" in response to societal shame that patriarchal culture foisted upon homosexuals. It aspired to achieve freedom and equal opportunity in order to join the political mainstream on the same level as other groups in society. In seeking to liberate our country from the homophobia that discriminated against those whose gender identity did not conform to traditional heterosexual values, the Gay Liberation Movement also challenged the status quo of masculine identity. One of the ways it did this was by challenging the long established stereotype that any tolerance for homosexual culture must be an indication of homosexual proclivities. Historically, this precluded heterosexual men from playing any supportive role in being outwardly sympathetic to the gay community for fear of being labeled "queer" or "homo" themselves.

These five pieces of social change created upheaval within men's previously unchallenged perception of themselves and the world. It also required men to change that perception in order to "keep up" with the times, but that was a tall order to expect from the "good ol' boy" network in charge of the most powerful nation on the planet. Nonetheless, the *social equality genie* was out of the bottle, and there was no going back to the previous days of racial, gender, and sexual identity discrimination that traditionally empowered patriarchal ideology.

Women's Challenge to Men

I believe the Women's Movement that began in the 1960s was not only a Wake-Up Call for women to courageously confront the institutionalized bias that their lack of physical strength precluded them from sharing in. It was also a huge Wake-Up Call for men to stand down from imposing the patriarchal hypocrisy that defined male power and privilege. For men, the Women's Movement felt more threatening than liberating. Women in America began to seek their own personal and political answers to the questions of what it meant to be a woman beyond the survival roles that they had traditionally played in their service to men.

Women have had their own dilemma, not only of what thousands of years of living life through a survival-of-the-fittest mentality has done to them from the outside-in, but also the effects from the inside-out, based on how much they had bought into the second-class citizen propaganda. The good news, however, is that women in America have challenged themselves since the 1960s to heal the effects that this has had on their own self-image, as well as on the feminine psyche. This leap in social consciousness dared women to take responsibility for their own lives in ways that their survival mentality previously trained them to believe they could not. As a result, American culture is becoming a more balanced, egalitarian society, though much progress still needs to be made.

There are now countless Women's Studies, Psychology of Women, and Gender Studies courses throughout America's colleges and universities. The self-help book industry has exploded with thousands of book titles geared toward women's self-examination of their ever-evolving participation in the social, economic, and political power base of American culture. Little girls actually grow up believing it possible to become President of the United States without being laughed at or considered to be foolish.

At the same time, the Civil Rights Movement, the Women's Liberation Movement, and the Gay Rights Movement were a Wake-Up Call for men and the white, male-dominated power base of our culture. These movements showed us that the American value of "equality under the law" was fictitious as long as the law unfairly empowered or represented one group's interests over another. As a result, the might-equals-right-in-order-to-survive-paradigm has had to make room for a new standard where both men and women of every racial background and sexual orientation get to share the responsibility of shaping the social, economic, and political landscape of American culture using a framework of equality and partnership, rather than dominance and hierarchy.

Because women have courageously dared to challenge the status quo about their womanhood and feminine identity, men in America have likewise been challenged to chart a new and different path to their own manhood and masculinity, a path they have yet to fully embrace. Whether men knew it then or not, the social movements of the 1960s were the beginning of the end of their stereotype of manliness. Updating the masculine hard-drive to integrate some new program beyond traditional survival roles has proven to be challenging and elusive. It has been stressful on our belief system as men, not only because it has forced us to redefine the way we perceive women, but also because it brings into question the fundamental role we as men have played in the human survival drama since the beginning. For men, adjusting to all the social change of the 1960s has been a profound force exerted more from the "outside-in" rather than from the "inside-out." In other words, men's struggles with adapting to the new rules of "equality for all" – no matter the race, gender, or sexual orientation – came by way of the courageous and steadfast resolve of women, gays and lesbians, and African-Americans to no longer endure unfair and unequal treatment. This identity struggle for men did not come from some internal conflict or turmoil within themselves, because they have always held power and there has never been a reason to question or change that. The gatekeepers of the status quo are always the last to recognize a need for change.

The Women's Movement in particular dared to challenge men to view women other than through the survival filter of being "the weaker sex" whose lot in life it was to be dependent on and submissive to a man: barefoot, pregnant, and without aspiring to be anything other than that. There was no way that women could view themselves differently without it automatically and directly affecting the way men viewed *them*selves. So much of men's self-image as a result of the survival stereotype of masculinity had focused on how much bigger/stronger/smarter men were than women, that when women decided it was time to challenge that way of thinking, men were put in a position of having to reevaluate the paradigm of masculinity. This has catapulted men into an extraordinary and mystifying journey of change that has created more questions than answers regarding some new, as yet defined model of masculine identity. Gone are the days when men could assume that women would remain silent against oppressive and unfair treatment as they had since the beginning of time. Gone are the days when men could sit back and assume that they had no parallel responsibility to challenge themselves to grow beyond the ideal of manhood that their fathers and grandfathers had laid out for them. Gone also are the days when men could just sit back and remain emotionally passive and unresponsive in their relationships because *"that's just how men are."*

Unlike for women, there are still very few academic courses devoted to studying male psychology, and there are hardly any self-help book titles that challenge men to dive into a deeper concern of where and what their historic and cultural roles will evolve into. Even if men are still not sure of how "else" to be, the picture of manliness that has hovered over men since the beginning of time has started to shift direction away from the macho, emotionally distant, might-is-right stereotype that is equally as oppressive to men as it is to women. That paradigm just does not work anymore, and not only because it's a change that women want. Way beyond any picture of what women could imagine for men to become, it is men's ultimate responsibility to create that healthy, mature picture for themselves. To shift something that has been humming along in a particular direction for eons will, however, take a bit of time to redirect.

Wherever the motivation comes from, the most shortsighted thing that men could do with this challenge is ignore or minimize it. Both individually and collectively, men must do the work of digging for a deeper understanding of how to see themselves way beyond the protector/provider/procreator role that they so deeply identify with. Unless each man does that work for himself, he will remain a captive of the patriarchal, only-the-strong-survive, might-is-right system. Unless he does that work, he will continue to perpetuate an outdated and dismissive approach to relationships that holds others to an unfair and unjust standard that he is not willing to be held to himself. Unless he does that work, the misogyny, sexism, racism, and homophobia that plague America and cultures around the world will continue to thrive unchecked. Unless he does that work, he will miss the opportunity to grow into becoming a bigger and better version of himself as a man.

Survival-of-the-Fittest Folklore

Survival is such a potent and relentless force in the everyday psyche of human beings, that it has helped shape a very powerful social legacy for all of us. The tales of certain tribes conquering and being conquered by certain other tribes has created much of the world's oral tradition handed down from generation to generation. Stories of survival make up such a large part of the folklore of human culture that have not only served us as a way to proliferate and inhabit every corner of the globe, but also as a template for our respective gender identities. Both men's and women's halves of that survival legacy became the respective gender identity model for what it meant to "be a man" and what it meant to "be a woman" and, therefore, what it meant to be "masculine" and "feminine" for men and women around the world.

As we have all learned to depend on this innate drive to survive, humans are proudest of the ways they overcome adversity and live to tell its tale. It comes as no surprise then that the history and folklore of human kind is recorded as an epic testimony of respect and admiration for the *survival skills* each generation of each culture has innovated to thwart extinction by all kinds of threat to life and limb. So it is to this day when our high tech, up-to-the-minute-information-mentalities are bombarded with story after story of assault from deadly weapons, acts of terrorism, natural disasters, poverty, disease, war, traffic accidents, crime, homicide, suicide, nuclear proliferation – all threats to our survival. At one end of the survival folklore spectrum, the terrorist attacks of September 11, 2001 on New York City and Washington, D.C. have imprinted themselves onto our collective consciousness when we talk about life in America before and since "9/11." On the other end of the spectrum, popular reality game shows on television challenge contestants to see who can live and survive through our planet's harshest physical conditions alongside the belligerent and grating human interactions required in order to win a million dollar prize. The best and most popular human-interest stories are the ones that showcase some triumph of the human spirit over adverse physical, emotional, intellectual, and spiritual conditions. These stories document our evolution as humans and what our survival instincts have inspired in us to achieve.

This brings us to the issue of women who today serve in the U.S. military. As of January of 2013, women are able to fill front-line combat posts alongside men. In signing the directive that allows women to risk their lives to defend their country, the U.S. Secretary of Defense Leon Panetta said that women *"...have become an integral part of our ability to perform our mission, and for more than a decade of war they have demonstrated courage and skill and patriotism."* (Panetta, 2013) He also said that not everyone can meet the qualifications to be a combat soldier but that everyone is entitled the opportunity. So, even the survival folklore of our fighting forces has expanded to include the talents and courage of women. Never again will it be the exclusive domain of men, as was such a fundamental part of the warrior archetype for masculinity.

The Light Side of Survival: *Self-Preservation*

Even in the 21st century, fight-or-flight remains very much a part of our human drive-to-survive on a day-in and day-out basis. This survival-of-the-fittest imperative has been and will remain the most crucial gift we have inherited from the generations before us to help keep ourselves off the endangered species list. However, based on my observation of the influence that survival has on a man's self-concept and his sense of masculine identity, I think it is also very important to look at the overall picture of how survival has shaped our lives.

Like everything else in life, survival has both a light side and a dark side. Another way of saying this is that there are both gains and losses that survival offers us on a daily basis. For some time now, our survival instinct has trained our higher functioning brains to adapt and innovate our way to the top of the world's food chain. Our ability as humans to adjust and reorganize our physical limitations has refined our instincts as to what it takes to master the skill and art of *self-preservation*. Despite many life-threatening physical conditions that exist on the planet, humans have developed an amazing ability to endure and protect themselves from harm and death. Staying off the evolutionary menu means that we have learned our survival lessons well. So, the obvious reward is that we have gotten to stay around for a long time on the planet and in growing numbers.

The inherent human survival mentality also introduces a compelling bonding effect into social tribes. It has helped organize humans into shared-interest groups since the beginning of man's appearance on earth. This is the "tend-and-befriend" response mentioned earlier in this chapter that seems to be a more natural response for women than for men. Seeking ways to make a connection with others is what creates a tribe, which is as important a survival strategy as an individual fight-or-flight response given the strength and safety that comes from numbers. When trench buddies in a war or members of a sports team or a family group are subjected to a challenging or even life-threatening experience, they inevitably emerge from the experience feeling emotionally closer to each other. Surviving a traumatic experience as a group creates a trust and camaraderie that strengthens that group's identity. It solidifies the "team concept" and reassures every member that when push comes to shove, other members of the group can be counted on. A man's survival sense is also what drives his motivation to compete and excel toward "success." Business and sports are modern day examples of the ways that humans around the world access the same survival-of-the-fittest information wired into our DNA human schematic.

As a young nation, America was founded as an alternative to the tyranny of religious and political oppression. Today, our country has come to symbolize a place in the world that offers the unique opportunity of surviving in an environment of political, social, religious, and financial freedom. We have honed our survival skills to such a point that we are the wealthiest and most powerful military presence on the planet. We are a nation of sophisticated and cunning survivors, who pride ourselves on the way we have developed materialism and militarism into everyday art forms. We even glorify our sports heroes the same way that history books celebrate our war heroes. All of this comes from the self-preservation side of our survival consciousness.

Over the many epochs of human evolution, our story of survival has gone from keeping animal predators out of the cave to keeping human enemies away from our borders. As a species, self-preservation is something that we have fine-tuned and hums like the high performing engine that it is. However, as is the case for every aspect of Life, the light is always balanced out by the dark, and survival certainly has its dark side.

The Dark Side of Survival:
Suppression of Vulnerability

When humans are under stress and feeling susceptible to any type of physical or emotional threat, this fear of being an open and vulnerable target activates our fight-or-flight instinct. The automatic response of this survival urge is to shut down and prevent any further vulnerability. In switching off our feelings of vulnerability, this awakened drive for self-preservation also shuts down access to our feelings, which is a crucial part of what is needed to maintain close relationships. Not only do we shut down our connections to others when we move into survival mode, we also abandon our True Heart. So the dark side of survival is this *suppression of vulnerability.*

The challenge for all human beings is how to save this suppression of vulnerability for the moments of true danger when our lives are genuinely under threat and at risk. Unfortunately, this drive-to-survive gets triggered even when we have disagreements with the people we love and trust the most. The resulting knee-jerk suppression of vulnerability creates either conflict (fight) or distance (flight) when really what is needed at a moment such as this is the one thing that gets extinguished, which is to have a vulnerable and respectful dialogue about the differences any two people will run into sooner or later. What often prevents this from happening is the competitive survival itch we all have some amount of in our psyches.

It is this suppression of vulnerability that I believe evolved into a dysfunctional and oppressive piece of *patriarchal ideology,* where not only men held power and women were excluded from it, but the competitive need for more and more power compelled men to justify their "authority" to oppress women into subservience and hardship in order to maintain that authority. I talk more about this in Chapter 3.

Survival's Influence on Masculine Identity

As I have said, the standard of what men have been taught to believe masculinity should look like, walk like, and talk like has much of its foundation in the survival-of-the-fittest mentality passed down from previous generations. This built-in survival legacy generates a red-alert approach to life that is not easily switched off. More often than not, however, a man also unwittingly carries this approach with him into his interactions with his loved ones, where it gets triggered in emotionally reactive situations. When this happens, his instinct will be to shut down emotionally and become bulletproof rather than be open and vulnerable.

All of the activities it takes to survive – hunt for food, choose a mate, sire progeny, protect a family, protect a tribe, etc. – has evolved into the default template for masculine identity. This is similar to how women's template for femininity has evolved from how they gather food, bear and nurture children, socialize, etc. As we have passed down both the heroic and tragic stories of these experiences to our children in the form of our history, folklore, and oral tradition, it has also become our way of passing down the survival information we believe they need in order to stay at the top of the food chain. To have ever questioned either one of these standards before the latter part of the 20th century would have gone completely against our survival instincts as a species and could never have become a predominant part of the zeitgeist – not before certain sociopolitical conditions were in place.

Outwardly, countless generations of men before mine have used their prolific survival talents as the template by which to distinguish themselves and measure their own sense of manhood:

1. Survival is the motivating force for a man to be successful in his career, even to the point of sacrificing his personal and/or relationship needs.
2. Survival instinct is why men are diehards when it comes to competition, whether in work, athletics, or everyday life, and why they often use sports and war metaphors as a way to illustrate and make sense of their lives.
3. Survival instinct is the reason men sacrifice their own masculinity and become complacent, placating, and non-confrontational eggshell-walkers with others as a way of "getting along" without seeing how they sacrifice their personal integrity and self-respect in the process.
4. Up until the end of the 20th century, survival has served as the main blueprint out of which "masculine identity" has evolved, and it has defined hero-worship in this country.

While humans have adapted their physical and intellectual survival skills very well, as evidenced by our burgeoning population on the planet, it might also be valuable to consider the psychological and emotional toll that a survival mentality has imposed upon us. Putting it in terms of the good news and the bad news of a survival mentality for men: The good news is that it helps keep all of us alive; the bad news is that it keeps us *emotionally immature* because our survival instinct trains us to avoid feeling *any* kind of vulnerability – emotional as well as physical.

Emotional vulnerability is *not* from-the-head intellect or logic. It is from-the-heart access to the feelings, experiences, beliefs, opinions, and passions that define a person's life. "Going there" requires: 1) taking the time to get to know what True Heart reality lives inside of us, then 2) finding the words necessary to articulate that reality, so that we can 3) take the risk to open up and divulge that reality in a vulnerable and honest way to another person.

The challenge comes when a man's *emotional safety* is feeling threatened by another person, which can be provoked by anything ranging from a simple disagreement to a weird look to a verbal attack or criticism. In the face of these kinds of "threats," a man's survival fight-or-flight instinct can take over, immediately causing him to switch into either an aggressive, controlling attitude or one that is submissive and compliant. Either way, when he clicks into survival mode, he is definitely not emotionally open or vulnerable, *which means that he is not being authentic.*

While authenticity is not a requirement in the world of survival, this lack of openness severely limits the emotional connection between any two people in a relationship. And if fight-or-flight has been a man's default way of dealing with people for most of his life, his awareness, understanding, and appreciation of his emotional world is more than likely very under-developed.

While it may be obvious to some that in order to create an emotional connection with a person it is first necessary to be aware of one's own emotions, most men go into their love relationships with a very limited knowledge of their emotional range of feelings. This is the "paradoxical prison" that men inhabit as a result of not understanding the emotional price they pay for being so highly invested in their survival responsibilities to themselves and others. As a result, a low level of self-awareness and emotional intelligence has (sadly) come to be associated with masculine identity. Worse than this low expectation from the culture has been *how men have come to expect so little from themselves emotionally.* Unfortunately, the narrow masculine standard of how to "be a man" that is emotionally indifferent also keeps men indifferent to the feelings of others.

The Mask of Masculinity

In the 1994 comedy film called "The Mask," actor Jim Carrey plays a milk toast guy who ends up "winning the girl" by impressing her while wearing a magic mask. He is nebbish bank account officer Stanley Ipkiss who lives a frustrated and unhappy life of butt-kissing his knuckleheaded boss and rejection from beautiful women. As he contemplates jumping off a bridge to end it all, he ends up finding an ancient wooden mask floating in the river that gives him super-human powers and transforms him from an indecisive, boring accountant to a swaggering, zoot-suited demigod. When he wears the mask, he feels like he is capable of doing anything he's ever imagined. This includes becoming the object of desire by beautiful Tina Carlyle whom he feels confident around as long as he is wearing the mask. Of course, he ends up being revealed as the flawed, imperfect guy that he really is, but the real version of Stanley is all who Tina has ever wanted to know and love from the start.

Stanley Ipkiss is a great example of how I think many men have come to trust and believe more in a socialized persona of masculinity (outside-in) rather than an authentically constructed experience of masculinity that comes from personal awareness and insight (inside-out). His is the classic story of insecurity that results in some short-term gain, but inevitably gets him a truckload of long-term pain.

Putting down the mask and being authentic requires getting to that deeper, systemic, second-order change outlined in Chapter 2 of this book. Men's shift in perspective must come from a better understanding of their own fear-based and intolerant viewpoint of others. Authentic masculinity cannot come as a result of merely appeasing the masses with politically correct words. It must be a choice to transcend the narrow viewpoint of measuring other human beings as being either better or less than. It must come from a desire to value the unique viewpoint a man has of the world without the insecure need to feel superior to others in order to feel self-worth. Men must choose between an experience of masculinity based on authentic, male values that encourage men to be true to themselves versus one that is based on toxic values that create a false persona and serve men only to maintain power over others.

This persona is an inauthentic façade – a *mask*, if you will – that men use to keep from feeling and showing the vulnerability of their real emotions. This *mask of masculinity* does *not* represent the honest, authentic embodiment and passion – the True Heart – of a man. Over the millennia, men have come to identify with this masculine persona to the point that they assume the mask actually represents what it truly means to "be a man," but the mask has come to represent the role of the arrogant male privilege rather than that of an imperfect man who has shortcomings and weaknesses as well as strengths. To keep the mask in place, men have had to link themselves to and feel at one with the toxic masculinity that has traditionally kept political, financial, and tribal power in their hands. This world of the male prerogative is the paradox that keeps men in prison.

Since gender roles are now a bit different for men and women at the beginning of the 21st century as a result of the social upheaval of the second half of the 20th century, men may have *theoretically* begun to support a more consistent, less hypocritical standard of social equality. Yet, it remains to be seen how good of a job men are doing at *observing themselves differently* in much the same way that they have been forced to alter their view of others. This is necessary in order for men to specifically define the differences between what feels manly and masculine today and what felt manly and masculine to their fathers' generation.

We live in a society that is now continually integrating the lessons of the social movements of the 20th century that fought for equal rights. The tectonic shift caused by these campaigns not only called out the institutional prejudice that had long been the status quo, but it also called into question the aspects of masculine identity that relied on social inequality and prejudice in order to maintain political power. The biggest challenge for a 21st century guy is that, for the first time in human history, many of the major anchor points of the patriarchal version of manhood upon which the mask is based, e.g., domination and oppression of women, racial prejudice and discrimination, and homophobia, no longer serve as the assumed standards by which men measure their masculinity. Putting down the mask and giving himself permission to know and show what really ticks on the inside of his chest *without judgment* is a huge step to take.

Here is what I believe is the most recent phenomenon that men struggle with today: The same survival instinct that his forefathers used as a filter to feel manly has passed-on a legacy of anxiety and fear in the male psyche that is so subtle, so insidious, and so automatic that he hardly notices how it has shaped his present-day sense of what feels masculine. Simply said, it goes something like this: Despite their reluctance to do so, it behooves men to take a hard look at the very real damage that the male heart, psyche, and soul has had to endure for identifying with the same toxic legacy that has wreaked its own unique havoc on women. Every man I talk to, whether clients or personal friends, has a story of how he heard the messages loud and clear of *don't cry, don't be a wuss, don't feel your feelings, don't ask for help, don't be incompetent, don't be vulnerable... because any of that means you're weak, inadequate, unmanly, cowardly, effeminate, blah, blah, blah.*

As the subtitle of this book suggests, not only is "healthy masculinity" *not* a contradiction in terms, it's actually the get-out-of-jail-card that can free us from the confines of the prison of toxic masculinity that men are all sentenced to as boys. The importance of making this distinction cannot be understated in light of the high incidence of divorce, physical and sexual violence toward women, and male depression and suicide in

21st century America. For any man reading this book who is confounded by the whole "emotional intimacy with a woman" thing, creating a successful connection with her must start first with *understanding yourself better,* which then allows you to participate at a more honest and mature emotional level with the woman you love.

Alexithymia

There are men who clearly have problems and are in great emotional pain, but they still insist that they have no problems and no idea what is wrong. This is called *alexithymia.* It's a condition of not understanding feelings, which precludes being able to describe those feelings to others. Men with alexithymia may be quite capable of describing their physiological responses to events, like sweaty palms or increased heartbeats, but are not capable of describing their emotions as happy or angry or sad. They are quite stoic and avoid forming relationships. There is also research that demonstrates considerable overlap in symptoms between alexithymia and Asperger's Syndrome. (Fitzgerald and Bellgrove, 2006)

Affective Deprivation Disorder (AfDD) is a phrase coined by researcher Maxine Aston to describe a relational disorder in which emotional needs are chronically unmet by the partner of someone who has low emotional intelligence or alexithymia, which in turn creates a sense of emotional deprivation in the relationship. (Aston, 2007) While there are shared traits between alexithymia and low emotional intelligence, men who have difficulty with emotional intelligence do not necessarily have alexithymia. My understanding of alexithymic individuals is that they are deeply disconnected from their emotional world. They have no grip at all on what they are experiencing internally, even in the midst of a life crisis.

In this book, I am referring to the general population of non-pathological men. I can usually tell the difference between men with alexithymia versus those with fear of emotional vulnerability. Despite the lack of awareness of their feelings, when I ask most men to "check in with themselves" internally, they can usually describe some type of unease, tension, anger, or anxiousness. Or they report that some part of their body is feeling tense, tight, or rigid. This means that, unlike men with alexithymia, they have some familiarity with their emotions, even though they are not skilled at articulating them.

A Man's Childhood Wound

A crucial piece of awareness comes in the form of being able to trace present-day personality traits back to whatever emotionally significant experiences occurred in a man's childhood. The lingering, unhealed wounds of fear, pain, anger, sadness, or shame that were inflicted onto any young human being's heart continues to exert its dark influence into adulthood until a conscious choice is made to recognize and resolve their influence. The goal of exploring and identifying a man's childhood wound is *not* to blame his parents for how he turned out as an adult. *The goal is to pinpoint the original belief system he created about himself as a result of whatever way his parents showed him love.* The way they nurtured him is how he learned whether or not he was *worthy of being loved.* The reason this is so important is because to a child, survival is less about receiving food and shelter and more about trusting that someone will love him enough to *help him survive*. As infants, humans' survival is dependent upon the care and protection from parents. To a child, *survival is the same thing as love*. A child is wired to operate on the belief that *"If I am loved, I will survive. If I am not loved, I will die."* So, if a child is ignored, neglected, mistreated, criticized, or undervalued, that child will grow up not believing he or she can trust or count on anyone else but himself/herself to survive. A child must be able to *trust* that when he or she cries from pain or hunger, that someone will respond to that cry in a nurturing or soothing way. If an infant boy is deprived of a nurturing response to his hunger/pain/fear, his unformed, primitive psyche will activate his fight-or-flight instinct. If it happens often enough throughout his young life, he will associate a cause and effect reasoning to this lack of receiving nurturing/love with some shortcoming on his part. This is the emotional wound that serves as the foundation of a man's "Inadequacy Myth" of "not being enough". Being the resourceful survivors that human beings are, when children do not receive a nurturing or loving response from their caretakers, they take on a persona (mask) to alter or cover up their authentic personalities in order to get some kind of positive, loving response. In short, they become a different version of themselves in order to somehow "deserve" and obtain their parents' love.

This unfortunately leads to the lack of self-worth and lack of self-respect that many men struggle with. It then morphs into a lifelong quest to feel adequate and competent in terms of being a protector, provider, and procreator. Part of this is his need to "be man enough" to attract a woman's love. The question that formulates for a man in his head, which will be explored in Chapter 6, quite often has him wondering, *"Is there someone who is capable of truly, honestly loving me?"* But what is really going on in his heart underneath all of that is the more important question of, *"Do I believe that I am truly, honestly worthy of being loved for who I really am – flaws and all?"* This is a pivotal question in a male's personality development into adulthood because it shapes the emotional intimacy that he is capable of creating (or not) in a relationship. The belief a man develops about himself in childhood as deserving love or not is what he carries forward into his adult life and brings to his intimate relationships with women. This is not conscious, of course. It is the way he was "wired" to believe about himself as a boy that is *forever in place in his psyche until he does the work necessary to re-wire it.*

I can look back and see that my parents loved me very much. However, they had difficulty communicating that message to me in a way that was consistent and obvious. In my formative years as a young boy, there were many mixed messages they sent me that confused me as to whether or not they loved me. I know now that they showed me love in the only way they knew how, which was how they were shown love by their parents. The problem was that – at least for me – the message did not translate very well into me feeling loved. I have no doubt that they did the best they could to bestow upon me what they were capable of feeling. I also know they both came from environments where love was shown in either very aggressive (fight) or very passive (flight) ways. Because I responded in the only way my young heart and mind could as a young boy, I grew up feeling misunderstood, unappreciated, and unworthy of their love. That does not mean that they did not love me. It means that I was not capable at the time of understanding that they felt the best way to show me their love was to train me to be a capable survivor. This meant that their "instruction of love" to me was more about fight-or-flight than about how my unique character – flaws and foibles notwithstanding – was deserving of their admiration and love. Teaching a kid about fight-or-flight does not send a message of unconditional positive regard. It instead sends a message to "toughen up," "don't show weakness," "don't be a sissy," "don't cry," "don't be like a girl." These messages were also mixed in with other messages like: "you are always wrong," "you're stupid," and "what you need is not important." I know for a fact that they were raised with these same exact messages, so they parented me in the only way they knew how.

The good news is that they also taught me how to be a great survivor! The bad news is that I grew up believing that in order for me to feel worthy of "being loved" by them or anyone else, I needed to alter my personality. The message I received as a child was that who I really was did not merit their approval/admiration/love, so I took on a persona that I hoped would get their positive attention. I became really good at wearing a mask that, at the very least, quieted down their criticism of me. This is how I became a "people pleaser."

Even though I now know that my parents showed me love when I was a little boy, I also know that I grew up feeling that the real, genuine, flawed, mistake-prone kid I was only got their disapproval and judgment. As an adult, I still struggle to this day with that insecurity, but I know it has more to do with my "wound" than about whether or not I am worthy of anyone else's love. My wife loves me wholeheartedly, flaws and all. So, I know I am loved. I trust her love. Whether or not I believe that I'm worthy of her love has been my personal challenge to overcome. As my sense of authenticity, personal integrity, and self-respect has grown over the years, I'm finally trusting that I'm worthy of being loved, whether anyone else actually loves me or not.

Life Beyond Survival

Nothing gets in the way of self-awareness and self-esteem more than a preoccupation with figuring out how to survive. A man's fight-or-flight tendency can create a limited awareness of his life wherein his commitment to keeping himself and his family alive can also lead him to the monotony of punching a clock, staying distracted about work while he is around his family, zoning out in front of the TV, and going to sleep just to get up and do it all again the next day.

This tendency has set the bar very low for men to the point that they have become content to aspire to the mediocrity of an emotionally ignorant life. Yes, a man's need to "remain alive" always has been and always will be his most important priority. He will always need his survival instincts to be running in the background to sniff out his susceptibility to dangerous situations. The problem occurs when this survival approach becomes the **only** filter through which he looks at his life, especially in his personal relationships.

As a result of many technological advances from medical breakthroughs in treating and eradicating disease to increased worldwide food production to heightened awareness and access to healthier lifestyle choices, life in the 21st century has provided the opportunity to focus on increasing the *quality of our lives.* The challenge for any man is in the way he gives himself permission to see his life through some sort of thriving perspective beyond just doing whatever it takes to remain alive. A survival mindset rarely allows or requires any ethical, truthful, or forthright approach to decision-making in order to see that new day. In fact, honesty, integrity, and genuineness can actually get in the way of survival. But aspiring to walk the talk of *living an authentic life* that comes from knowing and feeling self-respect and personal integrity is still a mystery to most men because it requires a deeper level of emotional maturity than what is currently being taught or role-modeled by our culture.

No wonder men struggle with and are confused by how to create day-to-day intimacy with their partners that isn't just about sex. Intimacy requires an awareness of and sharing of the authentic, vulnerable, personal feelings that underlie our behavior and interactions with others. All of that goes against men's primitively ingrained hyper-vigilance to thwart any personal risk to life and limb. Remember, that *survival has less to do with staying in good health and more to do with staying alive – even if it means just barely.* Where in the culture can a man see examples of how he can do any of this differently than what men have been doing for millennia? *His parents and friends?* Perhaps. *His political leaders?* Not likely. *Celebrities in the media?* Absolutely not.

His dilemma then is this: How does he change the one thing that limits his ability to find happiness and self-fulfillment when it is the one basic thing that he believes he needs, and his culture tells him he needs, to stay alive and be seen as a "real man"? The healthiest counterpoint to his survival instinct that safeguards and promotes his authenticity, personal integrity, and self-respect is his *emotional vulnerability*. Vulnerability, however, needs to be a *conscious choice.* Otherwise, survival rules his life, and his life becomes a case of "the tail wagging the dog." When he *chooses* to be vulnerable, he can courageously open up to himself and others. This is what creates emotional safety and trust with another person. He frees himself from the prison of emotional ignorance. If he is not consciously choosing to be vulnerable and open, *his fear of being vulnerable takes over and he protects himself by retreating into his survival mentality.*

While it remains a crucial part of our humanness to protect loved ones using our survival intelligence, it is equally instinctive for us as humans to grow and flourish beyond our limited survival skills of "just getting to tomorrow." A man may not feel the same sense of gut-level urgency from this *drive-to-thrive* that he does from his *drive-to-survive,* but it still requires a shift from a focus on *quantity* (doing whatever it takes to live to see another day) to a focus on *quality* (choosing to act courageously in accordance with his True Heart). Because every man is a multidimensional being, his attention to all aspects of his personality, especially those aspects he is less familiar with, would serve him well. This role confusion is also responsible for the well-documented and inevitable train wreck that we call *male mid-life crisis.* Until men are able to transcend their limited survival thinking, they are doomed to repeat the mistakes that have led to their unhappy life conditions.

SIGNS You Are in SURVIVAL MODE

- When you finally see that there is not much difference between your survival instinct and your masculine identity;

- *When you realize that your personality is wired more for FIGHT by being: aggressive, criticizing, blaming, controlling, mean, spiteful, shaming, abusive, or lacking in empathy;*

- When you realize that your personality is wired more for FLIGHT by being: submissive, indirect, passive-aggressive, withdrawn, avoidant, victim-like, deceitful, manipulative;

- *When you realize that you either argue to prove that you are "right" (fight) or walk on eggshells in order to "not make waves" (flight), rather than resolve conflicts or differences;*

- When you finally see how your reactions to stress tend to be all-or-nothing, or black-or-white;

- *When you cannot help but personalize everything your partner says to you;*

- When you use the words "never" or "always" to describe how you or others approach any situation;

- *When you finally realize that you have had some level of fear, pain, anger, sadness, or shame in your heart that you ignore and try like hell NOT to feel;*

- When you finally realize that the painful experiences you had in your childhood still influence and color your behavior to this day.

Chapter 4

TOXIC MASCULINITY

"The tragedy of machismo is that a man
is never quite man enough."

- Germaine Greer

What I appreciate about the above quote from Germaine Greer, an Australian journalist and pioneer of the Women's Movement in the early 1970s, is that she succinctly captures how machismo confines men to the prison of inadequacy in their own minds. Healing the hole in men's hearts and souls will be challenging without first trying to identify what this quote refers to. It is the premise of this book that, as a result of the close association that has evolved over the millennia between the survival instinct and masculine identity, a type of social ideology long ago took root in men's self-concept that hinders both their *intra*personal as well as their *inter*personal development. Some of the descriptors that have come into use to define this ideology are: patriarchal, macho, misogynistic, chauvinistic, sexist, racist, and homophobic. All of these terms share similar definitions in that they refer to an aggressive, cultural bias that elevates the value of white male privilege while devaluing all others who do not fit into that category. These terms only partly describe what is being referred to in this book as *toxic masculinity*, however. There are also passive elements that define toxic masculinity. These are avoidant, timid, placating, unassertive, submissive, unresponsive, and passionless.

While a man's survival instinct is something he can never delete from his human wiring, he must become more aware of the limits it places on the quality of his life. This identity paradox is crucial for men to recognize in order to rehabilitate and modernize the foundation of a masculine identity that can reflect 21st century values. Nevertheless, the fight-or-flight filter through which a man leads his day-to-day existence is difficult to approach with objectivity. It is challenging for a man to somehow "step outside of himself" and get an objective perspective of how he acts when he gets stressed out in order to observe himself and assess the choices available to him at any given moment. The dose of cortisol manufactured by his adrenal glands in these challenging moments keeps him highly tuned in to his immediate environment in order to make a choice between either fight-or-flight.

Whenever he views his choices in that moment as being limited to either fight (move toward the source of stress in order to overpower or control it) or flight (move away from the source of stress in order to avoid its threat), he will be caught up in his kill-or-be-killed survival instinct to get through the situation. Until he can grasp how heavily he relies on that survival filter to make multiple life decisions, it will be difficult for *quality* to deliver its beauty and wisdom into his life.

While all living organisms on the planet are primitively wired to survive, the higher functioning human brain eventually learned to exercise free will and make choices for adapting to survival threats in many ingenious ways. Survival became a fight-or-flight dance that went hand-in-hand with both individual and group needs. Creative strategies of exerting dominance over others, even if there was a disparity in physical strength, were always part of the survival imperative. Inevitably, a powerful intellect became as important as a powerful body. Outsmarting a saber-toothed tiger became the best way of surviving an encounter with one. Likewise, surviving conflicts with other humans evolved into strategic exercises, as well as physical confrontations.

As the human mind developed both the light and dark sides of the human psyche, we became as adept at instigating tribal living as we did at instigating tribal warfare. Both became crucial pieces of the human survival drama. It makes sense then that fight-or-flight has played such a crucial role in shaping human personality types.

The Passive Guy

One part of toxic masculinity that I notice in men's personalities is what I call the "Passive Guy." Passivity is another version of the "flight" aspect of survival's fight-or-flight urge. There are any number of traits that describe a man with a passive personality. He says "yes" when he really means "no"; he avoids conflict and confrontation, which means he's afraid to speak his truth; he hates to disappoint or hurt others; he doesn't like to "make waves"; he has a hard time making decisions, especially weighing in on a decision that may be unpopular. He may be timid, submissive, unassertive, compliant, unemotional, detached, apathetic, uninvolved, or passionless.

Much different from "Aggressive Guy," Passive Guy is quite often disguised as "Laid Back Guy." In other words, when push comes to shove, I observe that many male clients who describe themselves as being "laid back" are actually afraid to express an opinion that might cause conflict or evoke a negative response from others. This comes up for male clients all the time as they recount to me how they have learned to just keep their mouths shut and not rock the boat when their wife or girlfriend has a strong opinion about something. These are the fellows that are quiet or say "yes" when they really mean "no." Whenever a guy admits to me that he "hates confrontation," I know it means that he's afraid to speak his truth because he hates to disappoint, anger, or hurt others. Digging deeper, what I often find is that the guy's passivity is really about *his lack of confidence in his own ability to express a different opinion than someone else's and know how to get his own needs met.* This guy often feels bowled over by his wife or girlfriend because he doesn't know how to articulate his feelings in a way that she can understand. So, here is another example of how a man's lack of familiarity with his emotional world keeps him ill equipped to express his own wants and needs in a healthy, respectful way. The "story" he then creates in his head about her is that *"she is incapable of appreciating what I need"* rather than *"I don't have the guts to say how I really feel because I don't want to deal with her reaction."*

The saddest thing for me to hear from a client is that he has learned to "eat it" because it's not worth the aggravation that usually ensues to stand up to her usually well-thought-out opinions. What I observe is that he's just reluctant to get out of his cocoon of comfort and stand up for himself because he believes that he doesn't really deserve to have what he wants and needs. In the long run, this "avoider" type of guy does not understand how much damage he does to his own integrity as well as to the integrity of the relationship by not speaking up. This is a great example of emotional immaturity and insecurity in that he conducts himself more like a wounded little boy who is afraid of the authoritative "parent", rather than being the grown, adult, mature man that needs to deal with the grown, adult, mature woman that is his wife.

I grew up as a Passive Guy. I learned early on that whatever it was I had to say from the authentic part of myself was not appreciated or valued. I also learned later on that I had a lot of internal, built-up resentment as a result of feeling that what was important to me was not important to anyone else. As an adult, I would blame others for not appreciating me, but the truth was that no one really could appreciate who I was because long ago I had stopped showing anything deep about myself. The other thing about being Passive Guy, though, was that I could never really admit that I was angry or resentful because that would go against my persona (mask). And I had put a lot of energy into convincing others and myself that the mask was the real me.

I certainly wasn't Aggressive Guy. That was my father, and I had promised myself as a boy that I would never be like him. The problem was that Passive Guy is just as unhealthy as Aggressive Guy. Of course, like most Passive Guys, I covered that persona up with another mask of Laid Back Guy. It's not that I wasn't laid-back. That has actually always been my natural speed. But I ended up using my laid back persona as a way to avoid being real with people. I avoided showing myself because I was afraid of being judged as "not enough."

The funny thing was that hiding out only kept my Inadequacy Myth of that feeling of judgment alive inside me. I never even gave myself the opportunity to be accepted for who I really was. So, even though people were not judging my "inadequacy" because I wasn't revealing it, I still felt inadequate! In living this way, I avoided dealing with the very real fear, pain, anger, sadness, and shame of my life. Laid Back Guy was my vehicle for staying in denial.

Because of this, I also sometimes became "Passive-Aggressive Guy" because the only way I could give myself permission to express my anger was by being indirect. This was as dishonest as the way my father would inflict his alcoholic rage on me. I finally realized that keeping all of my insecurity hidden from others, stable as it may have felt, also kept me from being authentic with others. Hiding out kept me from ultimately knowing whether or not my True Self had any value in the eyes of others. I disempowered myself by giving power to a lie I had bought into as a child.

The Aggressive Guy

The "fight" aspect of survival's fight-or-flight instinct produces the other part of toxic masculinity that I call the "Aggressive Guy." The personality traits that describe the character of this aspect of survival are all associated with aggression: controlling, criticizing, humiliating, hostile, violent, assaultive, attacking, bellicose, belligerent. Aggressive Guy to me is the example of pent-up, un-vented, stifled anger that is expressed at one end of the behavior spectrum as violent and abusive and at the other end of the spectrum as overly opinionated, controlling, and disrespectful. Whatever his unexamined wound was with the family situation in which he grew up, he takes it out on the people around him in his present-day life. It is this aggressive characteristic of survival's dark side that I associate with *toxic masculinity*. My belief is that this survival-based aggression that men have lived with since time began is what has also shaped and fueled the landscape of patriarchal ideology that is present around the world.

Research done in the animal kingdom on what is called *dominance hierarchy* by Harvard School of Public Health research scientist Jennifer Yeh explains the social structure that develops in groups when certain individuals are dominant over others and, therefore, able to claim access to better resources in the form of food, mates, shelter, and other desirable commodities. (Yeh, 2002) Dominance hierarchies, according to the research of psychologist and author Denise Cummins, are ubiquitous in the societies of human and non-human animals. She says that social dominance hierarchies shaped the evolution of the human mind, and hence, human social institutions. In human socio-economic and socio-political systems, dominance hierarchies include monopolies, monarchies, social stratification, caste and class systems, sexism, and racism. In each case, social, political, and economic power fall disproportionately into the hands of some members of a society at the expense of others. (Cummins, 2000)

University of Wisconsin research professor Gerda Lerner writes in her book, *The Creation of Patriarchy* (1986), that the sexuality of women, consisting of their sexual and reproductive capacities and services, was commodified even prior to the creation of Western civilization. The development of agriculture in the Neolithic period fostered the inter-tribal "exchange of women," not only as a means of avoiding incessant warfare by the cementing of marriage alliances but also because societies with more women could produce more children. In contrast to the economic needs of hunting/gathering societies, agriculturists could use the labor of children to increase production and accumulate surpluses. Men, because of their physical dominance, imposed their right to essentially possess or "own" women. Then, women themselves became a resource, acquired by men much as they also acquired land. Women were exchanged or bought in marriages for the benefit of their families; later, they were conquered or bought in slavery, where their sexual services were part of their labor and where their children were the property of their masters. In every known society, it was women of conquered tribes who were first enslaved, while men were killed. It was only after men had learned how to enslave the women of groups that could be defined as "strangers" that they learned how to enslave men of those groups and, later, subordinates from within their own societies. (Lerner, 1986)

The bottom line here is that both Passive Guy and Aggressive Guy are expressions of the dark side of a survival mentality in that they both suppress their own vulnerability. Passive Guy is just as toxic as Aggressive Guy. His passivity is just easier to handle and not as obnoxious as his aggressive counterpart. Both of these guys are afraid and emotionally insecure, which spawns jealousy, possessiveness, and the need to control a woman in order to manage their anxiety of "not being man enough". They have both adjusted to this fear and pain in different ways. One is angry and overt about proving his adequacy by not letting anyone ever screw him over. The other is quiet and timid about making waves so that he doesn't have to get out of his laid back comfort zone and actually muster up the courage to speak his mind, despite whatever response he gets. Both personality types serve as the subliminal breeding ground for patriarchal traits that have morphed into the assumed picture of what it is to "be a man".

The Patriarchal Legacy

The fight-or-flight instinct naturally organizes every species of life on earth into a survival-of-the-fittest hierarchy that is necessary to ensure the survival of that species. Animals have their own pecking order to ensure that they stay alive. Similarly for humans, a pecking order or socializing principle has evolved in us to ensure our safety and survival. As early man assembled and coordinated in a way that was focused around the survival of the tribe, it meant that the physically demanding tasks would need to be carried out by the men. They would hunt for food, protect the food stores, and protect the women, children, and elderly from physical danger. Women's survival role, however, has always been just as crucial and indispensable as men's. Women would bear the children, anchor the family social system, and gather the wild-growing food. Because women were physically not as strong as men at protecting and hunting, men took over as the brokers of power when it came to managing, systematizing, and codifying the needs of groups or tribes. This came from the instinctive drive to suppress any type of vulnerability in order to survive, so men not only suppressed this in themselves, they also suppressed it in those who were physically more vulnerable than them, i.e., women and other physically weak men. In a world where "only the strong survive," the human reliance on physical strength and authority evolved into what we call a *patriarchal* approach to organizing human society, which has also led to the domination, exploitation, humiliation, and even destruction of the physically weak and vulnerable.

Webster's *Encyclopedic Unabridged Dictionary of the English Language* defines "patriarchy" as: *a form of social organization in which the father is the supreme authority in the family, clan, or tribe and descent or lineage is determined only within the male line, by the children belonging to the father's clan or tribe.* (Webster's 2001, p. 1057) Bell Hooks is a writer, feminist theorist, and cultural critic who has written extensively on feminist issues and how women have been oppressed by patriarchal power. Her definition of patriarchy paints a more defiant picture of the cultural impact of its ideology: *"Patriarchy is a political-social system that insists that males are inherently dominating, superior to everything and everyone deemed weak, especially females, and endowed with the right to dominate and rule over the weak and to maintain that dominance through various forms of psychological terrorism and violence."* (Hooks, 2004, p.18)

This suppression of others created the hierarchy that became a significant piece of the platform upon which masculine identity developed that has been in place in every corner of the globe since humans evolved from primates. Competition evolved out of our survival instinct as a way of measuring and demonstrating that power to other human beings. Through the filter of survival, competition quite naturally ranked the order of physical prowess among men in all cultures. As another version of me-against-the-world thinking, it's telling that many men revere their competitive nature as an expression of their masculine identity. As a piece of masculinity, there is nothing wrong with wanting to be a "winner" or wanting to excel at something, especially when competing in a contest or running a business. But as an approach to working out conflict or managing differences in any kind of relationship, it more often than not creates a "win/lose" dance that: a) keeps men seeking to assert and maintain a superior attitude over others, and b) limits their understanding of how to strengthen the quality of those relationships. This is the survival paradox that I believe men have been trapped by in their limited development of masculine identity. On the one hand, a man feels the primitive urge to be physically powerful in order to survive and keep his family and tribe alive. On the other hand, if he shows any of the vulnerability along the way that is required to maintain relationships, he fears he will be deprived of power and privilege and possibly risk death. Not only has this created a hierarchy among humans for who would possess power, but it has also institutionalized the oppressive, shame-based stereotype that men of *all* races have had to "live up to" and measure themselves against.

Because of this, such terms as *patriarchal* and *macho* have become pejorative labels that apply to masculine self-concept in many cultures. For example, the term *machismo* may have its own particular meaning to any particular culture, but suffice it to say that it has become synonymous with an unhealthy paradigm where a man expresses his manliness by avoiding any and all appearance of weakness, vulnerability, emotions, or sensitivity. To do so would put his reputation of strength and power at risk. To do so would sabotage the control and authority he feels entitled to over his family or "underlings."

To do so would activate an enormous amount of internal shame and humiliation. This closely parallels the fight-or-flight mandate of a man's survival instinct to avoid risking any physical danger. It is no wonder that men have learned to trust and retreat into their heads more than into their hearts.

My survival-focused father was the poster-child for misogynist and sexist behavior. He was a product of his survival-focused, patriarchal upbringing. He could never be wrong. He could not imagine women ever being equal to men. He would lecture at me to be an honest person, but he lied about his own behavior and could never be honest about the obvious pain he inflicted on our family. He avoided showing any type of vulnerability. He was condescending and self-absorbed. He was unable to take constructive criticism, but his ever-present rage infused all of his comments toward others with judgment and disapproval.

I can look back now and see how wounded my father was as a boy at the hand of his own enraged, alcoholic father, which became the legacy he would hand down to his three sons. This wound followed him into his adulthood and into our lives. I can also see how most of the men of his generation had their own version of that same indoctrination to themselves as men. It trained me to avoid being open and vulnerable in my own life. It also trained me to mistrust men, as well as my own masculinity.

If the weapon of patriarchy is the use of strength to control and humiliate, then a man must also reflect on the extreme manifestations of human behavior that come from this need to suppress vulnerability, such as: sexism, misogyny, objectification of women, rape, sexual harassment, physical abuse of women and children, homophobia, slavery, racial prejudice, ethnic superiority, and gang violence, just to name a few. (See a more complete list of patriarchal symptoms on pages 225 and 226 of this book.) All of these demean and disempower anyone, male or female, not considered strong enough or powerful enough to warrant being feared.

Traditional masculinity has trained boys to associate their ability to survive with traits of this oppressive paradigm. The lesson has been that the stronger and more savvy the survivor, the more manly the man, and vice versa. A man learns early on that his proficiency in this realm not only conveys his high masculine status to the competitive eyes of other men, but that it is what makes him the most attractive to a potential mate. For our ancient caveman kinfolk, it was crucial for them to assimilate a level of strength, cunning, and power because they were vulnerable to many hostile adversaries, as well as to long-toothed, meat-eating predators. Both men and women were on the same page back then about how to view and appreciate each other's survival skill sets.

Not so in the modern world.

Patriarchy's Oppression of Men

It's not a huge leap to see how an ideology that glorifies power, wealth, and sex could be responsible for the oppression that women in cultures all around the world have felt. What is not so obvious, however, is how this same abusive and controlling system originating from a survival instinct has also oppressed and victimized men. I consider patriarchy to be an "equal opportunity oppressor." The confusion has been how a man can even recognize his built-in patriarchal proclivities when he has never known that his *personal sense of masculinity* can be distinguished from the system of male privilege and power that has also shaped his self-concept. *A man's blind spot is that the same patriarchal system that has been oppressing and victimizing women has also been oppressing and victimizing himself as a man.*

This in no way absolves any man from the responsibility he needs to take for any of his own oppressive or disrespectful behavior towards women. What is important for him to understand, however, is that he himself has also paid a high price at the hands of the patriarchy and, therefore, needs the motivation to aspire to something much higher than the baseline survival mentality that he calmly identifies with.

Part of the unconscious patriarchal legacy that a man learns as a young boy is to dole out this criticism to others in order to a) put himself in a one-up position of feeling powerful, which in turn b) insulates him from feeling his own shortcomings. As a result, men have great difficulty admitting when they have a fear or a lack of ability regarding anything challenging in their lives. The cultural imperative for a man is to live up to a standard of adequacy that is so unrealistic that *it is difficult for him to keep from judging himself as being inadequate* when he feels his very human limitations. This becomes the Inadequacy Myth in his head that he starts to believe about himself that is written about in Chapter 1. The way the "no wimps" mandate compels us as men to steer clear of showing any emotional vulnerability is much the same way that women are constantly bombarded in our culture by the unrealistic messages and images of what constitutes feminine beauty. If the weapon of the patriarchy is the use of humiliation to disempower the less physically strong, then the message to men from the patriarchy is *your value as a man comes from the way you dominate and control those who are less strong, especially women.*

Feminists began to use the word "patriarchy" in order to point out the way that both women *and* men were subjugated by what educator and author John Bradshaw describes as the *"...blind obedience – the foundation upon which patriarchy stands; the repression of all emotions except fear; the destruction of individual willpower; and the repression of thinking whenever it departs from the authority figure's way of thinking."* (Bradshaw, 1994, p. 49)

Bell Hooks also gives a voice to how men have been oppressed by the patriarchy in significant ways. In her book, *Feminist Theory: From Margin to Center,* she talks about how patriarchy stigmatizes men to "become and remain emotional cripples" and that "men are still imprisoned by a system that undermines their mental health." She goes on to say that, *"The first act of violence that patriarchy demands of males is not violence toward women. Instead,* **patriarchy demands of all males that they engage in acts of psychic self-mutilation, that they kill off the emotional parts of themselves.** *If an individual is not successful in emotionally crippling himself, he can count on patriarchal men to enact rituals of power that will assault his self-esteem."* (Hooks, 2004, p.32)

However, because patriarchy is an expression of fatherly or masculine authority, an easy assumption to make is that patriarchy and men are one and the same thing. But in order for both men and women to have a clear understanding of why men have become who they are, it is crucial to make the distinction between individual men and a male-dominated, patriarchal social system. This is another way of stating the theme outlined in Chapter 3 of this book of the need for men to distinguish between their survival instinct and their masculine identity.

Little girls identify with their mothers, as well as with the cultural standard of femininity, in order to get an idea of who they are as females and to feel a sense of self-worth. Similarly, young boys identify with their fathers, as well as with the cultural standard of masculinity, to get a sense of who they are as males and feel a sense of self-worth. There is no way for a young boy to avoid being influenced by the fatherly authority that the current masculine culture offers him. Whether it is considered to be "healthy" or not, he will organize his sense of how he is masculine by comparing himself to any number of different male influences in his environment and either move toward that example or push away from it. First and foremost is the influence of his father or whatever male figure that raised him. Secondly, the male peer group that he grows up around will have a significant influence on the shaping and development of his masculine identity. In the absence of either one or both of these influences in his young life, a boy will always be at the influence of his immediate family, community, or ethnic cultural standard of what is expected for a boy to become a man. Even if there is an absence of a prominent male figure in his life, that absence will also influence his personal sense of masculinity. No matter how robust a mother's efforts are to fill both parental roles when there is no father figure, a boy's masculine identity will be shaped by his father's absence.

The primary motive of patriarchal power is the use of shame and humiliation to degrade the intrinsic value of those who are less physically strong. Boys utilize this strategy among themselves to challenge each other's manliness. The more a man tries to live up to the "manly" identity prescribed by the patriarchal paradigm, the more he is capable of victimizing and oppressing others. Or he could find himself on the receiving end that oppresses and relegates less physically powerful men to a subordinate rank on that hierarchy. Either way, a man must *"engage in acts of psychic self-mutilation"* and sacrifice his own self-worth and self-respect. By living up to what has now become a stereotype of masculinity, men have trained themselves in a very strange way to act as "obedient children" to some figurative patriarchal father by carrying out this very dangerous legacy. It is a legacy that keeps men in conflict about their respect and compassion for others, and disconnected from their true nature as caring and feeling human beings. When the survival instinct of "every man for himself" gets triggered, a high quality, emotional connection with a loved one can plummet far down the priority list of what a man instinctively values.

As men, we have endured our own form of hell at the hands of the patriarchy that has carved fear and humiliation into our masculine hearts and souls. We have actually come to believe that in order for us to feel and appear manly, we must deny our own vulnerabilities, especially our emotions, to the point that we feel ashamed about that very human part of ourselves. Ironically, with this has also come the tendency to notice and criticize these attributes in others. Good examples of this are the most common judgments that we hear when boys feel vulnerable: "Boys don't cry," "Don't be a sissy," "Suck it up and be a man."

Until men summon up the courage to identify patriarchy's toxic and dangerous effects on their personal sense of masculinity, they will remain victimized by it and will allow themselves to stay under the control of its toxic ideology. Despite the ages-old patriarchal influence on men to treat women like second class citizens, doing so is actually a choice and becomes more a commentary on a man's character than the fact that he can't help himself because "that's just what men do."

It is important for men to courageously recognize the system of institutionalized gender prejudice that have given birth to the pejorative labels of "male chauvinist," "sexist," "macho," and "racist" in order to identify the worst examples of patriarchal behavior. However, since men have been the power brokers who historically have made all the rules, made all the money, and controlled social change, it has felt threatening to most men to allow such a recognition.

A survival mentality does not allow for an understanding of what a *life of quality* feels like and walks like and talks like. It does not value or prioritize the skill and virtuosity of the human experience required to assimilate self-knowledge and self-worth. As men, it keeps us bleeding from the agony of our inadequacy that reminds us of how we are "not enough."

There I was – my terrified seven-year-old self – standing in front of my boozed-up father, who was yelling at me for pissing him off because I didn't take out the trash again. The menacing look of rage on his face only seemed to intensify the stink of his alcohol breath puffing and wheezing down on my guilt-ridden conscience. I remember how I would stand there, my two hands clutching each other behind my back as my knees shook, wondering how close I could get to counting to ten on my little fingers before getting whacked. Wondering if I could get all the way to six or seven became my pathetic goal, as if achieving some number greater than two or three before he hit me would be some kind of moral victory. And it wasn't as if my actual guilt or innocence for whatever lapse in judgment I had wandered into even figured into this dance I had with him. His rage was omnipresent and ever imposing, kind of like a light switch that was permanently broken in the "on" position. This meant that I had to constantly be on "red alert." My survival radar was finely tuned to every look and nuance of his presence in our house in order to make sure I could anticipate even the slightest excuse he could use to lob his rage-grenades at me. It wasn't that I was very successful at avoiding them, however. I was a typically inquisitive kid, but my questions and curiosity only seemed to provoke his impatience with my lack of knowledge about life. Somehow, he expected me to already know the answers to my own questions about the world, and my questions meant that I was "stupid," as he had no problem reminding me. Thinking that I could control his alcoholic spewing was part of the self-centered delusion I constructed for myself as a way to survive the misery. I essentially had to break the switch for my own survival radar wiring into the "on" position as a way of coping with that constant threat. "Survival mode" became my default approach to every aspect of my everyday life.

I had many moments of those "not enough" feelings throughout my childhood. I know now that I was feeling the shame of inferiority as a 5 year-old of not wanting my parents to know that my body was in pain from appendicitis; as a 10 year-old listening to my father slur his disapproval at me in front of my friends; as a 15 year-old hearing my girlfriend tell me that she liked another boy; as a 17 year-old hearing my basketball coach tell me I wasn't good enough to make the school team; as a 20 year-old struggling to keep my grades up in a university *curriculum I didn't belong in. The "failings" of my young life seemed to haunt me like a ghost determined to keep me from forgetting my lack of value – especially as a man. Otherwise I would be smarter, richer, stronger, handsomer, and sexier. I would not have weaknesses, limitations, struggles, questions, and dilemmas. Because I was at best inconsistent with **any** of those traits, I put on my own mask of what I thought would appear masculine to others. Not surprisingly, it was a survival mask fashioned from the toxic world that I grew up in.*

SIGNS You LACK COMPASSION for Yourself and Others

- When you realize that there is a part of you that believes the lie that you are "not man enough" or "not good enough" and therefore "not lovable enough";
- *When you realize how you verbally criticize others for not living up to your unrealistic expectations of them;*
- When you compare yourself to others and judge yourself negatively as a way of beating yourself up;
- *When you are more invested in winning arguments and being right rather than being open to learning from other people and being respectful of their different opinion;*
- When you cannot seem to "let go" of resentments/ grudges toward others;
- *When you hold others to a standard of behavior that you yourself are not willing to live up to (double standard);*
- When you verbally "beat up" others rather than try to put yourself into their shoes and imagine what might be going on for them;

- *When you realize that the quality of your Life is controlled more by the critical voice in your head than by the compassionate voice that comes from your True Heart;*

- When you feel the need to justify your choices and convince others of the value of those choices, rather than trusting what you know to be true for you in your own heart.

The Toxic Personality

While any number of traits can contribute to a toxic personality, there is a specific personality trait that I have observed in men that serves as a "vehicle" to accommodate a toxic version of masculinity, which is *narcissism*. According to the *Diagnostic and Statistical Manual* of psychological disorders, the narcissistic traits of a person include:

1. Has a grandiose sense of self-importance.
2. Is preoccupied with fantasies of unlimited success, power, brilliance, beauty, or ideal love.
3. Believes that he or she is "special" and unique and can only be understood by, or should associate with, other special or high-status people.
4. Requires excessive admiration.
5. Has a sense of entitlement.
6. Takes advantage of others to achieve his or her own ends.
7. Lacks empathy.

8. Often envious of others or believes others are envious of him or her.

9. Shows arrogant, haughty behavior. (DSM-V, 2013)

An important distinction must be made between having a few of these narcissistic personality traits and having what is referred to as a Narcissistic Personality Disorder (NPD). Most people have a few of the self-centered tendencies that show up on the above list. However, the diagnosis of NPD occurs when a person shows a pervasive pattern of grandiosity, the need for admiration, and a lack of empathy as indicated by five or more of the above traits. According to the DSM IV-TR, between 2% and 16% of the population in clinical settings (between 0.5-1% of the general population) are diagnosed with Narcissistic Personality Disorder (NPD). Most narcissists (50-75%, according to the DSM-IV-TR) are men.

We must also carefully distinguish between the narcissistic traits of adolescents, which can be seen as an integral part of their healthy personal development, and the full-fledged disorder. Adolescence is about self-definition, differentiation, separation from one's parents, and individuation. These inevitably involve narcissistic assertiveness, which is not to be confused with Narcissistic Personality Disorder. (Vaknin, 2007)

San Diego State University psychology professors Jean Twenge and Keith Campbell write: "*Narcissists don't have a problem with everyone, or with people that are different. They have a problem with people who may reject them. They have a problem with heterosexual women, because those are the people who might see through them, reject them and not give them the attention and adulation they feel they deserve.*" (Twenge & Campbell, 2009)

Not surprisingly then, narcissism is associated with a number of interpersonal problems. Although people scoring high in narcissism make positive first impressions, people interpret them more negatively in long-term social interactions.

Two by-products of narcissism that provide fuel for the misogyny that remains in our culture are *exploitative-ness* and *entitlement*. An illustration of this came in the form of a tragic event that occurred on May 23, 2014, when a 22-year-old man with a sketchy mental health history decided to express all of his personal rage through a misogynistic rant that ended in mass murder and suicide. He aimed his twisted agenda against University of California Santa Barbara college co-eds. He blamed them for not being attracted to him enough to want to date or have sex with him and for desiring other men over him – men he deemed to be not as desirable as he. Ultimately, he killed six people and wounded 13 others before shooting himself in the head. The 141-page manifesto that he left behind painted a stark picture of a man who hated women, as well as the men they were attracted to. (Ellis and Sidner, CNN, 2014) He apparently could not help but feel victimized by women's lack of interest in him, which ran counter to his narcissistic fantasy of feeling entitled to exploit women sexually. He believed that he had a right to expect women to view him as the object of their attention and sexual desire, and when that did not happen, he elevated himself even further to believe that it was his right to annihilate them and their snub of his desirability. Was his pathological behavior a result of his twisted, misogynistic masculine identity, or was it a result of his unstable mental health? His was a lethal convergence of misogyny, mental illness, and access to guns. To attribute this heinous act solely to mental illness or a lack of gun control misses the opportunity to address the most toxic piece of the puzzle, which is to start talking and educating people about how alive and kicking the patriarchy still is in the 21st century.

While his "mental illness" may ultimately be shown to have influenced his choice to pick up a gun and murder people, the misogynistic chip on his shoulder was sick enough to explain his shockingly deadly behavior. The sexist vitriol that he spewed in his manifesto was an exaggerated version of the cultural misogyny that pervades everyday life in America and most of the rest of the world. Even the argument that would question whether this was an act of blatant misogyny, given the fact that four of the six people he shot and killed were male, is misplaced. The point here is that those four men were just as much victims of misogyny as the two women he murdered. As I have articulated previously in this chapter, patriarchy is an equal opportunity oppressor.

The problem is that the everyday sexism/misogyny that a man lives with is supported by his ignorance. Every day, women are on the receiving end of catcalls, leering, groping, and objectification by men. Every single day, women must be on survival red-alert in order to anticipate any possible sexual harassment or violence when they walk to their cars alone in a parking garage or walk down the street at night or get grabbed or poked or prodded in public by strangers who are physically larger and stronger. There are even so-called "pick-up artists" on the internet who advise men who are desperate for companionship on how to get a woman's attention in ways that use physical force and disregard gaining her consent. (Collins, 2014)

It misses the point for men to react merely from a personal rationalization of "not all men" do this. *Women understand that not all men do this.* The point for men to understand is that the cultural and global misogyny/sexism that the legacy of male privilege has kept alive for thousands of years still exists to this day, and it plays itself out in ways that men need to pay attention to in order to help change it.

There are many more examples of this type of tragedy that occur in our culture that could be enumerated here, but the point is that men must become more aware of how their attitude toward women affects how much women feel safe around them. Men can be insensitive when it comes to empathizing with what women go through regarding their own survival needs in certain situations. For example, a man rarely needs to have a contingency plan in his mind regarding where he walks, what he wears, what time of day it is, or how he scans for people who approach him to assess a level of threat. A woman on the other hand always has to take all of this into consideration in order to avoid a potential physical assault that could happen anywhere at any time. Men (including myself) do not understand how oppressive this is, but it is indeed the sexist type of masculinity that men "live up to" that has provoked this much of a survival response in *all* women.

Dysfunction is the ongoing dynamic of a *toxic relationship.* Any relationship that has either physical or emotional abuse as any part of its dynamic is by definition toxic. The type of individual who needs to exert complete power and control over the other is a toxic individual. The type of individual who allows him or herself to be overpowered and controlled by the other is a toxic individual. This type of relationship parallels more of a parent-child interaction rather than an adult-adult partnership, where both people share power. It is not unusual for couples to struggle at times with issues of one being overly controlling of the other. However, in the case where one person absolutely insists on being in control of all or most aspects of the relationship, the toxicity of this kind of dysfunction launches the couple into dangerous territory that creates aggression, drama, and abuse.

Healthy relationships are environments that offer emotional safety and trust for either individual to be authentic and vulnerable. A healthy relationship provides mutually respectful treatment that is loving, kind, and compassionate. On the other hand, toxic relationships are dishonest, distrusting, and insecure, and they tend to leave people feeling unsafe and manipulated.

The Hostile Statistics

As long as men are emotionally immature, they will struggle to empathize with what women endure regarding everyday survival. This is because men are not at physical risk everyday the way that women are. For a man to listen accurately to what a woman's fear and rage are about requires two things from him: First, he must listen to her pain without becoming defensive and attempt to put himself into her shoes for a moment to wonder how she must be feeling. Second, he must have a conversation with himself, and ideally with other men, as to how and what he can do to fight this ideology of male privilege and power that is deeply embedded in our society. If we as men don't speak up to the change that we each need to make, we *are* each a part of the problem, whether or not any of us have ever raped, harassed, or abused a woman.

The following are the gory statistics for any who wonder if the patriarchy is truly still alive and well today:

- More than 1 in 3 women will experience rape, violence, and/or stalking at the hands of an intimate partner in their lifetimes.
- 85% of intimate partner violence victims are women.
- About 3 women are killed by their partners every day. 1 in 13 murder victims are killed by their intimate partners.
- Domestic violence is the leading cause of injury to women between the ages of 15 and 44. One in 6 women with bone or joint fractures is a recent victim of abuse.
- Violence is often paired with controlling behavior: Women whose partners are jealous, controlling, or verbally abusive are significantly more likely to report rape, physical assault, and/or stalking from their partners.
- A domestic abuser who has access to a firearm is more than 7 times more likely to kill his partner.
- Between 2009 and 2012, 40% of mass shootings started with a shooter targeting his girlfriend, wife, or ex-wife. In nearly 60% of mass shootings during the same time period, the gunman killed a current or former spouse, partner, or other family member. In at least 17 incidents, the shooter had a prior domestic violence charge.
- The leading cause of death for women at the work place is homicide, most often at the hands of an intimate partner.

- While the rate of intimate partner violence declined by 64% between 1994 and 2010, most of that decline came before 2001, and since then, the decrease has slowed and stabilized, while the overall crime rate has kept dropping.
- Domestic violence support services get more than 75,000 requests for assistance on a typical day, but in 2013, they had to turn away more than 9,000 people as a result of budget cuts. (CDC, 2011; NCADV, 2014; NNEDV, 2013)

Go to the Dark Side

Like it or not, ALL humans have a dark side – even you. This does not mean that you have a vicious or savage facet to your personality (unless, of course, you do). It merely means that you have more than likely had emotional experiences of fear, pain, anger, sadness, and shame in your lifetime that you have ignored rather than attempted to heal. Avoiding these feelings has been *exactly* what you have been trained to do as a man in order to demonstrate your manliness, so it is more the rule than the exception. However, denying these feelings has also compartmentalized a part of yourself away from your awareness of your personal identity. It is called the "dark side" or "shadow side" because you do not let it see the light of day. This means that until you bring these emotional experiences to the light of your understanding and knowledge, they will continue to shed darkness onto your life in many ways that you are not yet capable of controlling. Staying ignorant of your fear, pain, anger, sadness, and shame empowers all of these feelings to exert control and influence over your day-to-day life. Your lack of emotional awareness is what keeps your blind spots in place and makes your life feel unfulfilled and miserable. Having the *willingness* to explore and embrace the unhealed wounds that these feelings represent in order to heal them will bring to light all the ways that they keep your life small.

Looking at your dark side first requires you to access the courage you may have come to believe you don't have. Embracing our dark side inevitably uncovers the depth to which we feel "not enough". This feeling of inadequacy is at the heart of our insecurity, and it has become the repository of our ignored fear, pain, anger, sadness, and shame. Until we "lean in" to understand and forgive the moments in our life when we felt scared, hurt, angry, sad, and ashamed, we will be stuck in our *not enough-ness*. You'll know you've accessed your courage when the tail is no longer wagging the dog, i.e., when your unexplored dark emotions no longer keep you from living a courageous life. This will empower you to face all of your adult responsibilities and relationships in honest and honorable ways.

❖ ❖ ❖

SIGNS of Your Own TOXIC MASCULINITY

- When you realize how oblivious you are to your own emotional world, which undermines your self-respect, integrity, and self-worth, and also keeps you emotionally reactive to others;
- *When you realize that your lack of emotional maturity keeps you powerless in relationships and severely limits the courage*

and honesty needed from you to be a trustworthy, fully-participating adult partner with the woman you love;

- When you realize how much the unhealed wounds from your childhood of fear, pain, anger, sadness, and shame put you at risk for bouts of depression and anxiety;

- *When you realize that your emotional ignorance makes you incapable of feeling empathy and compassion for yourself and others;*

- When you realize how this emotional immaturity has spawned the oppressive treatment of others in the form of misogyny, sexism, racism, and homophobia, and how this may have shaped some of your own personal beliefs and judgments about people who are female, different color/culture, different sexual orientation, and different religious belief.

Chapter 5

HEALTHY MASCULINITY, HEALTHY MEN

"You have to grow from the inside out. None can teach you,
none can make you spiritual.
There is no other teacher but your own soul."

- Swami Vivekananda

The fact that men have evolved over many millennia ignoring the value of personal emotion that lives in their True Heart speaks volumes about the psychological detour that has defined masculine identity through the filter of survival. Ultimately, the fight-or-flight mentality has made it difficult for men to appreciate their own uniqueness from a place that is not ego-based. It also explains why men have struggled to modernize the definition of masculinity so that it accurately reflects the beauty and wisdom of the male soul.

Many manly traits such as physical strength and dominance, competitive superiority, and financial accomplishment demonstrate a man's suitability for female attention. These are the traits that men seek to augment in their personalities if at all possible. Then, there are the "unmanly" traits that men avoid, such as wincing from pain or cowering from fear or tears from sadness – all expressions of emotional vulnerability.

This avoidance of vulnerability is what *keeps men from knowing the authentic and genuine truth that is a unique expression of who they are.* This is how men avoid exploring what is in their True Hearts. Having a limited understanding of what a man actually feels is also what hinders men's ability to empathize with others, because empathy requires an ability to relate to what another person might be feeling at any given moment.

Work Life/Family Life Imbalance

One of the paradoxes I consistently observe is how a man will bust his backside to work long and hard hours at his job, only to feel unappreciated when his wife or girlfriend complains that working so hard keeps him from spending quality time with her and with the family. On the one hand, he feels he is "doing his job" for the survival of his family. On the other hand, he feels hurt and undervalued for *being the kind of man that he learned how to be,* which doesn't seem adequate or "enough" for his loved ones if they complain about his lack of participation in family life.

Typically, when a man gets feedback that he is somehow "not enough," he instinctively does what feels manly, which is to *try harder by doing more to keep everyone else happy.* In addition to all of the tasks he already has at work, he may also try to accommodate the requests from his family to spend more time with them. Because he has only a limited amount of time and energy, it becomes more and more difficult to fit all of it into his busy schedule. The model of traditional masculinity that men access in a moment like this does not offer ways to take care of themselves physically, emotionally, intellectually, or spiritually.

Instead, it will compel a man to dig the hole of stress deeper by trying to "do more", all the while not revealing his stress and pain to his loved ones because that would project an image of him being "not enough" or inadequate as a provider.

This level of pressure can only be internalized and sustained for a limited time before it starts to "leak out" onto the people around him in the form of frustration and anger. His dilemma is that any distraction from "doing his job" of taking care of everyone around him would be more evidence that he is inadequate as a protector/provider. By the time he realizes that he has succeeded in taking care of everyone in his life *other than himself,* the collateral damage to himself and to his emotional connections may already be transparent to everyone but him.

Men and the Process of Change

When it comes to the evolution of a man's identity over the course of his lifetime, two important environments shape his personality. He is a product of the external influence of the people and cultural milieu he was raised in, as well as the internal, personal reality that has been his mental, emotional, physical, and spiritual makeup. He has a need to express all of this as a way of *being himself.* As he grew up, the nexus of these external and internal influences combined to give him a sense of his unique, authentic personhood.

He has also had to contend with the inescapable passage of time that has forced both his body and his mind to mature and thus, change. These changes represent the maturation that every human being must adjust to and embrace as a part of life. Change represents growth. Discovering how a person's unique identity can benefit from the process of change, however, is what maturity is all about.

The change that comes from deeper emotional maturity guides a man closer to knowing his authentic self.

What feels tragic and unnecessary is how a man's *emotional world* is not considered an important enough aspect of his personality to warrant just as much attention and awareness as his physical and mental worlds. Clearly, a man's emotional intelligence has effectively been "trained out of him" by a legacy of masculinity that has normalized the avoidance of emotional vulnerability as a manly trait. The best reason for a man to change is from his desire to grow, *not* from the pressure or politics of "trying to please others." As was expressed earlier, the process of personal change is synonymous with the process of personal growth. One cannot happen without the other. If a man avoids being emotionally open and vulnerable, there is no way he will learn about who he really is beneath the mask he wears and how to appreciate the gifts he was born with. Without this depth of self-knowledge, he will not possess the ability to make an authentic, emotional connection with another person, and he will be severely limited in his ability to empathize with and have compassion for others.

A man must demonstrate this change or new type of behavior *for himself,* whether or not anyone else is aware of it or can appreciate it. Legendary UCLA basketball coach John Wooden said, *"Character is who you are when no one is watching."* It is a man's responsibility to himself and his loved ones to define his character around speaking the truth from his True

Heart. By facing the fear that would normally make him avoid vulnerability, he gives himself the gift of knowing his own courage.

The survival mentality that a man lives his life through on a day-to-day level keeps him playing more of a "role" equated with *what he does*. Living authentically from his True Heart is a much deeper expression of *who he is*. Shifting away from this survival approach to everyday life is not easy, and does *not* mean that he has to delete it from his consciousness, as if it were even possible to do that! We all need to have access to our survival skills every day of our lives to be okay out in the world. But a man can learn to distinguish his survival skills from his healthy masculine traits so that he can then familiarize himself with the vulnerability needed to be honest and real. He can do this at the same time that he protects and provides for his loved ones. That will only happen, however, once he gives himself permission to stay connected to his True Heart while also maintaining access to his survival nature whenever he needs it. I am not saying be one way or the other. I am saying a man can and needs to be both.

The challenge for men to change is in a) objectively identifying the repercussions of the self-centered, fear-based elements that define traditional masculinity, and b) courageously defining a new version of masculinity that includes emotional maturity. A new zeitgeist every few generations forces human beings to awaken from their slumber of ignorance. Though change is never easy, the male side of the human psyche equation is desperate for liberation from its ignorance, and the growth that is called for today offers the hope of freedom for men.

Transformation vs. Stability

Answering the Wake-Up Call outlined in Chapter 2 and making the choice to change is the first important step for each man toward creating a healthier version of masculinity for himself and for the planet. Waking up to the need for change starts men on a pathway into the heart that, while unfamiliar at first, will receive so much positive reinforcement that they will be able to keep their eyes on the prize of a deeper experience of authenticity, personal integrity, and self-respect. This path will also, however, reality-check their need for a quick fix, because this is the path of the adult, mature man who understands the importance of making tough choices that initially may create short-term-pain that inevitably leads to long-term-gain. Changing for the "right reasons" will, at times, challenge every man's resolve to change at all. However, the rewards of taking this leap of faith into the territory of his heart are well worth the risks. When talking about the process of change, it is important to point out the difference between the two types of change that are possible.

First-Order Change

First-order change refers to doing either more or less of something we are already doing. It is behavioral change, which means that it is always reversible and non-transformational (Bergquist, 1993). Because first-order change is an alteration in behavior only, it merely creates stability. This is also called "change without difference." (Goodman, 1995) First-order changes can be implemented from a person's current knowledge and skill set, which means that there is no new learning curve necessary. For example, changes in day-to-day scheduling of drop-off and pick-up of kids, meal times, family vacations, or date night are all reversible and changeable without a need to acquire new skills. Change like this is necessary when busy lives are dependent on the cooperation of all members of a team.

Second-Order Change

Second-order change is a decision to do something significantly or fundamentally different from what has been done before. The process is irreversible. Once you begin, it's impossible to return to the way you were doing things before. (Bergquist, 1993) Second-order change is a new way of seeing things. It is change that not only affects a part of the system, but also changes the system itself. (Watzlawick *et al*, 1974). Second-order change is what we call *systemic change* wherein a comprehensive, fundamental alteration in values, beliefs, culture, and behavior at all levels of a system occurs. Second-order change represents transformation to something quite different than the previous condition. (Waters *et al*, 2004) The importance of knowing the difference between these two types of change cannot be overstated. First-order change relates to creating stability, while second-order change relates to creating transformation. This is illustrated by the often-quoted proverb: *"Give a man a fish and you feed him for a day; teach a man to fish and you feed him for a lifetime."*

Consider the example of how a man's willingness to move from first-order to second-order change can make a huge difference in an intimate relationship. A client I will call Emmett came into my therapy practice because his wife had threatened to leave the marriage if he did not "get professional help." After she threatened for months to leave the marriage, he finally agreed to come in to see me. In our first session, he began to paint a picture of the relationship for me. I learned that he and his wife had been having communication problems off and on throughout their 15-year marriage. He admitted that his wife's major complaint about him had always been that he rarely, if ever, shared any kind of emotional details or experiences about his life with her.

When Emmett was a child, nobody in his family talked to each other that way, so he was always confused about how to carry out his wife's request. Over the years, as she asked – even begged – him to share more of himself with her, she became more critical as he remained quiet. He said he felt "henpecked" and unappreciated by her for how hard he worked to support the family. This all reached a painful peak in their relationship when a year before he came to therapy, he became flirtatious with the wife of a couple in their circle of friends. This woman returned the flirtation, and they ended up seeing each other a couple of times on the sly, although he insisted it was non-sexual. Emmett's wife caught wind of this dalliance from one of their other friends, and she confronted Emmett and the woman, demanding that their extramarital activities stop. Emmett swore to his wife that he and this other woman only talked to each other and never got physical. He admitted to me that he felt like he could talk to this other woman about personal things that he could not share with his critical wife. Predictably, Emmett's wife was heartbroken, and he felt ashamed and remorseful about his behavior. He promised to never contact the woman again.

In the meantime, Emmett's wife's anger and feelings of betrayal intensified, and she became even more critical of him, despite the fact that he honored her request to stop seeing the other woman and despite the fact that he tried to convince his wife he wanted to make their marriage work. These efforts were Emmett's attempt at first-order change to repair the wound he created in his marriage. Justifiably, his wife needed something much more substantive from him than promises she knew he could break at any time.

He became more frustrated because he felt that she should appreciate his effort to follow through on her conditions and automatically trust him again. He could not yet understand that what she needed was to trust that he was changing at a deeper, systemic level. What she needed was for Emmett to be more forthcoming about the reasons for his behavior, not because it was what she wanted, but because he was growing enough to want to share himself with her at that deeper level. She needed to trust that he could speak to her from his heart rather than just from his head. He had no way of knowing what this meant.

Like my other client, John, it became obvious that Emmett was in my office only to placate his wife so that she would stay in the relationship and stop complaining. By coming to see me, Emmett was still attempting to demonstrate his trustworthiness to his wife by using first-order change. This type of change was simply behavioral, which meant it was also reversible. He could at any time stop coming to therapy and not be in conflict with that decision. The only change that had occurred up to that point for Emmett was saying "yes" to coming to therapy instead of "no." He had not yet gotten his Wake-Up Call.

Understanding that what his relationship needed was for him to participate in a deeper and more authentic way, I let Emmett know in the first session that unless he could find some reason to be in therapy for himself and his own personal growth, his therapy sessions would have little to no value to him. Some men are relieved at this suggestion and admit that they have known for some time that they needed help but were too ashamed to admit it. As it slowly sinks in for a client that he might actually gain something from therapy that could make him happy and fulfilled, he starts to see the importance of switching to a second-order approach to regain the trust of the woman in his life. This is a moment of deeper awareness that quite often becomes the man's Wake-Up Call.

Emmett's deeper moment of awareness came as a result of his wife moving out of the house. Because she sent him a concrete message, he finally experienced his fear, pain, anger, sadness, and shame in a concrete way. He could see that he was only changing in a way that he hoped would get her to "settle down" and quit nagging him. Once she moved out, he saw how shallow his efforts had been. He began to see the trust-building process as requiring more than just changing his behavior to placate his wife's anxiety. He started to understand that there was something missing in his own value system that made it okay for him to cheat on his wife in the first place. Although this was new territory for him emotionally, he began to see how it could not only make him a better partner to his wife, but also help him hold on to his personal integrity as a man. If a client is truly motivated to change, he will embrace this approach and stay in therapy to learn more about himself and what motivates his behavior. If not, he will leave therapy after a short while.

As a man "wakes up" and gives himself permission to dive deeper into second-order change, the journey toward his True Heart begins. He learns how to see the events of his entire life story through a different filter – one of compassion and empathy, rather than one of criticism and judgment. He can look back and appreciate not only the successes that have helped him feel good about his innate abilities, but also the losses he has endured throughout his lifetime. He can begin to feel gratitude for the preciousness of every moment he breathes. The painful lessons of life offer him the perspective of learning what choices have worked for him and which ones have not. Embracing his human-ness means that, while he may make decisions that sometimes fail, he is not a failure. In other words, feeling his inadequacy at doing any one particular thing, which all men feel sooner or later, does not mean he is inadequate as a man.

In reviewing these pivotal moments in his life, he learns to feel compassion for himself as he accepts that he made the best choices he was capable of making at the time. This offers him *the opportunity to forgive himself* of his transgressions throughout his Life that he has previously chastised himself for. It also gives him *the opportunity to forgive others*. Of course, men need to also understand that forgiveness has less to do with letting someone else "off the hook" and more to do with freeing themselves from the agony of having been taken advantage of or overpowered. Forgiving others is a way for a man to free himself from the prison of victimhood and reclaim the power he felt was taken from him.

What this requires from men, however, is a very unnatural thing to them. The freedom that results from forgiving himself and others demands that he *embrace* – rather than avoid – the fear, pain, anger, sadness, and shame that his choices have created over the course of his lifetime. To be able to integrate all of these very human feelings by *leaning into them* is what frees him from the prison of his denial and ignorance. Learning the life lessons from these so-called "negative feelings" gives a man the opportunity to finally "fill out" the whole emotional range of his heart and soul. In doing this, he hopefully discovers the value and beauty of his True Self by learning the unique landscape that is his emotional world, both the dark side as well as the light side. It is from this humble awareness that he can begin to bring a deeper, authentic version of himself to the woman he loves and become emotionally present in that relationship.

Developing an Objective Perspective

The process of second-order change requires a degree of objectivity from us in order to be able to "see ourselves". If we could take a couple of steps out of our bodies, then turn around and look back at ourselves, we would be able to observe our behavior and the motivating forces behind that behavior. Witnessing ourselves from a distance gives us an *objective perspective* about how we are thinking, feeling, and behaving at any given moment, but also can help us to recognize similar experiences from the past that have shaped our personality.

For example, it is very common for a client who experienced physical or emotional abuse in his youth to become emotionally

131

triggered today if there is even a hint in his life of someone treating him in an aggressive or abusive way. Helping him gain an objective perspective of himself helps bring to awareness the fight-or-flight defenses that keep him shut down emotionally in his present-day life and relationships. As a result of this awareness, he can develop the ability *to choose to stay open emotionally* and connect with loved ones rather than shut down and isolate.

Another way of learning this objective perspective is to get feedback from a helping professional who is trained to observe these patterns in order to help you make sense of this new emotional awareness. It is crucial for you to know when you are behaving from a place of authentic awareness and truth versus from the *cultural expectations* you have integrated into your personality about what "being a man" means. This kind of emotional awareness and vulnerability may elicit memories of a whole array of feelings and experiences that you may have done your best since childhood to "sweep under the rug" and try to forget. For instance, if your anger and frustration usually get triggered when you feel inadequate and unappreciated by the woman you love, you might end up questioning the viability of the relationship. Without some kind of objective perspective or feedback, your fight-or-flight impulse could be to leave her without ever learning the value of navigating that moment in a healthier way. While this can be the catalyst for a couple to decide to get into couples counseling, most men are reluctant to start the therapeutic journey to self-awareness on their own and commonly enter therapy at the urging or threat from a loved one. This is part of the first-order change versus second-order change intention that must be understood and explained at the beginning of therapy. As I have said, a man's participation in learning how to change his behavior in a relationship must come from his desire to change himself from the inside out (second-order change) rather than *for her* from the outside-in (first-order change). Despite however demanding and unfamiliar this may be for him, it's the key to developing emotional maturity as well as a healthier version of masculine identity.

The Importance of Self-Care

An important thing that a man needs is to learn how to *take better care of himself,* but this does not usually show up on his radar screen until he feels the impending doom of an imminent loss. This is a moment that he is constricted by his lack of knowing an alternative role model for masculinity that includes self-care as an active trait. And because self-care requires a degree of emotional maturity, this is a very common dilemma for men who identify with traditional masculinity traits.

What I mean by self-care is the effort a person makes to attend to his or her own personal well-being and overall health at physical, mental, emotional, and spiritual levels. All four of these essential aspects of the human condition need to be shown caring attention in order for a man to achieve balance in his personality. Surprisingly, when I ask the men in my private practice whether or not they feel like they know how to "take care of themselves," they answer affirmatively. However, when I ask what it actually means for them to take better care of themselves, they inevitably describe the maintenance of their physical bodies and mental capacities. When I point out that there may be a lack of balance in their lives because they are unaware of and ignore their emotional makeup, they reluctantly concede this but remain skeptical of the value of such awareness. When I suggest that this lack of attention to their emotional health may be having a negative effect on their day-to-day happiness, they give me a look that is both skeptical and curious. This tells me that they are caught between the potential shame of revealing themselves and the potential relief of what I am suggesting.

It is a novel perspective for any man to consider that the way he treats or mistreats the person he loves as being a reflection of his own internal sense of self-worth and self-respect. Unless men give themselves permission to take care of their own emotional and spiritual health, they will forever be limited in how they create emotional and spiritual intimacy with the people they love.

My suggestion that men need to integrate self-care more into their definition of healthy masculinity will automatically be at odds with traditional masculinity. It's important to understand that the self-care that feeds a man's heart and soul is completely different from the narcissistic self-focus that feeds a man's ego. They are at opposite ends of the spectrum of what masculine identity could be. One is healthy, and one is toxic. The self-centered, ego-based model of traditional masculinity extorts a huge personal price on a man's self-worth. It keeps him emotionally and spiritually disconnected from himself. It keeps him imprisoned by the fear of inadequacy that haunts his self-confidence. The edict of traditional masculinity for men to "be enough" by dominating others in any number of ways is also what makes them insensitive partners and keeps them clueless about how to create emotional intimacy with a woman.

Self-care is a much different thing than being self-centered. Being self-centered does not require any kind of courageous risk-taking that reinforces a person's self-respect. It's actually a way to hide out and avoid revealing a man's True Heart. As a result, being self-centered allows a man's fear of inadequacy to keep him small, invisible, and out of integrity with himself on the inside while wearing a different mask on the outside for others to see. Self-care, on the other hand, demands that a man has the guts to speak his personal truths – even in the face of disagreement or criticism – in order to create an environment on the outside that is a reflection of who he is on the inside.

Often, a man's ego thrives on "being all he can be" because he's a great problem-solver. Yet, in moments that it is necessary for him to be accountable for his shortcomings, his self-centered ego can become fearful of being seen as inadequate because he in fact does make mistakes and does not "have all the answers". Rather than taking care of himself by opening up and admitting his limitations, if he shuts down, distracts, lies, or uses his anger to gain control of a situation, he misses an opportunity to really take care of himself by building trust with others. A man's emotional honesty is the most important thing that his loved ones can hear from him because it is *the* thing that maintains mutual trust and respect in a relationship. When a man holds his integrity to be a non-negotiable part of his character, he does the absolute most he can do to take care of himself and of his loved ones.

What Men Need – Without Being Needy

This brings us to the topic of the importance of knowing the difference between what a man *wants* and what a man *needs*. Because men avoid the vulnerability required to feel emotions, they also avoid identifying/recognizing the essential emotional needs all humans have – including their own. Men are very much aware of the *physical needs* that make up their personalities. *Just because they may be unaware of – or in denial of – what their emotional needs are does not mean that they don't have emotional needs.* These emotional needs are just as crucial to a man's daily life as are his physical and intellectual needs. The challenge is to distinguish an emotional need from being emotionally "needy." There is a huge difference, but because men actively avoid emotional vulnerability in the first place, they in essence "have no choice" but to relate to their emotional world in immature ways – one of which is to be emotionally needy. What this means is that men relate to their fear, pain, anger, sadness, and shame in the way an insecure, emotionally-deprived child would – which is to approach a loved one with an expectation that it is that other person's job to soothe the unmet needs of that child. *Being needy* means we have the expectation that it is someone else's responsibility to alleviate the stress of our feelings.

Having needs is a whole different thing that has little to do with another person and absolutely nothing to do with being needy, but it's a really important aspect of human personality that must be acknowledged and dealt with in a healthy way. All humans have the basic needs of feeling safe, feeling loved, feeling valued, feeling connected, feeling joy and happiness, feeling a part of something bigger than themselves,

136

and feeling that their lives have meaning. Expressing any of these needs requires vulnerability and reveals an important piece of a person's emotional make-up. Expressing a need does not mean that someone else has the responsibility to fulfill it. Expressing a need simply reveals a piece of personal truth. It's an authentic utterance of a person's insides that bestows the inner beauty of one person to another. When men learn how to express a need without succumbing to their shame and their aversion to vulnerability, what they will get in exchange will be a wonderful gift of courage and self-respect. Bringing those needs to an intimate partner requires that a man:

1) wake up enough to explore his own world of feelings and needs,

2) bring that world to his partner and learn how to represent it and stand up for it,

3) be interested in and ask her about her world and what she needs,

4) work with her to create a shared world that represents both of their interests/truths/needs and supports an equal partnership.

It is also important to distinguish between a *want* and a *need*. Often in their effort to find happiness, my clients make great strides toward attaining the things they *want* in their lives without necessarily attaining the things they need. *A "want" is something I aspire to have that fills an empty space in my external, **material world***. Many men base their sense of self-worth on accumulating material things that are an indication to them and others of success. Acquiring "stuff" plays out the survival imperative of providing for family and loved ones that can definitely add to their sense of happiness and well-being. The limitation is that until a man can identify and strive to achieve *what he needs*, there remains a confusion and lack of contentment about his so-called "life purpose." There is certainly happiness to be gained from acquiring what he wants in the external world. But the real challenge comes during his mid-life years when he wonders why he has an empty feeling in his gut about what his life has been about.

*A "need" is something I aspire to have that fills an empty space in my **heart and soul**.* A need is a response to feeling some unsettling emotion like fear, pain, anger, sadness or shame. Revealing a need or admitting to an aspect of one's life that feels unfulfilled is, by definition, a vulnerable thing to do. This is the biggest difference between a need and a want. For example, I may *want* to win the lottery, but what I really *need* is the security and stability that winning a lot of money would bring. On the outside, I may *want* a successful career, a big new home, and a happy family, but what I really *need* is to feel the love, safety, and self-worth that those things would provide for me on the inside.

As a man becomes more aware of his own emotional world, he automatically becomes more aware of his own wants and needs. This then gives him the capacity to *empathize* with the woman he loves. His ability to put himself in her shoes for a couple of minutes and at least wonder what is happening for her emotionally comes from him having a familiarity with his own feelings. Again, learning how to articulate his unmet needs shifts him from focusing his attention on something he lacks in his environment to revealing an emptiness or void that lives inside of him. When a man shares such an honest picture of his True Heart, *this gives him the capacity to better understand hers.*

But to even suggest this scenario runs totally contrary to what toxic masculinity has taught men to believe about what it means to be manly. The mistake a man makes is to assume that he already knows "what women want" based on cultural cues he has decoded from his everyday life. This usually means he focuses on a woman's material wants (as opposed to her needs) in order to "win" her affection. When she ultimately realizes and articulates that her emotional needs are not being addressed, his feelings of inadequacy get triggered because he has never been aware of the importance of knowing the difference. As a man starts to identify the landscape of his own emotional world, he will be become more and more adept at creating and sustaining an emotional connection with the woman he loves.

The Need for Emotional Maturity

The truth is that everyone has his or her own unique experience of reality that is different from everyone else's on the planet. No two people will ever have the exact same experience or interpretation of the exact same event. The specific fusion of circumstances and events that each man experiences starting at birth serve to construct a framework of feelings, passions, and beliefs that define his unique personality. This serves as the *personal truth* that is as inimitable and specific to each and every man as are his fingerprints. When I work with male clients and help them reframe the full range of their feelings to represent an expression of their distinct personal truth, it somehow "gives them permission" to become vulnerable to feeling those feelings. My belief is that personal truth is an organic assertion of emotional maturity that serves as the core of Healthy Masculinity.

When we talk about emotional maturity and emotional intelligence, these interchangeable terms refer to character traits that traditional masculinity has never embraced and offered men as a standard to live up to. As a result of this, men have learned to avoid knowing a crucial piece of their reality by ignoring their emotional world. This lack of familiarity and comprehension of emotion is another way of describing *emotional immaturity*. This lack of maturity automatically creates a life of emotional reactivity where a man cannot help but feel defensive and criticized when getting feedback about his behavior. Because this defensiveness triggers his survival instinct, he is more likely to experience this as an attack on his character or as a lack of appreciation for his efforts. Emotional maturity on the other hand would give him an ability to be less reactive in order to explore the underlying emotional reasons that motivated his behavior.

Without emotional maturity, there can be no authenticity, personal integrity, or self-respect in a man's life.

This would give him the opportunity to be accountable for his behavior in a mature, adult way, rather than in a childish, self-justifying manner. Qualities like accountability, emotional honesty, personal integrity, personal truth, authenticity, empathy, dignity, self-respect, self-worth, and self-esteem have never been part of the definition of what it means to "be a man" from the perspective of traditional masculinity.

The above qualities are impossible to integrate into a man's sense of masculinity as long as he unconsciously lives his life through a survival filter. Ironically, all of these qualities already exist in a man's True Heart. They can only be accessed, however, through the emotional awareness and vulnerability required to explore the whole range of what is possible for him to feel in his heart. This includes not only his feelings of happiness, joy, pleasure, and well-being, but also his feelings of fear, pain, anger, sadness, and shame.

Salovey and Mayer first formulated the concept of *emotional intelligence* in 1990. They defined it as "the subset of social intelligence that involves the ability to monitor one's own and others' feelings and emotions, to discriminate among them, and to use this information to guide one's thinking and actions." (Salovey and Mayer, 1990, p.187) They came up with a model that identified four different factors of emotional intelligence that involve the abilities to:

1. Accurately perceive emotions in oneself and others, including non-verbal signals such as body language and facial expressions.
2. Use emotions to facilitate thinking and help prioritize what we pay attention and react to.
3. Understand emotions and realize that the emotions we perceive can carry a wide variety of meanings.
4. Manage and regulate emotions and respond appropriately to the emotions of others. (Salovey and Mayer, 1990, p.195)

In 1995, psychologist and *New York Times* science writer Daniel Goleman wrote a book called *Emotional Intelligence* that makes a strong case for emotional intelligence as the strongest indicator of human success. He asserts that people with high emotional intelligence tend to thrive more at balancing their lives between work and play, as well as between meaningful relationships and flourishing careers. (Goleman, 1995)

Men's lack of emotional intelligence has, unfortunately, created a lame stereotype of masculinity that is highlighted in the media in degrading ways toward men. We see men portrayed as immature, bumbling oafs who are inept when it comes to matters of the heart and only have clichéd appetites for sports, sex, and beer. Many men willingly accept this stereotype because they've been culturally trained to set the self-awareness bar very low by believing the myth that emotions are "what women do." This is a cop out, and it is disrespectful to women when men talk about emotional expression in this condescending way. What's more important, however, is that this is a sad sign of *a man's lack of self-respect.*

It seems reasonable to expect 21st century men to no longer be blindly influenced by the propaganda from previous generations of men who would question a guy's manliness simply because he might feel a need to "talk about his feelings" or get tearful in a genuinely sad or happy moment. Does a man's dread of being thought of as a "pussy", that misogynistic epithet all men fear to hear, grip his self-concept so much that he chokes in shame about all the ways he knows himself to be less than adequate? Is his nostalgia for John Wayne or other kick-ass hero types his attempt to hold onto some ideal his father wanted for him that never played out in reality? How is it okay that the phrase "men's emotional intelligence" is ignored and snickered at instead of becoming some piece of a man's ambition for personal excellence? Does he really think so little of himself as a man that he is somehow not capable of feeling and expressing his true, authentic feelings? Or that showing the courage – yes, the balls even – to stand up for what he feels and believes in is somehow less than manly? The importance of striving for and embracing emotional maturity/intelligence cannot be overstated. Without it, a man's self-respect and *his ability to love others are severely undermined.* In fact, it becomes difficult, if not impossible, to achieve.

A Man's Emotional Awareness

Emotional maturity comes as a result of a two-part process: 1) How a man finds the interest and motivation to identify the emotional "components" of his heart. 2) How he finds the courage to become vulnerable and openly share those feelings with someone he trusts and loves.

Emotional Maturity = Emotional Awareness + Emotional Vulnerability

Though many men struggle to gain an awareness of what they feel, it is possible for them to identify some type of emotion as a result of their interactions with other people when they finally pay attention to their "insides". This first step is very challenging for guys who rely primarily on their intellect in order to live a life that is logical and rational. However, once they make an effort to "get out of their head" and "into their heart", they discover that they can indeed begin to keep track of and feel the fear, pain, anger, sadness, and shame of many experiences over the course of their lives. As a man's emotional awareness begins to awaken, one of the biggest challenges will be for him to allow himself to *feel emotion* without judging himself as being weak or inadequate.

Because one of the myths about manliness is that emotional intelligence is not as valuable as mental intelligence, men grow up being emotionally unconscious and, therefore, emotionally immature. This bias created the stereotype that emotion is the non-logical human stuff better suited to feminine sensibilities. Because emotion is something that cannot be "solved" or "fixed", it is easier for men to gravitate to the joyful, peaceful, pleasurable, fun-loving end of the human emotional spectrum. As a result, men make the mistake of assuming that their responsibility to creating a life of happiness depends upon their ability to focus their lives toward that one end of the spectrum, toward the so-called "positive" feelings while avoiding the so-called "negative" feelings of fear, pain, anger, sadness, and shame. While it makes sense to want to live a happy and positive life, it also means that men inherit a limited capacity to handle uncomfortable feelings other than to rationalize avoiding them. It also means that men have very artfully evolved a lifestyle that avoids confronting the truth of the whole range of their emotions. And, of course, the price men pay for buying into this myth manifests when they try to create emotional intimacy in a relationship that has grown past the initial sexual chemistry. While it is challenging for my male clients to identify their feelings, most of them at least have a working knowledge of their anger. Getting them to explore their fear, pain, sadness, and shame is a bit of a stretch, but inevitably they allow themselves to get in touch with the life experiences that have elicited those feelings.

A Man's Emotional Vulnerability

The second requirement of emotional maturity is even more challenging than the first. Emotional vulnerability exposes a man's "insides" in a way that reality checks the mask or persona he normally shows to the world. By revealing what he feels, a man paints an accurate and real picture of who he is in his True Heart. *Showing a feeling is the same as divulging a piece of personal truth.* This is a courageous act that demonstrates a level of understanding and acceptance that a man has of his very human existence. By giving himself permission to do this, he "shows up" in a fully present and authentic way in his life. In this way, a man takes charge of his feelings rather than allowing his feelings to take charge of his life. This is what emotional maturity is.

Unless a man knows the whole range of his emotional world, he will not understand how his fear, pain, anger, sadness, and shame can cause him to avoid both conflict and connection with the woman in his life. For example, as I wrote about in Chapter 1, shame has a huge influence on a man's feelings of being "manly". Whether or not a man grew up with childhood experiences of feeling inadequate, if he feels criticized or judged as an adult, chances are high that the sting of embarrassment and humiliation will draw him back into his "cave" to lick his wounds. These moments of feeling inadequate that trigger the pain of his shame – of not feeling "good enough" or "man enough" or "love-able enough" – are what shape a man's decision to be vulnerable or not to others. It becomes a choice to either fight-or-flee in reaction to this pain. Unless he can learn to handle this moment differently, i.e., become vulnerable to someone he trusts, he will miss an opportunity to connect to that other person by expressing the pain of his shame, which is the best way for that pain to heal. If this is already an unhealed childhood wound stuck in his psyche, this lifelong pain more than likely has shaped him into being a very proficient "survival guy" who is stuck in his head and avoids his heart. This makes him more likely to create a codependent dance with his partner.

Research professor and author Brené Brown writes about the benefits of *vulnerability* in a very articulate and understandable way. She says that vulnerability *"...is not weakness. Vulnerability is the core, the heart, the center of meaningful human experiences."* (Brown, 2012) It is no exaggeration that most if not all of my male clients have a very limited understanding of what emotional vulnerability actually is – much less how to do it. The act of being vulnerable is the conscious choice to put aside all pretense and persona in order to reveal or share a very personal, authentic piece of personal truth to others. What makes revealing this truth feel vulnerable is that it is usually a feeling that comes "from the heart." It isn't an intellectual thought "from the head." It isn't a judgment or criticism of another person. It isn't an intellectual discourse of advice offered as a solution to someone else's problem. It is a confession of our imperfection. It is an admission of our fallibility. It is a declaration of our human-ness. For humans, there is a huge difference between what lives in the head and what lives in the heart. Usually, what is shared from the head reveals little about who a man is or what he is experiencing or feeling. The feeling of vulnerability is a genuine attempt at being real or "naked" with another by disclosing some unique or even intimate, personal, emotional experience about oneself that would not otherwise be known by that other person. It's usually some aspect of a man's fear, pain, anger, sadness, or shame, but it can also be his joy, hope, pleasure, or happiness. I have learned that *expressing what I feel inside my heart is also a simple and direct statement of who I am as a man.* And it is this type of openhearted disclosure that lies at the core of what I refer to as *self-care.* It isn't only a sign of vulnerability. It is also evidence of a level of *emotional maturity and self-awareness.*

So, the challenge from the *outside in* for a man has always been the indoctrination by his culture, family, and community into the belief that showing vulnerability is a sign of weakness and inadequacy. The challenge from the *inside out* is how to trust that the experience of emotional vulnerability could have value for his sense of masculinity. He will only begin to retrain his awareness to include this deeper type of honesty if he understands that it is in his best interest to show deeper parts of himself. Because of their emotional immaturity from having been taught as boys that knowing their feelings has no value, it is difficult for men to manage the shame that is triggered by that feeling of inadequacy. This shame is powerful enough that it shuts him down to any type of emotional openness.

It is a sad thing when a man hides behind his mask of invulnerability during moments of stress in a relationship, thinking that this is his best option. I understand that my suggestion to open up and be vulnerable as a remedy to relationship angst is completely counter-intuitive to what we have been taught to do as men, but growing up emotionally is the best thing a man can do for himself and his relationships. Hiding behind a mask requires no courage at all and automatically creates distance with others. The short-term gain of this approach is never worth the long-term pain that it creates. This is where men fumble the ball when it comes to figuring out relationships, because it inevitably leads them to living a lonely life.

As my clients explore and define their unique and authentic feelings, one of the more important object lessons I address is the "personal price" they pay by staying attached to this very limited survival perspective of themselves. They are protectors and providers who focus on a myriad of things-to-do in order to be effective, such as *"I've gotta make money, I've gotta find shelter, I've gotta feed my family, I've gotta have all the answers, etc."* But this lack of vulnerability creates a version of masculine identity that is more like an emotionally immature child than of a mature, adult man. This lack of emotional maturity weighs heavily on the identities of adult men because it prevents them from managing their adult lives and their adult relationships as just that – mature, adult men. It keeps men locked in their grown adult bodies while functioning emotionally as little boys. The irony is that the cultural standard that supports ignorance of emotional honesty in order to appear "strong and manly" is exactly what trains men to remain as wounded little boys. The really scary but obvious fact is how this version of masculinity is still used today to organize political, social, and economic power. The learning curve here for men is that this cultural myth not only leads them away from knowing their own True Hearts, but it also fails to train them how to recognize and understand what others are feeling.

As I look back on my childhood, I can see how my lack of emotional maturity was shaped by the way I had learned to mistrust my feelings.

Nowhere in my environment was there a role model who showed me the importance of my emotional world. In fact, the environment I was surrounded by taught me: a) to avoid feeling my feelings because that is "what women do," and b) to be wary of any male who was emotional because it more than likely meant that he was a "queer." This misogynistic, homophobic version of masculinity taught me to feel superior to anyone who would not conform. The irony, of course, is that in the meantime, I had a raging storm of fear and pain and anger and sadness and shame brewing inside me that I kept to myself to avoid the humiliation that would have been heaped upon me by my family and friends if I were to ever reveal it. I had no vocabulary to express whatever emotional intelligence I may have been capable of.

Unfortunately, the confusion that came with not knowing what to do with the emotional storm inside me redirected all of my unexpressed emotions toward my self-concept. By not expressing the feelings outwardly, all I could do was grit my teeth, hold them in, and let them kick me in the ass every day of my life until I got the Wake-Up Call. My self-worth took the hit. I lacked self-confidence. I had no idea what to really believe in other than what I was told to believe. Being raised in the Catholic Church also seemed to dovetail quite easily with my fear and guilt-based upbringing since the Church has been the bastion of patriarchy for over 2,000 years.

My parents, teachers, and others preached to me about how important it was for me to "tell the truth," but these were also the same people who said one thing and did another. They judged and criticized the truth as I saw it. For years, I was angry at how they treated me, but that kept me in a victim mentality that got me nowhere. As a boy, I was taught in many different ways that it was crucial for me to AVOID my emotional world. My father demonstrated that to me by never showing me any emotion other than his anger. My mother supported that by not ever expecting any emotion from him other than his anger. My friends, relatives, teachers, and coaches thought nothing of humiliating any male of any age – including myself – who cried or displayed emotional vulnerability. The movies, television, radio, newspapers, books, and magazines that influenced my life all supported the same message that "real men" are defined by their lack of emotional awareness and expression. As a result, I felt inferior, isolated, unfulfilled, and figured that that was all I could expect out of life.

Here's the part that confused the hell out me throughout my childhood: Despite how personally criticized or humiliated I felt by my parents, I also knew that they loved me. I knew that they were showing me love in the way that love had been shown to them. I knew that my father was being the man that his father had taught him to be. I knew that he felt it was his job to pass that on and teach me the same lessons. I knew – despite his need to drink in order to dull all the pain he felt from his own Inadequacy Myth instilled from an abusive, alcoholic father – that he was doing the best he could with what he knew to be true. This helped me forgive them once I became an adult, but I grew up with a very mixed message from my parents of how worthy I was of their admiration and love. At the time, I also knew other kids who had it much, much worse than I did.

At the age of 35, I realized that the wounded, immature Little Boy inside me (that I call "Henry") was unfortunately large and in charge of my adult life. So I started looking and asking for help. I read books, I went to seminars, I got into my own personal therapy, I joined men's groups, and I learned how to be okay with the fact that I didn't already know everything there was to know about being a man. As a guy myself, I relate to how difficult it can be to respond whenever someone asks me to share what I'm feeling. Like most guys, I had no *way of grasping the underlying feelings of my life experiences. I was great at talking about my life at a surface level, but I didn't know how to identify and articulate how important events really affected me in my heart, guts, and balls. Until I entered into my own therapy, I had no conscious understanding of my fear, pain, anger, sadness, and shame — even though I know I experienced them all throughout my life in different situations. Today I can look back and see how scared I was of any kind of deeper contact with other people because I did not know myself nor did I like myself very much. I even remember a job interview I had at 28 years old that at the end of the interview the woman told me that I did not once look into her eyes throughout the whole interview. Even that comment did not sink in till years later when I was able to see how scared I had been my whole life to give anyone an opportunity to really "see me". I knew nothing about my True Heart. Because I had such a lack of emotional knowledge and maturity, not only was the mask of masculinity that I wore mundane and uninteresting, but this lack of self-awareness also severely limited my ability to create a deeper, intimate connection with a woman. I can look back on my young adult years and see that this deficit of self-knowledge more than likely made me a very boring relationship partner with very little to offer in the way of personal perspective of my life experiences.*

Today, I'm actually grateful to everyone who influenced my personality the way they did because it created a fire in my belly to know and speak my truth without needing anyone else's approval. By realizing how deep of a personal price I paid by subverting my uniqueness to their criticism, I now see how my patriarchal upbringing has given me a fierce perspective on how NOT to treat other human beings. It also has taught me that the cultural indoctrination of what constitutes masculine identity is in serious need of conscious retooling.

<u>SIGNS</u> You Avoid Being <u>EMOTIONALLY VULNERABLE</u>

- When you realize that your need to avoid conflict or confrontation by keeping quiet is actually because you are too afraid to hurt, anger, or disappoint others by speaking your Truth;

- *When you realize that your lack of openness is a sign of a lack of self-respect and a lack of courage because of your unwillingness to let the people you love see the "man behind the mask";*

- When your embarrassment about something causes you to hide out from being seen as inadequate;

- *When you recognize how strongly you advocate against using "emotion" by which to make decisions;*

- When you realize you have little familiarity or understanding of your fear, pain, anger, sadness, or shame, much less the guts to show any of it to your partner;

- *When you believe that showing emotion to be a "feminine" trait or a sign of weakness;*

- When you rage at someone without also letting them know the fear, pain, anger, sadness, or shame that put that rage inside you in the first place;

- *When the "story" in your head about her is that no matter how much you bust your ass, it will never be enough for her.*

❖ ❖ ❖

The Need for Authenticity, Personal Integrity, and Self-Respect

The natural by-product of emotional immaturity is a lack of authenticity, personal integrity, and self-respect. Therefore the best reason for a man to "grow up" emotionally is to explore and define his own experience of these qualities. Gaining an appreciation for these qualities will in turn help men bring new substance and value to the definition of masculinity that can reflect a higher moral code of behavior to himself and others. As a man challenges himself to see his life experiences and observations through the filter of his True Heart, he will personify this higher "man-code".

AUTHENTICITY - is the quality of being genuine, reliable, trustworthy, and real. It is a reflection of an emotionally relevant and responsible way of life.

PERSONAL INTEGRITY - is the quality of being honest and willing to stand up for the strong moral principles that define one's uniqueness.

SELF-RESPECT - is having pride and confidence in oneself. It is a commitment to oneself to behave with honor and dignity.

As I have said, a man's emotional ignorance keeps him in the dark about his internal moral compass. His authenticity, personal integrity, and self-respect are the core values that define his character and real self but are only accessible through his True Heart. Because of this, it is incumbent upon a man to learn how to take a stand for his essential core and "claim" this distinctive piece of his personality. Of course, he must do this without imposing it onto others; without keeping it hidden from others; and without expecting anyone else in the world to agree with it or even like it. It is his and his alone to value, because if he doesn't believe his core values to "be enough", no one else will either.

One of my main challenges as a clinician has always been how to motivate a client to follow through with new behavior after he leaves a session and goes home to his wife or girlfriend. This is a prime example of the need for second-order change on his part. In other words, following through on his commitment to change *for himself* depends upon his courage to interact differently with the people he loves. If he is still afraid to disappoint or anger others when he speaks his truth, he is still finding his way to face the fears at home that he came into therapy to address.

Of course, any new behavior is not without its shaky moments. On the one hand, a man's authenticity, integrity, and self-respect are how he connects with his True Heart. On the other hand, there is still the part of him that he grew up believing was not worthy of love and admiration either from his parents, his peer group, or his community. This internal battle is actually a good sign, because it challenges a man to clearly see the difference between his old identity and the new one he knows he must attain in order to set himself free from the paradoxical prison. This is the reason it is difficult for my male clients to follow through when they leave my office. Their childhood fears/wounds still unconsciously run their lives. They are: a) terrified of bringing their True Heart forward because this puts them at risk to b) feel another awful experience of rejection and unworthiness if there is any form of criticism or judgment from their loved ones for being real.

Even *the possibility* of that happening challenges him to either avoid vulnerability or to be consciously courageous.

I think most of the men who walk into my office are looking for something similar, which is to quell the lifelong demons that haunt their hearts and minds. Once a man is able to see that his childhood wound has created his Inadequacy Myth to believe he is "not enough", he can start to see why he avoids vulnerability or confrontation or walks on eggshells or feels helplessly henpecked. His journey then can become less focused on trying to change his wife's criticizing behavior and more about trying to see at a deeper level how he: a) still does not believe that his flawed, imperfect self is worthy of love or "man enough" to be loved, and b) is still afraid to show this part of himself to others. Soon enough he learns, however, that to finally, truly feel loved in this lifetime, *he must find some way to take the risk and show her his True Heart.* Otherwise he will forever wonder whether or not she truly loves him for being the authentic but imperfect, mistake-prone human that he is, rather than the inauthentic masked-man he has always shown her.

When he finally understands what is really at stake, he will start to see how the reward of risking vulnerability is a way to live from his True Heart. Again, this in no way is about him somehow "proving" to her that he is lovable. His worth, value, and lovability as a man are just facts. *He does not ever need to justify or rationalize or convince anyone about any piece of his True Heart for any reason.* While it may feel good to get the approval of others, it is important for him to *rewire his belief* that his value as a man comes from being approved of and acceptable to his parents, friends, and loved ones. This only created his codependency on others rather than creating a trust of the unique authentic voice that lives in his heart, his guts, and his balls. The rewiring involves switching his sense of self-worth to come more from the inside out than from the outside in.

But this is a slow process that first requires he do a lot of individual work on himself to strengthen his foundation of self-worth and self-esteem. Once he gets emotionally stronger, he can start to have conversations as an emotional equal with the woman he loves in which they can agree on how to create a safe environment for *both of them* to become emotionally vulnerable with each other. From this point on, the stage is set for him to venture forth and take the risk of bringing more and more of his True Heart to her. It also is what I believe to be the transformation necessary to turn toxic masculinity into healthy masculinity. (*Note: There are just two situations besides psychopathy in which I have seen this NOT work, i.e., long term infidelity and unaddressed childhood sexual abuse in the history of either partner.)

What I learned in my own childhood was that – because my parents were not capable of understanding the genuine and real kid I was – I was always confused about who I was at a genuine and real level. Despite them warning me to never lie, I can look back now and see that I was always lying in some way, shape, or form about who I was. When I wore my mask of being the "good boy", they accepted me. So, even though I know now that they showed me love in the best ways they were capable of, I grew up believing that my True Self was not lovable. Therefore, I had no reason to trust or value my integrity. As a survival-wired guy, I learned to morph my personality into someone more suitable to the sensibilities of others in order to obtain their approval. I believed that as long as I wore my mask and didn't disappoint others, I would be worthy of their and someone else's love.

*This is, of course, my childhood wound. In my adulthood, I have come to realize that the one thing I really need in order to heal that wound is to truly believe that I **deserve to be loved for exactly who I am without my mask** – even with all my flaws, deficiencies, shortcomings, and defects. But it has also been the thing I have feared the most to explore because being authentic and keeping my integrity makes me vulnerable and puts me at risk. If I show my authentic, genuine, True Self, I run the risk of perhaps feeling the pain of rejection and criticism like I felt from my parents – only this time it would be from my wife. This would not only be devastating to me, but it would also prove that my parents were right! So, the risk of being vulnerable by living life from my True Heart is formidable.*

Discovering and embracing my integrity forced me to take the risk to see if my authentic, yet flaw-filled version of myself was indeed worthy of someone else's love. Even though I knew that my wife loved the "real me" (otherwise, why would she have married me?), I could feel a deep fear that if she knew all the parts of me that I myself didn't love, she would jump on the rejection bandwagon and bail. It has required deep vulnerability from me to show her my True Heart – the part of me that my parents rejected. Thankfully, she has seen the real me and assured me that she is not going anywhere! In the field of psychology, we call this having a "corrective experience." Because of this corrective experience, I not only trust now that she truly loves me "warts and all", but more importantly, I have learned that even if she did not love me, that the authentic guy that I truly am is deserving and worthy of love.

SIGNS You Are OUT OF INTEGRITY With Yourself

- When you realize that you expect the woman you love to just know – i.e., read your mind – as to what your needs are in a relationship because you either don't know or are too afraid to tell her;

- *When you realize how much you walk on eggshells around your partner because you are afraid to hurt her or piss her off or disappoint her;*

- When you realize that you are more invested in telling her things that will impress her or get her to love you, rather than speaking your Truth;

- *When you realize you have a belief about love where you think it's your job to "make her happy" in order to "prove" that you are worthy of her love;*

- When you realize you have become okay with ignoring (selling out) your own wants and needs in order to placate her so she will quit complaining and view you as being "good enough/man enough/lovable enough";

- *When you "stay in your head" and try to rationalize only by logic the reasons you live your life the way you do;*

- When you use the smoke screen of "being a positive guy" as a way to avoid having the guts to talk about your fear, pain, anger, sadness, and shame with her;

- *When your use of alcohol, drugs, food, sex, gambling, or work become sedatives for you to tranquilize your dark side;*

- When you use the smoke screen of *"I'm just being honest"* as an excuse to judge and criticize others, instead of saying how you really feel;
- *When you use the smoke screen that "She won't listen to me" – i.e., agree with you – as an excuse to justify not being truthful with her;*
- When you consider the possibility that you may have some amount of misogynist, racist, and/or homophobic prejudice inside you, but are too afraid to admit it to yourself or others.

STAGE ONE of a Man's Maturity:
Identity vs. Confusion

Because the men who come into my practice span the whole age range of decades from 20s to 80s, I have had the opportunity to observe the developmental stages of maturity for these men as they explore their masculine identities. Ninety percent of the men who come into my practice are there initially to address their relationship issues with or without their female partners present in the room. It becomes obvious, however, that their relationship problems not only come from their lifelong history of troubled relationships, but also from the combination of their individual personalities and the emotional blind spots as men that they have accumulated over the course of their lives.

I appreciate the model offered by developmental psychologist Erik Erikson in the 1950s on the psychosocial development of human beings as a framework to help men explore and construct a healthy expression of masculine identity. Erikson believed that a person's identity is impacted and shaped by social experiences throughout a series of eight stages across the whole lifespan. He is probably most famous and notable for coining the phrase "identity crisis." (Erikson, 1950)

According to his theory, human beings experience conflict throughout their lives, and they have the ability to either grow or fail as they deal with those conflicts. Each of the eight stages he proposed represents opportunities for a person's identity to either mature and prosper or struggle and decline. Erikson's model of the human life cycle serves as a template for the male clients in my practice as they embark on a journey toward emotional development. In particular, three of Erikson's eight life-cycle stages provide a chronologic and strategic "map" for a man to grasp the big picture of his emotional world. (Erikson, 1959) These three stages orient him to: a) where he has come from, b) where he is right now, and c) where he is going, in the pursuit of his emotional development.

For my purposes, Erikson's stage of *Adolescence* (12-18 years) will be referred to as "STAGE ONE of a Man's Maturity" because it includes the age when adulthood begins, which is late adolescence. "STAGE TWO of a Man's Maturity" (*Young Adulthood*, 18-40 years) will be explored in Chapter 6 of this book, and "STAGE THREE of a Man's Maturity" (*Middle Adulthood*, 40-65 years) will be explored in Chapter 7. These three stages are not only broad enough to cover the predominant age range of my clientele, but they also span the developmental issues that men struggle with throughout the course of their adult lives from adolescence through young adulthood all the way through middle age. Each of these stages poses a specific existential question, and the answer provides a "snapshot" of a man's emotional maturity.

While the age ranges mentioned above provide a general framework for each stage, they are not hard and fast definitions. More important than the age of the individual is the way he tackles the developmental question that helps him to achieve clarity at each stage. A man's experience at any particular stage is also highly dependent upon the way he has answered the existential question from the previous stage.

"Who Am I?"

According to Erik Erikson, the ideal time frame for a male to explore and uncover his personal identity and authenticity is during his adolescent years. This is the time of life when a young man needs to reexamine his sense of self and investigate his independence. In figuring out how an adolescent fits in to society, he must find a way to come to grips with the insecurity and confusion that are a part of transitioning from childhood into adulthood. (Erikson, 1968, p.128) His experimentation with roles, rules, and social expectations help him to establish a direction for himself in life, as well as a sense of his uniqueness. This is why the major existential question of the adolescent stage is *"Who am I?"*

Ideally, if a young man is allowed and supported to explore this new phase in order to discover what feels authentic and true to his own sensibilities, he will form a strong sense of self, as well as independence and control. If not, he will more than likely develop an identity crisis or "role confusion." This happens when his lack of identity and independence makes him question who he is and where he fits in society, as in *"I don't know who I want to be when I grow up."*

This is the stage of a young man's life when he starts to pay attention to his gender identity and all the social expectations he must conform to in order to show that he "fits in" to his male culture. These social cues come from his peers, his family, and from the traditions and values of masculinity in his community that have been handed down for many generations. One of the confounding pieces of masculine identity that men struggle with, however, is the fact that developing a true sense of self requires an honest, authentic expression of his feelings, not just his thoughts. In other words, as I've said, a man's true identity lives in his True Heart, not in his head. As a boy is taught to ignore what is in his heart, he is kept from knowing who he really is as a man.

Because boys grow up in a culture that shames them for vulnerably expressing the reality of their emotional world, it's rare that boys truly achieve a healthy and compassionate sense of masculinity during adolescence. This is confirmed to me on a daily basis in my psychotherapy practice when I talk to male clients of every age who report that during their adolescent years, they were taught a lot about how a man achieves strength through having power and control in his life. On the other hand, they were taught almost nothing about how to achieve strength by being vulnerable and having compassion for others. Whenever I ask a client if he ever asked himself the question, *"Who am I?"* at **any** point in his life, I am met, almost without exception, with a quizzical look as if I had just said something in a foreign language. I point this out to highlight the fact that this same unanswered question, and what it represents, haunts men for the rest of their lives until and unless they proactively address it.

Being unaware of his identity also puts a man at risk of not knowing "who is driving the bus," so to speak. As a metaphor, I liken the act of driving a bus to how a man manages his daily life. If his life is "the bus," it becomes crucial to know exactly which part of his personality is doing the driving, i.e., making the daily decisions of his life. When it comes to making choices about his adult life, it behooves a man to make sure that the mature, adult part of him is "driving." For example, his relationship with his wife is an adult relationship that needs the mature, adult part of him, the Mature Man, to participate and partner with her in their decision-making. Undoubtedly, when he feels stressed out or exhausted, the immature, child part of him, the Little Boy, tends to "take over" the interactions and decision-making with her. At this point, just as easy as it would be to guarantee that a child trying to drive a bus would crash it, so goes the parallel for the immature boy in any man trying to make adult decisions in his marriage, in his career, or in any of his adult responsibilities. This is why it is crucial for a man to know his authentic self so that he can consciously make adult choices and avoid "crashing the bus" in his adult endeavors.

It's also important, though, for a man to know when to allow the young and immature part of himself to inform his choice making. For example, when he allows himself the time to have fun and relax, it can be very rewarding for the Little Boy part of him to "come out and play." Both the boy and the man are integral parts of any man's personality/identity. There is room for both on the bus that is his life, but it is crucial for him to have the adult aspect of his personality "driving the bus" that is his adult life. This is why it's important for a man to know the difference between his mature and immature natures, which further informs him about the answer to the question, *"Who am I?"*. Just as it would have been unrealistic for me to expect my young daughter to be able to take on adult responsibilities, a man cannot expect this immature, naïve, reactive, wounded part of himself to be able to make responsible, healthy adult decisions about his life.

This brings us back full circle to the importance of self-care by noticing how a man's decision-making can come from either the part of his personality that is mature and capable or from the part of him that is immature and reactive. The former will lead a man to what is in his own best interest. The latter will more than likely elicit a fight-or-flight reaction from a survival stance. He needs to ask himself: *"Is it the Mature Man in me who is driving the bus that is my life? Or is it the wounded Little Boy?"* The challenge for men that I observe is how this lack of self-knowledge creates confusion about how to relate to a personal experience of masculinity. Does a man relate to masculinity through the filter of the Little Boy, which takes him directly back to the old paradigm of traditional masculinity? Or does the Mature Man strive to explore and embody some new version of masculinity that originates in the authenticity, personal integrity, and self-respect of his True Heart?

Despite this conundrum, it is most important that men continue to ask themselves the question *"Who am I?"* for the rest of their lives. I say this because asking the question is more important than figuring out the answer. The mistake that I find most people make when wondering to themselves *"Who am I?"* is that they quickly come upon an answer and then stop asking themselves the question. This locks them into a definition of themselves that does not continue to evolve and grow. As a man continues to ask himself this most important question, he will always stay open to learning about a new piece of his identity. Ongoing personal growth is the true nature of human evolution.

As a man comes to know himself better, he quite naturally will become more capable of creating higher quality relationships through this bigger and better version of himself. The foundation for any healthy relationship requires the balanced health of both individuals. Until now, emotional health has not been a potent or accessible ingredient for men to bring to relationships. As Erik Erikson theorized, bringing a deeper knowledge of one's self to a relationship helps create mental, emotional, physical, and spiritual intimacy in an exceptional way. The next chapter will explore how this healthier version of masculinity can help create deeper intimacy between two people.

❖ ❖ ❖

The 7 Signs of an EMOTIONALLY MATURE MAN

1) I no longer worry about pleasing my parents or living up to their expectations of me. I have more of an adult-adult relationship with them now and am able to have empathy and compassion for them because I see the very human flaws that have created each of their own Inadequacy Myths.

2) *I now understand that the version of masculinity taught to me by my father was synonymous with his survival instinct.*

Therefore, by inheriting his "legacy of masculinity", I have limited my own experience of being a whole person by negating and ignoring what lives in my own True Heart. I did this as a boy because I could not prevent my need-to-survive from defining me as a male the same way that my father's need-to-survive defined him.

3) My authenticity, personal integrity, and self-respect have become more important to me than maintaining any kind of "mask of masculinity" to get another person's approval or love.

4) *I accept that my emotional world is the doorway to my authenticity, personal integrity, and self-respect, which requires my courage to both explore and express.*

5) I have learned that my willingness to be emotionally vulnerable – challenging as it may be to sustain – helps me create closeness and trust in my relationships.

6) *I accept that knowing and sharing my emotional world not only takes care of my relationships, but it is also one of the best ways for me to take care of myself.*

7) I understand that the one thing I need the most – *which is to believe that I am worthy of being loved even if no one else loves me* – is also the one thing I learned to avoid figuring out because I've been too afraid to risk being rejected if I show someone the "real me" that lives in my True Heart. Because of this, I have relied heavily on my survivor mentality to "get by", but have also consistently kept true intimacy and love away from me in order to avoid feeling that potential, devastating pain of rejection. Because this is my absolute worst fear, the most courageous thing I can do is to make a

choice to live my life beyond my fight-or-flight prison by risking to let someone see my True Heart in order to feel truly seen and loved – flaws and all – by that other person.

Chapter 6

HEALTHY MASCULINITY, HEALTHY RELATIONSHIPS

"When the power of love overcomes the love
of power, the world will know peace."

- Jimi Hendrix

Retooling masculinity into something healthier is challenging enough, but how to bring that newer male perspective to an intimate relationship is another thing altogether. As social expectations evolve to expect men to appreciate their emotional world, they must bring this new perspective to their partners as a way to *participate emotionally* in the care and feeding of the relationship. Traditionally, men have deferred to the woman's emotional sensibilities to "carry the load" for the emotional side of the relationship. While women have played their part in allowing this to become the status quo of most relationships, it also has been a way for men to abdicate their half of the emotional responsibility to the relationship. In other words, men have become emotionally helpless as to how to pull their own emotional weight in the relationship. This dysfunctional dance has become frustrating for both men and women.

The bottom line is that until men develop an ability to contribute emotionally to their relationship, their wife or girlfriend will be left feeling alone in that responsibility, which goes against the equal nature of a partnership. As a result, because women are stronger and more self-reliant today, they are more inclined to seek an equal partnership with a man rather than one that is co-dependent. This has created a new phenomenon for women who are wondering where all the emotionally strong and mature men are to be coupled with, especially men who can handle a strong and self-reliant woman without needing to dominate, control, rescue, or abuse her. Similarly, they're looking for a man who has the courage to step up and help define the emotional needs of the relationship. What this has created is a whole new set of criteria for women to look for in men as potential life partners. These criteria ask men the question: *"Can you bring your honesty and vulnerability to the table that will help define your half of the emotional responsibility in this relationship?"*

Men, however, are still grappling with the shift away from living through a survival filter, so they are still struggling with how to partner with women by sharing power equally. Men have yet to embark upon their own journey of growth into a new paradigm of masculinity that includes their own emotional discovery and maturation process that is not based on holding power over others. To me, the evidence for this is the ever-present amount of social, cultural, and economic inequality that still exists in the form of gender discrimination in the workplace, misogyny, rape, domestic violence against women, and sexual harassment.

Men are also accustomed to putting on a persona to romantically pursue women, hiding their insecurities and flaws, but the tragedy occurs when they actually believe their persona is an accurate and authentic representation of who they are. In so doing, these flawless-appearing men have fed women's fantasies of finding "the perfect guy" in the form of the knight in shining armor, the savior, the rescuer, the caretaker, the prince, who could help her create the perfect relationship/marriage. None of these roles/masks/personas are authentic expressions of who they really are. Until men learn how to confront their fear of *not being enough*, they will continue to try to "live up" to women's fantasies of being the perfect guy by continuing to wear any of the above masks.

This puts men in a position of *jumping through hoops* for women in order to "prove" that they are "man enough." But all it does is set women up to be disappointed when a man inevitably falls from grace by being the very human guy he really is. Not only does this upset and disappoint the woman he tries to woo, but it also keeps him in his own jail cell of inadequacy.

As I wrote about in Chapter 5, vulnerability is a conscious choice to put aside all pretense and persona in order to reveal or share a very personal, authentic piece of your truth to another person. A man must have the courage to choose to be vulnerable, honest, and authentic, even if he doesn't live up to a woman's fantasy of who she thinks he *should* be. This is how a man gives up his balls, i.e., his personal power, in a similar way that a woman gives up her personal power by being submissive to a man. He must be honest enough to *not* try to live up to a woman's fantasy because a fantasy is dishonest, and it keeps his true nature hidden. It also creates immature relationships. It's really important for men to remember how human they are and how that humanness will always bring them up short of a woman's fantasy. So many of my male clients cringe at the ways they have disappointed the woman in their lives because they've tried to meet some unrealistic expectation she has of him. As I point out to a client in this situation, trying to live up to her fantasy is about *his* insecurity and is the opposite of self-care. He will strive to be perfect as she gives him feedback that he is imperfect. It's only a matter of time before he blows a gasket due to built-up resentment. The truth is that her feedback is correct. He is indeed imperfect, as are we all!

Any man's quest to be a perfect mate can be traced back to a childhood wound that was never healed. It is crucial for him to learn how to heal this wound by learning to trust that he is worthy of being loved as the flawed, insecure, mistake-prone, imperfect, real guy that he is, rather than seeking love and approval for being the fake guy who hides out behind some perfect-looking mask.

So, how confusing have relationships been for me? Enough that I stayed single until I was 43 years old. As I look back, I know now that I would have gotten divorced if I had tried to marry in my 20s or 30s. I knew enough then to know that there was a lot that I didn't know about what makes a relationship succeed and thrive. Even though my parents were married until they both died in their mid-70s, I knew that their version of marriage was one I did not want. Paying attention to the quality of their relationship was never a goal in how they related to each other. Their sense of "being a couple" had very little to do with healthy, respectful communication or fair fighting or emotional support. *Survival for them and the families they came from was the sense of purpose they learned from the Depression and World War II, and this shared approach to staying alive became the glue that kept them married for 40+ years. For them, survival had more meaning to their relationship than a higher quality of life. They weren't looking for anything more.*

I instinctively knew I didn't want that kind of survival relationship, but I had no idea how to do anything other than repeat what I observed in them. So, throughout my 20s and 30s, I played out my own version of survival relationships with women. Even though I did what felt natural for me as a man when I related to women, I can look back now and see that I had a huge gap in my awareness that kept me from knowing how to make an emotional connection beyond the shallow depth of my own personality.

There was something else going on that was getting in the way of my knowing how to connect with a woman at a deeper level. Despite my assumption that I had my act together, I wasn't relating to women from a sense of self-worth or self-respect. There was no way I could because I had no idea what self-worth and self-respect really meant. This was my paradoxical prison, i.e., looking for happiness but living my life through a survival filter that was wreaking havoc with my ability to create an honest and healthy relationship.

STAGE TWO of a Man's Maturity:
Intimacy vs. Isolation

According to Erik Erikson, the *Young Adulthood* ages between 18 and 40 span a period of time that centers on how a man forms intimate, loving relationships with other people. If he succeeds at developing a strong sense of commitment and care within a relationship, he achieves intimacy. If he fears commitment and avoids intimacy, he can become lonely, depressed, and feel isolated. It is the reason Erikson labeled this stage of psychosocial development as *Intimacy vs. Isolation.* He believed it was essential for people to develop close, committed relationships with others and that we are not developmentally "complete" until we are capable of creating intimacy, no matter how "successful" we are in our careers. (Erikson, 1959) The lessons learned in the previous stage of *Identity vs. Confusion* posed the question *"Who am I?"* and will help determine what will be learned in this stage. If a man has not developed a strong sense of identity during the adolescent stage, he will usually fear a committed relationship and may retreat into isolation. A recent study conducted by members of the psychology department at the University of Virginia found that parents who exercise psychological control on their teenagers actually hinder their child's ability to develop close relationships in adulthood. (Oudekerk *et al*, 2014) This to me supports Erickson's chronology of development where healthy *Intimacy* is achieved as a result of healthy *Identity* first being developed. The implications of this may only be subtly felt, but the ramifications are far-reaching. Not having achieved the emotional foundation that is necessary to create emotional intimacy follows a man for the rest of his life, despite whatever subsequent developmental stages he lives to experience.

"Will I Be Loved, or Will I Be Alone?"

Many men who come into my practice are chronologically way beyond their adolescent and young adulthood years, but still struggle with this very important aspect of relationships, which is how to create emotional intimacy. These middle aged and older aged men have achieved many amazing things in their lives. Despite whatever measures of success they have used to feel good about their accomplishments, they come to see me because they very humbly understand that happiness still eludes them. It is as if they have avoided recognizing some deeply buried treasure within themselves that is just waiting to be discovered. Their ignored emotional worlds are rich with experiences that, while emotionally challenging and perhaps even unbearable, offer each of these men a perspective of themselves that no one ever taught them had value. What distracts men away from this inner treasure is their ever-present fight-or-flight emotional reactivity. This is definitely NOT a sign of personal inadequacy. It is merely the manifestation of socio-cultural conditioning that challenges all men at the moment. If you accept the challenge, you can significantly improve the quality of your life, as is outlined in this book.

Our conscious awareness of our so-called "inner life" helps us answer what author Sam Keen says are the two most important questions of life: *"Who am I?"* and *"Who will go with me?"* He also cautions us to answer those two questions in that particular order. (Keen, 1992) Erikson himself suggests the same. He stresses the order of importance of identity formation in adolescence as the foundation for creating a successful relationship in young adulthood – that finding "The One" *first requires a man to know who he is himself.* I have observed, though, that because the human survival imperative of fight-or-flight has defined masculine identity for men since the beginning of time, men have come to expect and even take pride in operating in an emotional vacuum, thus avoiding building the foundation of self-knowledge that leads to creating relationship intimacy.

Like most of my male counterparts, when I was growing up, I was a typical, impressionable flunky of traditional masculinity. I had been trained my whole young life, unbeknownst to me, to regard and treat women as second-class citizens. Of course, intellectually, I thought that I regarded women as equals and appreciated them as wonderful creatures of God. But when it came down to it, when it was necessary for me to be respectful and honoring, I can look back now and see that I had a very limited understanding of how to do that. Given where I came from, I guess it makes sense, but for someone who worked very hard to NOT turn out like all the adult men I grew up around; it's a very humbling admission. In retrospect, I can see that I focused too much on what NOT to be, i.e., my father, so I neglected to put energy into figuring out who I really was.

I rarely saw my father be genuinely humble and respectful to my mother. I almost never saw him honor her opinion as his partner. Respect was demanded from me, but never role-modeled to me by them in how they treated each other and in how they treated me. I never learned how to earn someone's respect. I never saw my father risk any kind of vulnerable expression of his own emotional honesty to my mother, my brothers, or myself. All of that would have gone against the grain of the man-code he felt compelled to uphold. Instead, what I got to see was an angry, scared, self-possessed man who demanded that the world inside his home revolve around him and his needs. Everyone inhabiting that world, my mother, two brothers, and me, was there to serve him. We were all required to surrender our personalities, beliefs, and needs at the door.

My mother also exerted an important influence on my perception of relationships. Rarely did I ever see her stand up to my father's narcissistic tirades. Her timidity toward his unreasonable expectations of us sent me a clear message that this was the way that men and women acted toward each other. I learned two things from them: 1) that the most effective way to get your opinion across to someone was to impose your will on that person, and 2) in the face of someone else's will being imposed, submit. This went on in front of my eyes every day of my young life. How could I have NOT inherited some or both of those traits? Much as I wanted to believe that I would not turn out that way, the truth was that it was the most concrete thing in front of me to learn about masculinity in my formative years. Like it or not, it was the only template available for me, and I became my own version of that. Nevertheless, I am by no means blaming my parents for how I turned out. While they were my original role models, I still made my own choices with regard to the man I thought I was and how I believed I should act.

The Lessons of Lost Love

A circumstance I see from time to time in my private practice is the *"I'm in between relationships"* situation. The client has either ended a recent relationship himself or been dumped. No matter how the relationship ended, it's a great opportunity for him to learn about the blind spots he has that got triggered and contributed to the demise of the relationship. With this information he will have a better chance at succeeding in his next attempt at love.

If the man ended the relationship, it's important for him to become aware of the part he played in the demise of the relationship. He is usually very aware of the part his partner played. But just because he may have ended the partnership, with the exception of cases where there has been infidelity, it does not mean that he didn't contribute to the dysfunctional dance. Even if he was cheated on, this usually happens because the connection between the couple was emotionally immature, which means that both people weren't doing their best to feed that connection. Of course, this does not justify cheating.

For the man who gets dumped by his girlfriend or wife, the healing process is a long, slow journey filled with self-doubt, shame, and feelings of inadequacy. There is usually much second-guessing and confusion about either feeling blindsided or about being in denial about the reality of his relationship. Regardless, what is most important is his ability to forgive himself for whatever "mistakes" he made and learn the lessons that will keep him from repeating those mistakes. Certainly, the cliché I hear often in this circumstance is that "things happen for a reason." The best and most obvious "reason" is that there is an important lesson to be learned. However, this takes a bit of time, and if the guy is chomping at the bit to get back out there and meet someone new to take his mind off of his pain, it rarely works!

If a man doesn't take at least three to six months off from dating after getting the heave-ho, he is destined to repeat the same mistakes he just made. Every man needs time to process the emotional hangover of being rejected. Jumping into a relationship with another woman only delays that process and actually prevents it from happening, which means he will fall into the same behavior patterns. For the men who open themselves up to learning from their mistakes, it usually requires huge discipline to not become distracted by another woman. If he does the work and gets the lesson, however, he can feel confident that the chances of repeating his previous gaffes are greatly reduced. Again, depending on how he is able to answer the question *"Who am I?"* he will be limited in his ability at creating emotional intimacy in a relationship.

Intimacy vs. Codependency

One of the ironies I have observed from working with male clients is that "being in love" is quite often the place that a man can both find himself *and* lose himself. Indeed, I can look back at my own life and see how love helped transform me from a boy into a man, at times willingly and at other times kicking and screaming all the way. While there are other arenas in Life where that transformation takes place for a man, the experience of opening up emotionally to a woman is where a man explores and discovers his deepest connection to his masculine self.

Healthy emotional intimacy is something altogether different from codependency, but there is a cultural bias toward "codependent love" that sends a lot of people into my office for help. Intimacy requires emotional maturity while codependency thrives on immaturity. Because no piece of American culture educates men to recognize and value emotional maturity as a masculine trait, the default paradigm of masculine identity in America teaches men to approach relationships as codependent, immature Little Boys.

In 1986, author Melody Beattie introduced the term "codependency" to the world in her book *Codependent No More.* She defined a codependent person as *"someone who has let another person's behavior affect him or her, and who is obsessed with controlling that person's behavior".* (Beattie, 1986) I have expanded that definition to a more usable one for myself with my clients: in a codependent relationship, expressing "love" means each person feels responsible for the other person's happiness and well-being. It is a relationship where each person is trying to please the other while ignoring his or her own need for self-care. If a man believes it is his responsibility to keep the people he loves happy, he will continually subvert his integrity and his own needs by not saying what is true for him. I call this "eating it," and all it does is build up resentment and become an excuse for him to justify not having the guts to speak his truth. Inevitably, this codependent behavior bites him in the behind because it creates mistrust with those around him who feel they cannot count on him to be honest.

On the other hand, intimacy, according to Erik Erikson, refers to a person's ability to relate to another human being on a deep, personal level (Erikson, 1959). It is the feeling of closeness created between two people who risk showing each other the whole range of what is in their True Hearts. Because the most important events during Erikson's Young Adulthood stage revolve around establishing authentic love relationships, the possibility of creating true intimacy depends on whether or not a man has already established his personal identity. The foundation for his commitment to true intimacy depends on the familiarity and openness he has with his emotional world. Without this ability to share emotional experiences with another person – what scares him, what hurts him, what angers him, what makes him sad, what embarrasses him – intimacy is very limited and codependency reigns supreme!

My client "Teddy" struggled with feeling unappreciated by his wife because he felt he was trying his hardest and doing his best to "show her love". He did this by working two jobs to feed her and their two kids, as well as by helping her manage the kids on the weekend. He believed the best way of showing her love was to fulfill all her requests and to "fix" whatever problems she would bring to him. Despite all his attempts and hard work at trying to make her happy, he was resentful and confused about why she would not do her part to make him happy by being more sexual in the way she did before the kids were born. Theirs was a codependent relationship that was slowing becoming toxic due to all the accumulated resentment they felt for each other. They came into therapy feeling confused, angry, and skeptical that they could save their marriage. As my wife and I helped them to see the dysfunctional dance they were doing, they were able to set their sights on learning more about emotional intimacy and what it required from each of them. For Teddy, he had no idea what it took to speak truthfully from his heart, especially if what he was feeling was any type of fear, pain, anger, sadness, or shame. He acknowledged that he hid his true feelings behind a mask of showing people how capable he was of handling anything that came his way because that is what his father taught him as a boy of how to "be a man". Slowly but surely, Teddy began to learn about his emotional world and became more aware of the feelings that were running his life. As he risked telling his wife about his anger and pain as to how she was treating him, and as his wife learned how to likewise communicate how she was feeling rather than criticize him, they were able to build the trust needed to be more vulnerable with each other with their true feelings. This gradually helped them forgive each other and brought them closer. Despite the skepticism they entered into therapy with, they hung in long enough to find the motivation and courage needed to be more honest with each other. The emotional intimacy they brought to the relationship automatically increased their sexual intimacy to a level they had never previously experienced.

Sexual Intimacy

Mature, emotional intimacy also requires mutual commitment from each person to have a sexual connection with only each other. However, if a man is sexually intimate and monogamous but without the shared emotional open-ness, true intimacy will flounder here as well. This type of connection between two people also gets deeper and deeper as the commitment to exclusive and reciprocal intimacy stays in place.

There is a survival approach to human sexuality that I think men profoundly identify with. It is the instinct to procreate and propagate our species, which we feel in our bodies at a primitive level. The challenge, however, is for men to know when to re-wire their sexual identity from "spreading their seed" to "settling down". By the time boys enter into puberty, they receive a plethora of messages from the culture as to what is expected of them sexually if they want to be looked upon as being *masculine*. However, there is very little input from traditional masculinity about what and how a man can integrate his sexual personality with his emotional maturity as a way of creating true intimacy.

Men's understanding of intimacy usually points them toward a narrow definition that has more to do with physical connection than emotional. Sexual attraction is definitely an important part of how two people find each other. From there, however, it is crucial for both people to also explore each other's mind, heart, and soul. The whole motive of mature love is to create a connection with a woman that is fulfilling at an emotional, intellectual, and spiritual – as well as at a physical – level. This balanced approach to connecting is a mature, healthy approach to generating intimacy with another. Successfully appreciating a woman at those four levels, however, means that a man must first know *himself* at emotional, intellectual, physical, and spiritual levels.

Fantasy vs. Reality

Whether most people know it or not, they carry in their minds a fantasy of what a relationship could look and feel like that would make them happy. Many things influence a man's dreams and wishes for relationship bliss. There is nothing inherently wrong with having some happy-ever-after ideal. The problem occurs when a man finally realizes that the person he has chosen does not fill out the picture of that fantasy. This, of course, is unavoidable. The fantasy comes from the Little Boy part of him. Dreaming of an ideal outcome that makes us happy is entirely different from actually learning what work is required to achieve true happiness. It's always sad for me when a client becomes skeptical and hopeless about ever finding love, or as many of them put it, finding "The One."

I often tell male clients that The One could be sitting right next to them on the couch in my office, but they would not recognize her. The puzzled look in response at least leads me to believe that I've gotten them to think about what finding a suitable partner might really mean. I point out that unless and until he knows himself better as a man, his chances of recognizing this person when she walks by are very slim. Recognizing The One really has less to do with who that other person is and *more to do with how he wants to feel himself when he is with someone special.* In other words, if he focuses on whether or not she lives up to some list of attributes he has in his head about the perfect girl, his insecurity will always trigger his disappointment in her. Sooner or later, she will fail to live up to his fantasy because of her very human nature.

But if he also knows in his heart *how he wants to feel when he is with a woman* (e.g., respected, cared for, loved, appreciated, understood, trusted, safe, excited, etc.), and *he is emotionally aware enough to know when he is feeling all those feelings,* his chances of finding and recognizing The One are much higher. This is because he will commit himself to something he can control, i.e., knowing how he wants to feel, as opposed to trying to commit himself to something he can never control, i.e., hoping that this other person will someday live up to the fantasy list he has in his head.

Without the awareness and tools required to create a healthy relationship, the picture in a man's mind of happiness will rarely match the reality of his daily interactions with the person he loves. What is required is learning the "work" of a relationship. A couple of other fantasies I hear all the time are the very childlike assumptions that: 1) true love should be all a relationship needs to thrive and should not require having to learn how to "work" at it, and 2) because we love each other, it means that we should automatically trust each other – even if we barely know each other. These fantasies are the evidence of the emotional immaturity that creates codependency rather than true love.

A Man's Relationship Blind Spots

One of my consistent, ongoing observations as a clinician is the high correlation between relationship dysfunction and lack of self-awareness, which includes a low level of emotional maturity, lack of empathic capability, and low self-esteem. What this means is that if a man does not know who he is, he is severely limited in his ability to create an intimate connection with another person in a way that is not sexual. If a man has learned to avoid his feelings, how can he value his emotional world? If he has never valued his emotional world, how can he truly trust what is in his heart or in the heart of his partner? If he can't trust what is in his heart, how will he ever access and appreciate his own authenticity? And because men have been trained since boyhood to not really embrace and explore who they are emotionally, men arrive into their adult relationships still missing these huge pieces of themselves. This lack of emotional intelligence also prevents men from learning how to express anger in a healthy, constructive, respectful way that is neither aggressive nor passive. The actual "identity crisis" here is due to the fact that the internal, immature, wounded Little Boy is trying to make the decisions needed for the life of a mature, adult man. This, unfortunately, is prevalent throughout every strata of our society – even at the political level of our elected officials.

I call these limitations of emotional awareness *blind spots* because they are highly influential forces on the lives of men, but men have no clue that these blind spots are shaping their decisions, their personalities, and their relationships. By definition, a blind spot is some personality trait that stays just outside of a person's peripheral vision or awareness, and it usually takes objective feedback from someone else to point out its existence. All men need some kind of objective perspective of themselves in order to "see" what may be lurking outside of their awareness.

Often, a man is able to become aware of a blind spot when he sees the results of his unconscious choice making. Because pain can get his attention in very concrete ways, the blind spot in him that inadvertently inflicts pain on others can be a very humbling revelation. As humans, it is part of our nature to perpetuate patterns until we receive feedback that it is creating stress or anxiety for others. Of course, the biggest blind spot for 21st century men has been the legacy of global, toxic, traditional masculinity handed down from previous generations that have evolved into misogyny, sexism, racism, and homophobia.

On the one hand, men rely upon the deeply hard-wired survival instinct within their DNA to overcome setbacks that threaten them on the road to succeeding in their careers. This can be a very good thing. On the other hand, they also unwittingly and unconsciously rely on this same hard-wired survival instinct whenever setbacks occur in their intimate relationships. In other words, his survival instinct kicks in whenever he feels physically or emotionally threatened or hurt. Relying on this instinct only creates more disappointment, anger, distance, confusion, and hopelessness in the relationship. Furthermore, because this survival instinct is also a very fundamental piece of who men are as human beings and how they express their masculine identities, it is difficult – if not impossible – to function without it.

While it may be second nature for a man to protect himself by using this same instinct to keep his business alive, the personal price paid when he brings it to his relationship is huge. That instinct is likely to make him hunker down with swords drawn and an *"I'm right, you're wrong, you are now the enemy"* type of attitude. This unfortunately can become the slippery slope to any number of types of verbal or physical abuse of women. And the worst part is that most men don't realize the damage caused by this attitude until it is too late and she is threatening to leave the relationship!

The bottom line is this: Bringing survival skills to a partner as a way of dealing with differences only pushes her away and can also end up inflicting pain. It is very common for one person's survival approach to resolving conflict to trigger the other person's survival defense, which relegates them both to creating a *survival relationship*. As the name implies, a survival relationship severely limits any chance at establishing emotional intimacy between two people. And when this pattern of interaction repeats itself over and over, the foundation of the relationship erodes, leaving no trust, no goodwill, and no hope of saving the relationship.

Many men also mistrust any decision that is made "from emotion." I consistently hear male clients and male friends criticize any opinion that has some emotional component to it, as if allowing feelings to inform an opinion can only weaken a person's credibility. According to traditional masculinity, "being emotional" is not something a "real man" does, so men attach a condescending, even sexist, judgment onto emotions.

This is another version of the equally sexist epithet that ridicules anything done "like a girl." How many times have I heard a male client apologize or feel embarrassed for crying or getting teary during a session! Not only do I consider it to be an appropriate display of vulnerability, but I also appreciate the display of courage and trust required for a man to give himself permission to be seen this way. This is a great example of a blind spot. The best way for a man to normalize and reframe this kind of moment is to explore his feelings of inadequacy at a deeper level of whatever shame he feels in his life for not "living up to" that worn-out, antiquated, obsolete stereotype of masculinity. It is only at a courageous moment such as this that he could begin to appreciate how avoiding his emotional world prevents him from knowing what is in his heart – from knowing his personal truth. As he grasps the importance of not limiting his self-expression to an outdated stereotype, he will begin to appreciate how vulnerability can be felt as a source of emotional strength.

Why Men Compartmentalize

Compartmentalization is a survival skill that can qualify as both good news and bad news to any guy trying to manage emotional overwhelm. It describes an ability to divide a suffocating amount of emotion into segments or parts in order to accomplish the task at hand. Because men have a limited capacity when it comes to managing their emotional world, they utilize compartmentalization very adeptly by putting aside difficult feelings in order to attend to immediate needs. This is definitely the good news of compartmentalization and defines, to a large degree, one of men's better talents when it comes to survival.

The bad news is that compartmentalization can also become a way for a man to emotionally hide out. It can be a liability when a man needs to define his feeling state at any particular moment, especially in his relationship with his wife or girlfriend. Until a man becomes more and more familiar with his emotional world, he will automatically compartmentalize as a way of regulating the emotional overwhelm that comes up when he explores his little known emotional history. It is not unusual for men to minimize their feelings because their capacity is so limited when they first start to become aware of their feelings. It's like trying to fit a gallon of water into a cup. In time, a man can increase the size of his "cup" to hold and manage more of his feelings in a healthy way. His ability to articulate those feelings can help to regulate the amount that builds up inside of him, which can also help him to stay emotionally "present" with his partner.

Fear of Commitment

When a man is not yet ready to commit himself to a monogamous intimate relationship, the best-case scenario is for him to be honest with a woman about his true desires and intentions before revving up any physical intimacy. This gives her the choice to jump in with him or not, given her own readiness to be in a committed relationship. Ideally, such a man would become involved with women who are similarly not ready to focus on one person. This of course requires a bit of discipline when it comes to feeling the fierce pull of sexual desire that brings two people together in the first place. The emotional challenge seems to come when a "quasi-commitment guy" develops an affinity for one woman more than any other and begins to pursue her.

Two years ago, a client I will call Malcolm came into my practice. He was the poster-child for bobbing and weaving around relationship commitment. He came in because he wanted to understand why he was feeling so hurt and confused from being rejected by a woman he had only been dating for 3 months. Because he could not commit himself to being monogamous with her, she broke up with him in order to find someone who was willing to commit to being in an exclusive relationship. Though Malcolm tried to convince me that at age 39 he believed he was not yet ready to "settle down", he was obviously deeply affected by being dumped by this "amazing woman". His worst fear was that she was The One that he let slip away.

Malcolm's blind spot (fear of commitment) is a very common story that I have heard over the years. He had an internal battle going on between his head and his heart. His head was saying that he didn't want to limit his "options" by being "tied down" to just one woman. On the other hand, he was hurting from the fact that he had unwittingly opened up his heart to this woman in what was for him a very deep way, but could not reconcile this with the critical voice in his head that was yelling at him to run away. So despite the great experience he was feeling in his heart at any given moment with her, his fear and anxiety of a future without "options" also kept his survival instinct activated and on red-alert. This kept him treating her one way on the outside while feeling another way on the inside. Back then he could not articulate this either to himself or to her, but the outcome was inevitable and it shook his foundation for the first time ever.

Malcolm had a very conventional interpretation of "commitment" that was defined by his fear as "limitation". He had always managed this fear of being limited to one person by avoiding exclusivity. He justified his lifestyle to me with, *"What if there is someone else out there who would be a better match for me?"* Because this woman who dumped him somehow found her way through his survival defenses and into his heart, however, he realized there must be something else going on for him that he was not aware of because he missed her so much. And missing someone was just not part of his makeup. Because he could not commit to this woman who rocked his world, he finally, after much digging and peeling back layers of an outdated belief system, came upon the realization that *what he really feared and felt deep down was that he was unlovable.* Unbeknownst to him, this was the Inadequacy Myth from his childhood that was the program continuously running in the background of his present-day life. This story of his inadequacy kept him at arms length with women because he never believed he deserved their love. On top of that, he was also very afraid to allow a woman to see his True Heart for fear that she would in fact come to realize and reject him for what he already believed about himself, that he was "not enough" to deserve her love. The pain he was experiencing now from this amazing woman's rejection was *exactly* the pain he unconsciously always tried to avoid by not committing to exclusive relationships.

This experience led Malcolm to realize the deeper truth he felt of not wanting to end up alone in his life, despite his fear of letting any woman see the "real Malcolm". The good news of all this was the fact that he was finally addressing the core issues of his personality that were keeping him alone in his life and which also reinforced his belief that he was not good enough, not man enough, and therefore not lovable enough.

As Malcolm became a student of his own life, especially about the fear, pain, anger, sadness, and shame that made up his dark side, he began to forgive himself for his inadequacies and accept himself more for the unique guy that he was. Instead of running away from and avoiding commitments, he learned to take more emotional risks with women by showing more and more of his True Heart to them. Doing this gave him the reality-check he needed so that he could learn firsthand that, if someone else could truly appreciate and love his authentic self, *perhaps he was lovable.* As he became more emotionally aware, he learned he could make a commitment to himself and his personal integrity to follow through on his commitment to others. When he finally took the risk to pursue a relationship with a woman he met and was attracted to, though it was scary at first, he challenged himself to be faithful and loyal to her exclusively. Even though that relationship only lasted for a year, he gave himself the gift of learning how to become *accountable to his commitment to himself to stay openhearted with a woman as a way of keeping his authenticity, personal integrity, and self-respect intact.* This taught him to trust his ability to take care of himself in a relationship, and is now in a new relationship that he looks forward to taking to even deeper levels of commitment.

Anyone can get married, but committing to a successful, long-term relationship also means making a commitment to learn the relationship tools to create healthy, respectful partnership. This includes, but is not limited to: how to feed the emotional and physical connection; how to keep the romance alive; how to respectfully communicate; how to "fight fair"; and how to agree to disagree. Conflict and adversity are unavoidable parts of every relationship. Learning how to manage each of those in a way that feeds the partnership is what commitment is *really* about. Unfortunately, many couples avoid learning these skills until too much damage has been done. Guys who resist learning these skills usually end up in my office only at the threat of their marriage ending. At that point, learning how to create and sustain emotional intimacy can be a very heavy lift. If he has gotten his Wake-Up Call due to being humbled by his blind spots and freaked out by the prospect of ending up alone for the rest of his life, he must have the willingness to learn how to rewire his system enough to breathe life into his emotional world without thinking that he will become less of a man by doing so. This is the doorway to his commitment to himself and to others.

Walking on Eggshells

If a man is unfamiliar with his emotional world, he essentially "wanders" into a relationship with a woman unprepared for what will soon be required of him emotionally. How is this NOT starting a relationship with a huge blind spot? Love requires that both people contribute equally to feeding the emotional connection between them. When a guy feels like he is at an emotional deficit compared to the woman he loves, how can he operate in the relationship as an equal? Because he doesn't know his own emotional world, he won't be able to empathize or understand what is going on emotionally for him and for her. In a situation like this he will more than likely learn to avoid "talking about feelings" by avoiding any triggering topics that compel him to *walk on eggshells* around her.

This describes one of my clients named "Ed" who came into my practice knowing that he was very emotionally limited. Predictably, Ed's relationship with his wife was one where he avoided participating in the emotional responsibilities of the marriage, assuming his wife would naturally take that on because as a woman, she was probably more aware of her feelings than he was. Ed didn't know he was doing this, which again is the definition of a blind spot, but he was effectively being controlled by two fears that were kicking his butt: Fear #1 – he admitted that he was afraid to show any emotional vulnerability to anybody that might trigger his shame of being seen as weak and unmanly; Fear #2 – he also admitted that he *hated confrontation,* and he considered any conversation that included talk about feelings with his wife as being "confrontational".

Both of these fears converged to keep a lid on Ed's sharing a whole range of important feelings (Fear #1) because he did not want to trigger his wife's anger or disappointment (Fear #2). So he would instead walk on eggshells around her, i.e., not say anything that might provoke a deeper discussion, even if he disagreed with her. Rather than weigh in on any number of real-life issues, Ed yielded to his wife's opinions that ended up defining many aspects of their marriage simply because he didn't have the guts to stand up to her if he had a different opinion than she did. This created resentment in Ed even though he played the "laid-back-dude" role of acting as if none of it was important enough to stress over. The reality was that he felt unappreciated and misunderstood because he somehow expected her to read his mind and know what he was feeling. I pointed out to him that if he didn't have the courage to talk to her about his built-up resentment, his wife would be left to decipher, unravel, and resolve all the challenging issues of the relationship all on her own. Walking on eggshells around her did two things: 1) it effectively "trained" her to believe that he didn't have any complaints about their marriage, which was not true, but he was too afraid to tell her something she might not want to hear, and 2) not talking to her directly about his feelings only motivated her more to talk about their lack of emotional connection, which is what he wanted to avoid in the first place.

Most guys start to walk on eggshells around women because they need to prop up the façade of being manly and "protect her" from a) any complaint he may have about her or about life in general in order to b) keep her happy and c) prop up the mask of masculinity he had constructed in order to appear bulletproof, so that d) she will stay attracted to him. This is how men try to justify that it is not in their best interest to complain about what's going on in their relationship. Saying something about his fear or pain or anger or sadness or shame would blow his cover of not really having it all together! It's a hole that men dig for themselves. Climbing out of that hole isn't easy. Ed came into my practice wanting to learn what he could say to his wife to keep her from complaining so much. Instead, he was shocked to discover that these and other unexamined fears were running his life. This was his Wake Up Call!

Ed finally made the connection in his brain that by not weighing in on his emotional needs, he effectively handed over the power of the relationship to his wife. By the way, his wife was never interested in running the whole show. She felt his emotional absence and knew that things would only get done if she stepped in and made most of the decisions by herself. By doing his laid-back-guy thing, Ed abdicated his responsibility, not only to his half of the partnership, but also more importantly to himself as a man. By not knowing and sharing his emotional honesty with the woman he loved, he betrayed his own integrity, his own truth, his own feelings, his own authenticity, and his own heart. *Walking on eggshells is not only a blind spot. It is how a man emasculates himself.*

A Lopsided Relationship

Unwittingly, when a man yields his emotional responsibility in a relationship to a woman, he forces her to be fully responsible for something that is by definition a two-person job. This is unfair and disrespectful. Ed set his wife up to fail because in strapping her with all the responsibility of dealing with the major decisions of their marriage, he created a *lopsided relationship*. He put her into the role of being the "parent" while he stayed stuck in the role of being a wounded Little Boy who could not be responsible for his own adult feelings, beliefs, and truths. In the partnership that was their marriage, he created a lopsided emotional dependency on his wife that quite often translated for Ed in his immature emotional system as "love," but it actually created a codependent relationship. While his wife early on may have even enjoyed this power differential that was in her favor, it inevitably became a burden that trapped her in one of Life's most depressing ironies, i.e., feeling alone in her most significant adult relationship. By the way, just because Ed's wife may have had a better understanding of her emotional world didn't mean she didn't have her own blind spots when it came to their relationship.

This emotional passivity on Ed's part, however, led to confusion and pain for him because he started to feel unappreciated for all the "non-emotional" contributions he felt he made to the relationship. This made sense given the fact that Ed busted his behind to provide for his family. He was also feeling that the marriage was lopsided, but from the different perspective of being the only one working and bringing in an income. He felt stressed about carrying all the pressure of having to make the money they needed to survive, because it was always just barely enough to get by. He admitted that he had never come out and said that directly to his wife because he didn't want to make her angry or disappoint her. He also was afraid to admit that he felt like he needed help in providing for their family, because this put him in contact with all of his feelings of inadequacy that he was always trying to hide from others. I pointed out to him that in a mature partnership, neither person can be expected to carry an unfair burden of responsibility. What Ed needed to learn was how his reluctance to risk saying his opinion out loud to her created an unfair burden on his wife and kept him in the immature Little Boy role that was his way to avoid dealing with the emotional connection. Though it took a while for Ed to "catch up" to becoming more comfortable with talking about his feelings to his wife, he began to experience the difference it made in how she was able to understand and appreciate who he really was and all he did for the family. He was similarly appreciative of what he learned about his wife and all she did on her side of the relationship. This open-ness between them not only balanced out their lopsided relationship, it also deepened and strengthened the quality of their marriage.

Accountability and Empathy

When a man doesn't know his emotional world, the tendency for him to clean up some inappropriate choice he made that inflicted pain onto a loved one is to either a) explain or justify his poor choice-making, or b) blame the reactivity of the loved one for him making the poor choice he made. All of this is an avoidance of *accountability*. Being accountable for making mistakes and bad choices requires the courage to be vulnerable enough to hear the other person's pain, take responsibility for any bad behaviour, express remorse, offer an apology, reassure the other that it will not happen again, and ask – NOT beg – for forgiveness.

Another example I see of a client trying to avoid accountability and find an easy fix for relationship problems occurs when he tries to convince his wife or girlfriend to *"forget about the past and just move on."* If solving interpersonal problems were simply a matter of having the willpower to "just forget" about the pain of the past, the divorce rate would be a lot lower than it is. As if it were even possible in the first place, trying to "forget" fear, pain, anger, sadness, or shame is unrealistic and naive. Accountability is how we put the past behind us and move on. Having the courage to acknowledge our shortcomings is what heals the wounds we have inflicted onto others. Accountability re-builds trust.

Unless a man can access and utilize his emotional maturity, he will not be capable of empathizing with his aggrieved partner and the emotional connection will stay derailed. In *focusing on the fix*, a man misses an opportunity to acknowledge the underlying emotional experience of his partner that may be more important to recognize than trying to "solve the problem". If he instead takes the time to explore and show interest in whatever feeling state created stress for her in the first place, he creates an emotional connection. It leads him to comprehend and become conscious of a level of emotional reality in his wife or girlfriend that is a sign to her that "he cares". This is what is known as *empathy*. As a man learns how to develop the ability to empathize with his wife or girlfriend, *he creates intimacy*. Empathy is the "glue" in a relationship that keeps the connection between two people solid and strong. It is the essence of thinking and acting like a "we" instead of thinking and acting like a "me". When a man is single, "me" thinking makes sense. Everyone does it. But once he is in a relationship, "me" thinking without regard for the other comes across as self-centered, competitive, and non-caring.

Thinking like a "we" also means to behave like being part of a couple even when alone out in the world. It means that a man "holds and carries" the woman he loves in his heart wherever he goes. It involves creating an atmosphere of cooperation with a partner in a way that allows both people to get their wants and needs met. It does not mean that he subverts his own wants and needs to hers in order to just "get along".

When a man refrains from saying what is true for him as some codependent "show of love" for his wife or girlfriend, he abdicates his personal integrity and responsibility to himself.

Gutsy honesty not only creates emotional intimacy with a loved one, but it also helps to answer the question *"Who am I?"* by compelling a man to dig deep into his heart and soul to reveal the authentic motivation behind his hurtful behavior. The courage required to being emotionally vulnerable in this way with his loved one is another way of revealing a part of who he is that he may not be very proud of. Nevertheless, this part of who he is has driven him to behave in ways that are detrimental to his relationship and his self-worth. As men, we must become aware of the behaviors that get triggered in us when we are in survival mode. These behaviors can be aggressive (fight) or passive (flight) toward the other person rather than vulnerable and honest, which is more difficult because it requires that we stay open and real with the other person.

SIGNS of Your BLIND SPOTS in a Relationship

- When you realize you cannot imagine how being emotionally vulnerable could ever be seen as a sign of strength rather than as a sign of weakness;
- *When you lack courage to tell her how angry and hurt you are by what she said or did;*
- When you believe that dealing with your fear, pain, anger, sadness and shame on your own can somehow be a good thing for your relationship;

- *When you believe that — because you bust your ass at work to make a living for the family — your wife or girlfriend should have few expectations of you as an emotional partner in the relationship;*
- When you choose to be in an intimate relationship but are unwilling to help create emotional intimacy by being sexually monogamous and emotionally vulnerable;
- *When you try to control your partner's behavior either passively or aggressively rather than be vulnerable by telling her how you feel and what you need;*
- When you realize how reluctant you are to express appreciation to your partner for even the little things she does, but feel unappreciated and unloved yourself that she doesn't notice and appreciate the things you do for the relationship;
- *When you realize you are carrying out the immature legacy of your parents who did not show you how to be a mature man in a relationship;*
- When you realize that your disappointment in your partner is a result of having unrealistic expectations of her;
- *When you finally realize that the Little Boy in you is much more in charge of making your adult life decisions than the Mature Man in you;*
- When you finally realize that there is some part of you that took on a sexist and/or misogynistic viewpoint of women – even if only subtle – that you now project onto your wife, girlfriend, or women in general.

Parent-Child vs. Adult-Adult Relationships

Having worked with many couples over the past 27 years, it has become clear that there are two "phases" that a relationship progresses through, if a couple can hang in long enough to get from the first phase to the second phase. The main characteristic of the first phase is that *the relationship is emotionally immature.* This means that once the "honeymoon period" is over, there is more and more: walking on eggshells around each other; disrespectful communication – especially when there is a difference of opinion expressed; win-lose arguments; fight-or-flight interactions; judgments and criticism toward each other; very little emotional vulnerability; feelings of disappointment based on unrealistic expectations of each other; mutual mistrust with no effort or desire to rebuild trust; and an absence of empathy. This phase is known as a *parent-child* relationship or a "one-up-one-down" relationship. One person assumes the *parent* role of the authoritative, controlling partner who takes charge of the details of any number of arenas in the relationship from the social schedule to the kids schedule to the bill-paying to the house chores, etc. This person also has the type of anxiety that compels him or her to control others, more so than the person in the *child* role.

The person in the *child role* is more laid back and easily amenable to the task-chore-calendar-finances management that the *parent* organizes. He or she does not complain a lot, is prone to tuning out the *parent* when there is tension, can become passive-aggressive as a way to express dissatisfaction and acquire power in the relationship, and is very reluctant to disappoint or hurt the *parent's* feelings.

Many couples switch roles back and forth. For example, it is not unusual for the woman to be in the *parent role* when handling the details of the family social calendar and for the husband to take on the *child* role. But they often switch roles when it comes to the financial arena, where the husband steps into the *parent* role and the wife steps into the *child* role. Whatever configuration occurs, the *parent-child* relationship is an emotionally immature dynamic that pushes couples into relationship dissatisfaction.

Virtually every couple that comes in for help is in the throes of dysfunction as a result of accumulation of unresolved fear, pain, anger, sadness, and shame throughout the course of the relationship. Once a couple gets past the honeymoon phase of their early relationship, the reality of their emotional immaturity creates all of the above issues. This is an important choice-point for a couple to seek outside help. It is very common for couples that get to this point of parent-child interactions to assume they are married to the wrong person and are hopeless that any type of change can happen. The relationship then devolves into separation or even divorce. This hopelessness is the main reason that the divorce rate has always been and continues to be so high.

Couples who seek help have the opportunity to grow into the *emotionally mature* phase of a relationship, which creates an *adult-adult partnership*. In this mature relationship, both people treat each other with respect as equal partners and express healthy, emotional vulnerability to one another. There is honest communication, mutual validation and empathy for differing opinions, mutual benefit-of-the-doubt given, no walking on eggshells to avoid confrontation, and mutual effort to work together as a team in managing child logistics, house chores, work schedules, social schedules, and exercise schedules.

Of course, this isn't an easy thing to achieve and requires a lot of work and practice. Both parties must work on managing emotional reactivity; proactive building of trust in each other; compassion for each other's childhood wounds; forgiveness; sincere expression of appreciation; support for each person's needs regarding physical health, including exercise, diet, and sleep; a healthy attempt at balancing sexual intimacy with emotional intimacy, and much more.

Configuring an *adult-adult* relationship is usually the goal of couples counseling, but it requires an equal amount of motivation and sweat equity from both people to change their *parent-child* dynamic into one that is *adult-adult*. The underlying requirement for this type of change is the willingness of both people to examine the emotional wounds that have created distance between them. Only then can they heal the pain and create closeness that comes from a compassionate and more mature understanding of each other. This type of relationship where both partners approach each other in an emotionally mature way makes emotional and sexual intimacy possible to be in balance with each other.

A New Kind of Protector/Provider Role

It is in a man's best interest to improve his role to protect his loved ones and provide for their physical and material well-being. While women have stepped into that role in more and more ways since the beginning of the women's movement, it is still a man's responsibility to participate in protecting and providing for the physical and material welfare of the family. However, the traditional paradigm of protector/provider is a survival-based model, which serves the important purpose of attending to a family's physical and material needs. I want to challenge men to see themselves as filling that protector/provider role beyond their survival instinct by also becoming more skilled at protecting and providing for the *emotional welfare* of their family. This would address the quality of a man's relationships.

This concept is very abstract for most men and can be confusing when I suggest it as a possible solution to relationship issues. Working his butt off to provide for and protect his family with the material things they all need does not necessarily mean that a man is also helping to increase the overall quality of life that his relationships need in order to thrive. The industrialization of the food industry made it less necessary for men to hunt for food, thereby reducing the need for one of the conventional ways that men displayed their physical prowess and survival ability. In today's world, a man's inherent drive-to-survive still compels him to display whatever strengths and talents he possesses as a prospective mate. Though men need to follow their instincts to protect and provide for their families, they need to adjust to the concept that women today see their role as being protectors and providers for the family as well.

Becoming more aware of his emotional world, however, equips a man to better provide and contribute to the emotional needs of his relationships. This in turn gives him a better awareness of how to protect the emotional foundation of his relationships from any threats – real or imagined. Both of these together create a higher level of emotional participation for a man in his relationships, which evokes a higher level of trust and appreciation for and from his loved ones. This is what elevates his relationships from a level of *surviving* to a level of *thriving*. It does, however, require him to learn a whole new set of skills when it comes to relating to his loved ones.

Men as Co-Caretakers of Relationships

So often women tell me that all they want is for their man to just "show up" in their relationship. The idea of "showing up" is one that strikes confusion in a man's mind because it is so formless and abstract to his concrete way of thinking. It takes a shift in his perspective to see that she needs him to reveal his emotional world to her so that she does not feel emotionally alone in the relationship.

A tricky piece of this puzzle is that women can only give men feedback from a female perspective as to what "showing up" looks and feels like. How can he truly be present if he shows up in a way that only makes sense to her, but not to him? And what are the ways that he already shows up that may make sense only to him and not to her? Are his ways of showing up not as valid and meaningful as the ways that makes sense to her? On the one hand, a man really needs to hear her perspective because it is valuable information about who she is and what she needs. On the other hand, she needs to do the same for him. If her input is the only reference for how they "show up" for each other, the relationship will again be lopsided. Therefore it is crucial that he hears her request and then offers feedback about what "showing up" looks and feels like from his perspective. This will help them forge an agreed-upon approach to showing up that could be satisfactory for both of them. By approaching the woman he loves this way, a man can step into the unfamiliar role of being a *co-caretaker of the relationship* in the best way possible – by participating in the relationship as an equal emotional partner.

<u>Ten Things Men Can Do To Become Better Emotional Partners In Their Relationships</u>

1. **Assume that whatever level of emotional immaturity you have is now officially an obstacle in your relationship with your wife or girlfriend.** Participating in your relationship as an immature wounded little boy and not as a mature, healthy adult man only compromises trust in your relationship and promotes distance between you both. Challenge yourself to "grow up" and bring whatever maturity you express out in the world to the woman you love. The worst way for an adult relationship to operate is with a wounded little boy (or girl) making adult decisions. This Little Boy within you will avoid being accountable for his actions. The Mature Man, on the other hand, will always walk a line of personal integrity, whether anyone else is watching or not.

2. **Showing respect to the woman you love is a sign that you respect yourself.** If there are ways that you are unfair or unkind toward her or act dishonorably toward your partner, see it as an indication of your own lack of self-worth. Similarly, if you walk on eggshells around

her and don't speak your truth, you probably lack self-respect. Assume it means that you have a blind spot when it comes to being a healthy emotional partner in your relationship. Then, do something about it! Read a book, go to a seminar, get into therapy, join a men's group, or talk to a clergy person. Get information that will help you examine the ways your personal belief system no longer serves you.

3. **Have the courage to tell her something you typically avoid telling her out of fear of her reaction.** While she might not agree with what you say and may even feel hurt or angered by it, she will respect you for taking the risk of being truthful with her. By maturely expressing what is true for you, even if it hurts her, disappoints her, or makes her angry or sad, *the relationship will benefit* from your courageous vulnerability. If she does not appreciate you being forthcoming, it means your relationship is definitely immature, and you both have a lot of work to do.

4. **When communicating with her, know the difference between expressing a feeling versus being judgmental.** Underneath every judgment you have about her, there is a feeling, so communicate *that feeling*. Beginning a sentence with the word "you" is a sure sign that you are delivering a judgment. Even starting a sentence with, "I feel that you are ____" does NOT express a feeling. It's just a tricky way of disguising your judgment of her. Expressing a feeling sounds like this: "I feel [angry, sad, hurt, scared, or confused] when you do ____."

5. **Give her the benefit of the doubt.** When she says something hurtful – which will happen at times – do not assume that she is intentionally trying to hurt you. If you feel hurt or angry from something she says, ask her directly if she is intentionally trying to hurt you. Chances are high that she is not, but it's important for her to know when she does. You could also show how much you care about her by asking whether or not you have done something to hurt her or make her angry. *This is a way to show empathy, which is a crucial aspect of any healthy partnership.*

6. **Think and act more like a "we" in order to balance out the ways you already think and act like a "me."** Because you are in a relationship, you MUST become more aware of your automatic, self-centered thinking. Developing an ongoing awareness of *what is best for the relationship* is a sign of the mature man in you stepping up and being present. For example, asking her what she needs when she's stressed out is a way of showing her love and respect, as well as showing her that you care about who she is and what's important to her.

7. **Carry the woman you love in your heart wherever you go.** Whenever you are alone out in the world, act like a man who is part of a couple – even if she isn't standing by your side. It's the wounded little boy inside a man who acts inappropriately toward other women. "He" is the one who projects his desires and fantasies onto other women about what he doesn't have, and his actions are totally destructive and disrespectful toward

you and your committed relationship. Rather than distracting yourself with thoughts of other women, be more accountable to yourself and to your partner by having an honest conversation about what you need in your relationship that you are not getting.

8. **Push your own comfort level by exploring ways of being affectionate with her that do not have sex as the ultimate goal.** Let her know that you are capable of giving her a neck or back massage without it needing to lead to sex. Be mindful of how the emotional connection between you is part of your sexual intimacy with her, and let her know that you understand that.

9. **Be supportive of her need and desire to grow as a person.** If she becomes happier with herself as a woman – even if it gets scary or confusing for you – it will definitely help the relationship in the long run. Ask her what she needs to feel that you are a supportive emotional partner for her.

10. **Do any and all of these things because they will make you a bigger and better version of yourself as a man on the planet.** Do NOT do any of them because they will get her to love you more. She will instinctively love you more *as you commit yourself to your own personal growth.* Tell her what you need to feel that she is a supportive emotional partner for you.

Chapter 7

HEALTHY MASCULINITY, HEALTHY PLANET

"Men must teach each other that real men do not violate or oppress women – and that a woman's place is not just in the home or the field, but in schools and offices and boardrooms."

-- UN Secretary-General Ban Ki-moon

When I first began writing this book a number of years ago, I was focused on offering insights that I presumed would be helpful to men and their relationships. The more I delved into the underbelly of masculinity, however, the clearer it became that men must not only do this work to better themselves and the way they treat their loved ones, but also for the numerous toxic consequences that patriarchal ideology has foisted upon human beings all over the planet for thousands of years. As an expression of survival's aggressive dark side, patriarchy's insidious, deadly reach extends out from individuals to families to communities to tribes to cities to homelands and to nations around the world, as well as to the planet itself. Patriarchy is an equal opportunity oppressor toward women, children, and men. It has polluted cultures, religions, businesses, and governments at every corner of the planet.

The overly developed sense of male power and privilege that has evolved out of the condescending ideology of patriarchy has its roots in the suppression of vulnerability that is the dark side of survival. It holds power by leveraging its superior physical strength to assert dominance over other nations in the form of war and to impose violence and control over the less advantaged. The unhealthy consequences of this authoritative legacy are evident at both local and global levels and are hostile relics that no longer make sense in a 21st century world.

STAGE THREE of a Man's Maturity:
Generativity vs. Stagnation

Erikson's model for human development focuses on contributing to society in the Middle Adulthood years from 40 to 65. The concept of *generativity* is about achieving some kind of "give back" in the form of socially valued work that will guide the next generation. People who fail to find some higher purpose in their lives tend to feel unproductive and stagnant. This book challenges the reader to make a difference in your own life by redefining your personal paradigm of masculine identity from a toxic one to a healthy one. Whatever commitment you have to your own personal growth, you will be able to use your journey of transformation in two important ways: 1) to contribute to future generations by actively teaching children – especially boys – a healthy version of masculinity that comes from your own journey toward authenticity, personal integrity, and self-respect; and 2) to campaign against the effects that toxic masculinity has had on the planet at any of the levels mentioned throughout this chapter. This developmental need for generativity calls for the end of self-interest. Because this stage compels men to give and care about something beyond their personal world, it's also a way for men to create a life that "has meaning".

Stagnation, on the other hand, can take the form of selfishness, greed, and lack of interest in what might happen in the future. The other term Erikson used for stagnation was *self-absorption*. This is another form of narcissism that challenges men during the middle-age years to serve some higher purpose beyond their self-absorbed ego. Bear in mind, however, that this is very different from seeking the deeper self-knowledge that answers the Adolescent stage question of *"Who am I?"* As is evident from Erickson's model, generativity is only possible once a person's true identity is in place. Until then, his life will stagnate in the confusion of trying to "find himself".

"How can I contribute to the world?"

This stage poses the question that comes up when we reach middle age maturity: *"How can I contribute to the world?"* Erikson explained that this existential question is at the root of mid-life angst, when people want to feel like their lives "have meaning". They attempt to contribute to society through the children they raise, their productivity at work, or by helping to create positive changes that benefit others. This is why Erikson labeled this stage as *Generativity vs. Stagnation*, when people want to give back to society in both individual and collective ways. (Erikson, 1959)

Men's "Crisis" At Mid-Life

My work with men of middle-aged years has benefited *in vivo* from Erickson's developmental model, especially regarding the importance of the sequential order of each stage. As clients challenge themselves to "stay awake" and grow, they quite naturally become aware of the progressive emotional growth that is needed before other things can happen. In this mid-life developmental stage, men tend to ask themselves some important questions, the answers to which are informed by their previous experiences. The stereotype of a man's so-called *mid-life crisis* does not just materialize out of thin air. Even if he feels blindsided by this new, unfamiliar urge to go out and buy a sports car, the anxiety of this "crisis" has been a number of years in the making and the result of being oblivious to the emotional highs and lows of his childhood, adolescence, and early adulthood years. If a man has lived his life under the influence of traditional masculinity like most men, chances are high that he will arrive at middle age a) not having been aware of his emotional experiences, wants, and needs throughout his lifetime, which b) has trained him to engage the world from behind the mask of his ego. During middle-age, this lack of authenticity can steer a man into feeling restless, on edge, and uncertain about himself, which can then stoke his overall anxiety and make him question his life's purpose. Even if he has accomplished all the financial and material goals he has ever set out to achieve, he may still feel a lack of fulfillment in his personal identity and start to question whether his efforts were worth the investment of blood, sweat, and tears – especially if he still feels "empty on the inside" at mid-life.

As he becomes aware of his need to address this lack of meaning in his life, it is actually a sign of personal growth because it means that he is slowly, but surely, "waking up." However, it can also turn into a learning curve that can wreak havoc on a marriage if a man continues to look outside of himself for answers that can only be found on the inside. In other words, there are two ways to deal with the inevitable mid-life anxiety we are all confronted with: 1) the immature way, which focuses on finding new answers by trying to rearrange his external circumstances, or 2) the mature way, which focuses on finding new answers by courageously inspecting his personality traits that have been shaped by both his light side and dark side.

SIGNS Your Life Feels Stagnant From LACK OF SELF-KNOWLEDGE

- When you realize that the un-acknowledged fear, pain, anger, sadness, and shame of your lifetime is starting to leak out onto the way you treat your loved ones;
- *When you assume that the lack of satisfaction you feel about your marriage must mean that you are married to the wrong person;*
- When your fantasies about other women entice you to question the realities of your marriage vows and tempt you toward infidelity;
- *When you realize how personally unfulfilling your job is;*
- When you keep attempting to scratch some restless "inside itch" by changing something in your

environment, rather than look to change something within;

- *When you start to question and regret certain choices you have made in your life as having been mistakes without looking at the underlying values and lessons you learned from each of them;*

- When you realize that besides raising your kids and busting your butt at your job, that you have not left any kind of "mark" on the world that could make it a better place or contribute to it in some positive way;

- *When you realize that you have become a bit cynical about the rest of the world and are more self-indulgent and self-absorbed than you used to be;*

- When you finally realize that the version of masculinity that you have related to your whole life has similarities to the patriarchal ideology that oppresses women, children, and men around the world.

First Things First

The middle-aged men in my practice seeking relationship help are essentially trying to figure out the answer to the STAGE TWO question of *"Will I love and be loved?"* They are aware of the emotional pain in their gut at the moment and are also very wary of the potential pain in their future if they do not figure out how to become better emotional partners in their intimate relationships. For the most part, these guys are not aware of their blind spots. So, while this STAGE TWO question is foremost in *their* minds, it isn't a huge leap for me to wonder whether or not they have even answered the STAGE ONE existential question from adolescence of *"Who am I?"* I mention this because these clients also inevitably reveal to me that they are already wrestling with the STAGE THREE question of "How can I contribute to the world?" even though they may still be trying to figure out the two previous stage questions. Again, it makes sense to me that anyone struggling with the *generativity* question will more than likely also be struggling with the *intimacy* and *identity* issues of the earlier stages.

This mid-life uncertainty happens when men have not adequately considered their emotional development until they reach middle age, when adult life has already been shaped by many years of emotionally immature decision-making. How could attempting to become emotionally mature at middle age *not* be a struggle when it was developmentally appropriate some twenty years before? Living an adult life "on the outside" while functioning emotionally as an adolescent "on the inside" would be a disturbing idea were it not such a common phenomenon for men in our culture. A phrase like "boys will be boys," as it applies to adult men, is tacit acceptance of a toxic version of masculinity that the world can no longer afford to endure.

Toxic masculinity will linger for as long as it takes men to finally have the courage to ask themselves the question, *"Who am I?"* and to continue asking it for the rest of their lives so that they will never again settle for living up to someone else's definition of what *being a man* means. Answering this question cannot be approached from solely an intellectual perspective because, while the mind is the repository of the accumulated data of the events of our lives, it does not contain the accumulated *experiences* of the events of our lives. The answer to the question of *"Who am I?"* must come from both the information our minds have acquired along the way as well as from the moments of personal experience that are stored in a man's True Heart. This balance of heart and mind coalesce the battle scars and hard mileage of his journey into his unique and unrepeatable personality. What compels many men to finally get to this quest, however, is the forced maturity of middle age that crawls through his psyche and seeks to kick down the doors of immaturity that have shut him out of a deeper experience of himself and others. How could this type of guy *not* struggle with creating intimacy in an adult relationship since he has little knowledge of his true identity? No wonder when I ask a man if he has ever asked himself the question, *"Who am I?"* he looks at me as if he has never thought to put those three words together in the same sentence! His initial answer usually paints me a picture of *"What I do"*. While it is crucial for a boy or man to figure out what he wants to "do" in his life as a career direction, focusing outwardly still directs him away from knowing *who he is on the inside*. Until a man can give himself permission to venture into his inner world to find his True Heart, he will struggle with knowing his authentic self.

This illustrates how emotional immaturity has become so much of a "normal" part of traditional masculinity that this delay in psychosocial development is hardly noticed. Women may have their own observation of this about men, but I think it's safe to say that most men function at an emotional level that is immature and under-developed. This makes it necessary for men to "catch up" developmentally if they want to finally believe that their lives have meaning.

What Men Can Do

It is crucial that men begin to see themselves as part of a larger, complex, global picture of life on Earth in order to actively participate in the healing of themselves, their relationships, and the planet. This all starts at "home." In other words, men must become fiercely motivated to know themselves in order to help change the world. To get a clearer understanding of what might be possible, I think it's necessary: 1) for men to realize the importance of healing the toxic aspects of masculine identity that limit their personal lives; and 2) to then identify the effects of toxic masculinity in their families, communities, and culture; and 3) apply some amount of personal energy toward "making a contribution" to the planet by taking a stand against it. The following are a few suggestions of what I think men can do to make a difference:

Fearless Fathering

To me, *fearless fathering* at the very least means that a man is vulnerable enough to admit to the mother of his child if he feels fear and confusion about child-rearing. I also call it *courageous parenting* when both fathers *and* mothers can agree to be living examples of accountability to each other in front of their children when negative consequences arise as a result of the choices they have made. This is the exact opposite of what toxic masculinity has bred into the male psyche for thousands of years.

I believe men have many unique challenges and opportunities concerning how best to offer a role model of accountability to their children. Given the ever-evolving role for "fatherhood", men are still adjusting to what constitutes effective fatherly leadership, guidance, and protection of their children because many of the child-rearing duties today are shared between both parents. This inevitably leads men to a new set of expectations about how to "show up" in their child's life. *"Fathers are extremely conflicted today,"* says Christopher Brown, president of the National Fatherhood Initiative. *"Many years ago, the father was looked at primarily as a financial provider. Now he's looked at in a much more holistic sense of what providing means. It's not just financial; it means spiritual and emotional provision as well."* Yeshiva University psychology professor Louise Silverstein suggests that redefining fathering to emphasize nurturing, as well as providing, will place attachment and connection at the center of gender socialization for men. Masculinity would then become much less oppressive for men and women. (Silverstein, 1996)

As a man opens himself up to his emotional world and finds the essence of his authentic self by asking himself that question *"Who am I?"* he will be more capable of recognizing his impact on the life of someone he loves. It is at this point that he will be capable of teaching his son or daughter how to recognize the oppressive influence of toxic masculinity on women and men and how important it is to stand up for an egalitarian approach to social gender roles. It is essential for fathers and mentors to teach young boys that women deserve respectful treatment as human beings with equal rights. They must also teach that this lesson goes beyond the family household. It must go into the school classroom, the gym locker room, sports teams, the job market, the church, the neighborhood, as well as cities/states/nations. Fathers and mentors to boys and young adult men must challenge them to be courageous enough to speak up against oppression in all the forms that it exists in the world today.

❖ ❖ ❖

Four Tips For Fearless Fathering

1) Show more interest, investment, and involvement in helping your sons and daughters develop *emotional intelligence* at an early age, along with their physical and mental abilities. Do this by discussing their personal experiences with them and encouraging them to express their unique points of view, including their feelings.

2) *Throughout adolescence, encourage your sons and daughters to develop gender identity based not only on their environment but also their inner experience of who they are. When they reach adolescence, explore the question "Who are you?" with them along with figuring out the answer to "What do you want to do for a living?" Challenge them to clarify their beliefs and opinions without humiliating or judging their character. Be a mirror that reflects back to them the value of their uniqueness and authenticity. DO NOT EXPECT them to be a reflection of you and your values. Let them make their own value choices throughout their lives to integrate and emulate what you have taught them.*

3) Teach your sons and daughters that becoming a man has everything to do with living a life of personal integrity and accountability and absolutely nothing to do with misogyny, sexism, sexual abuse, harassment, bullying,

racism, or homophobia. Challenge him or her to have the courage to speak out against any of these things in their environment.

4) *Be a role model for your sons and daughters as to how a respectful, emotionally intelligent man makes choices in his life that are informed by what is in his True Heart.*

As the father of a teenage daughter, I constantly question my decisions about how to guide her to a better understanding of herself without imposing my own filter about life onto her young sensibilities. My father raised me very differently. The only thing he could think of to offer me was what he knew best, which was for me to fit into his concept of how to be a man. While there are things I can look back on and appreciate about what he tried to teach me, I can also see that, because no one ever supported him to know himself as a boy, there was no way he could have known how to do that for me. So he expected me to take on his filter of how he saw life, rather than help me develop my own.

As my daughter's father, there are times that I struggle with whether or not I am making decisions that are in her best interest, as opposed to trying to subdue my own fear of the unknown. Yet, I also continue to trust (and hope) that no matter what decisions I make regarding her well-being, it's more important for her to observe me being accountable for my choices when I make mistakes than it is for me to try to justify my behavior to her. As a man, I take my role as a protector and provider of my family very seriously, even though there are ways I'm still learning how to best fulfill that role along with my wife, who also protects and provides for our family. I know that my fears about being a good father have their roots in my insecurity about how best to live my life with integrity as a man. My attempt at being the best role model possible as a father is to hope that my daughter can observe me face my fears and stand up for what I'm passionate about and feel deeply convicted about. I want her to see me take risks and fail and succeed and fail and succeed so that she will know that she can do the same with her life and still be okay. I want her to see me face my insecurities as a man and how I take a stand for something that contributes to our lives on the planet.

Whether it's good news or bad, I know there are ways she will end up emulating me, so I want to give her something of value to pursue, something that will contribute to her happiness, self-esteem, and ability to make a contribution to life. My hope is that as she sees me be willing to deal directly with both the light side and dark side of my own life, that it will inspire her to do the same for herself.

Deconstructing Patriarchy

In my view, men must focus on the visible and invisible mechanisms of power and influence that characterize the dominant-subordinated system of cultural oppression. Besides being oppressive to other human beings, patriarchy also robs masculinity of its dignity through the overuse and misuse of male privilege. The dark shadow of this age-old patriarchal ideology makes life miserable in so many ways for women and men around the world. Patriarchy is a derivative of toxic masculinity, but patriarchy is an equal-opportunity oppressor to all groups who do not possess political and economic power. As the dominant group, however, men must be the ones to step up and do their best to challenge the culturally installed, patriarchal status quo that still exists here in

America as well as around the world. Men must take it upon themselves to become more aware of all the ways women are subtly and overtly oppressed and be willing to do something about it. I am not saying that to accomplish this, men must become the subordinated, disadvantaged group themselves. Unfortunately, most men support patriarchal masculinity by not educating themselves about its presence in their family, in their community, and around the world.

Deconstructing patriarchy begins when any man has the courage to look at himself through a different filter of what it means to "be a man" than the one that traditional masculinity has forced down our throats through fear, aggression, and humiliation for centuries. This is not even a man/woman thing. This is about seeing the need for all humans to have the right to live a life of dignity and self-respect, not one where power and privilege of a certain group dictates how anyone else should live. Women in western culture have been working on their half of this deconstruction throughout the 20th and into the 21st century. It is time now for us as men to figure out our half and do what we can to further this most important cause. Unless we step up and participate in fighting the outdated cultural ignorance that oppresses us all, we only contribute to the further demise of our own dignity and self-respect.

"Think Globally, Act Locally"

In 1978, a French-born American microbiologist named Rene Dubos coined a phrase that became a popular idiom. As an advisor at that time to the United Nations Conference on the Human Environment, he urged people to "Think

Globally, Act Locally." This referred to his argument that "global environmental problems can turn into action only by considering ecological, economic, and cultural differences of our local surroundings." (Eblen and Eblen, 1994) His message was that ecological awareness and consciousness should start at home. Using this concept as a template, there is an opportunity here to transform a piece of the complicated human jigsaw puzzle into a healthier picture of tolerance and harmony for people around the world. The way that men can participate in this is two-fold:

"Thinking Globally" would mean, for example, focusing on issues such as the presence of gender discrimination, honor-based violence, human trafficking, or human rights violations at a national or international level. Many countries around the world operate heavily under the tyranny of patriarchal tradition that glorifies male privilege, influence, and power. These cultures, in turn, promote the inequality of race, class, and gender that produces environmental inequities and injustices for the less advantaged around the world. (Newell, 2005)

"Acting Locally" would focus at the individual, family, community, and municipal levels. It would start with how a man takes the initiative at a personal level to deconstruct the toxic masculinity that alienates him from his own authenticity, personal integrity, and self-respect that was outlined in Chapter 5. He could then choose to bring the benefits of that personal transformation to his immediate and extended family, then to his community by any number of ways of becoming involved at the local level.

Patriarchy in Everyday Life

The list that follows paints a picture of the many expressions of male privilege, influence, and power that exist around the world today:

Acts of Terrorism
Benevolent Sexism
Body Shaming
Catcalling
Child Labor
Child Marriage
Child Physical Abuse
Child Sex Slavery
Child Sexual Abuse
Cultural Suppression of Girls' Education
Dating Violence
Domestic Violence
Dowry Murder
Drug-Facilitated Sexual Violence
Employment/Salary Discrimination
Ethnic Superiority
Female Genital Mutilation/Genital Cutting
Gang Violence
Gender Discrimination
Gender Pay Gap
Gender Stereotypes
Gendercide
Gun Violence
Hate Crimes
Homophobia

Honor-Based Violence
Hostile Sexism
Human Rights Violations
Human Trafficking
Incest
Machismo
Male-Dominated Industries
Misogyny
Objectification Of Women
Physical Abuse
Pornography
Racial Profiling
Racism
Rape
Religious Intolerance
Sexual Abuse and Assault
Sexual Exploitation
Sexual Harassment
Sexual Violence
Shaming, Bullying, Hazing Language & Behavior
Slavery
Stalking
Street Assault
Street Harassment
Toxic Masculinity
Unrealistic Standards Of Physical Beauty

Whether or not the above is a comprehensive list of attributes of patriarchal culture, it at least paints a picture as to the presence and power of male power and privilege that continues to dominate the world.

My Challenge to the Reader

1) Pick *one* item from the above list to simply Google and learn more about that particular issue.

2) Implement *one* possible course of action, *however small or large*, to help reality-check, dismantle, or extinguish that particular issue at an individual, interpersonal, family, community, tribal, municipal, national, or global level.

3) Recognize in your own life how these patterns of male privilege, influence, and power express themselves as a part of your masculine identity.

4) Identify how these personal patterns affect the lives of the people around you.

5) Become conscious of the degree to which male privilege, influence, and power permeate whatever culture you live in.

6) Commit to speaking up against all forms of abuse and control over women no matter where you encounter them.

7) Self-assess your own behavior and prejudice toward women, people of color, or members of the LGBT community, and be willing to educate yourself about the injustices that have kept those groups at a political, social, and economic disadvantage.

The Whole Heart and Soul of a Man

It is my belief that as we give ourselves permission as men to occupy and understand the internal world of our True Heart, it also opens the door to a higher spiritual Truth for us – one that is very personal. As I said in the first chapter, the True Heart is a type of interface between the soul and the ego. In other words, when I allow myself to be emotionally vulnerable by connecting with my True Heart, I can make the choice to either "listen" to the voice of my ego or the voice of my soul. Having access to both aspects of my identity gives me the power to live my life in a very honest way – or not. Staying connected to my True Heart allows me to observe and understand my wounded ego from a viewpoint that is both objective and non-judgmental. It also gives me enough "clearance" from my ego to actually hear what I call the "intuitive utterance of my soul." Overall, this gives me the opportunity to actually choose to live any moment of my life – every moment of my life – as an expression of that utterance.

In connecting with that piece of myself, I have the choice to define my higher spiritual Truth in whatever way I wish. I can overlay the filter of an already established religious practice onto it and give it structure that comes from the mind and heart of some person considered to be "enlightened." Or I can roll the dice and use the knowledge that comes from my own mind and heart as a way to explore the Truth that lives in my True Heart. I personally believe that this is what the so-called divine prophets did to come up with their own versions of "God" or a "Creator." I also believe that these messiah figures tried to convey that *anybody* could achieve the same wisdom and insight if they looked inside themselves in a deeper way.

I believe that we are all naturally gifted with the wisdom and insight needed to connect to the higher spiritual Truth we are here to celebrate. It is up to us to find it inside ourselves. For me, accessing that information comes through knowing my True Heart.

Going For It

When we summon up the courage to explore our individual emotional worlds, we open up to the unique and exceptional gifts that make up our authentic selves. It is my hope that as a man, you now at least have a clearer understanding that this is possible for you. I also know that as a guy, the first question your mind will ask is, *"Well, how do I do that?"* I want to answer this question by suggesting that before jumping into the *how*, you give yourself time to consider the very different *what* that my book has put forward. The *how* will be much easier to digest once you more fully consider the possibility of seeing yourself through this unique and very different filter of your emotional world.

Your current sense of masculine identity has more than likely been in place for many years. Please do not expect to be able to change that belief system overnight. The change I am asking you to consider is not that you become a different person than you already are. I am asking you to deepen your knowledge and appreciation of *the man you already are,* but that you have been trained to ignore and keep hidden from yourself and others. My wish for you is to see that second-order change requires that you become even *more* of who you really are. This mask or ego that we as men have come to show the world only keeps us all disconnected from our True Hearts.

Traditional masculinity fully serves the dark side of the male ego. It does not support or even acknowledge the existence of our authentic self. This is a lot to overcome. The influence is everywhere in our culture for us as men to continue to act like wounded Little Boys. We are constantly bombarded with direct and indirect messages to "be a man" by avoiding our emotional world. But the sad irony is that the version of "being a man" by the standard of traditional masculinity means to live your adult life as an immature, wounded Little Boy. The only thing that keeps this craziness in place is the draconian and outdated belief system that power and privilege are the birthright of those who possess greater physical strength.

Patriarchal culture is set up to constantly oppress and humiliate those who are disadvantaged and ignorant so that they conform to its ideology. I am asking you to consider the possibility that no matter what your status in life is as a man, that you and your loved ones still qualify as being a target of these patriarchal principles. That until you take the time, effort, and courage to pro-actively define yourself by a different standard of masculinity than the one that is culturally-installed to dominate and look down on others, you are in effect supporting that very system. You are more than likely very attuned to looking for feedback from others about yourself. Fine. It's what we all do as humans. However, it is time to look for and find the value of your uniqueness that is innate and instinctive to your heart – *despite what others think.* I'm asking you to trust that the more you allow yourself to feel what is in your True Heart – both the light side of joy, happiness, pleasure, satisfaction, and gratitude, as well as the dark side of fear, pain, anger, sadness, and shame – the more you will come to know your authentic and genuine self. It's important to explore the possibility that you could make an inward change that would help you evolve into a bigger and better version of yourself as a man.

Do not take my word for any of this!

You must try this all out for yourself:

- Become a student of your own life, and observe all the ways you act and react to circumstances that occur.
- When a relationship issue arises, make sure it's the mature Man-in-you who steps forward and opens up. Otherwise, it will be the immature Boy-in-you who either shuts down and runs away or tries to control the situation.
- Consider the possibility that embracing all of the feelings you were taught to avoid – fear, pain, anger, sadness, and shame – could somehow teach you to live a more courageous Life.
- Challenge yourself to summon the courage required to explore those feelings.
- Take the risk to tell the woman you love about what has scared you the most in your life.
- Have the guts to let her know when she hurts you by telling her directly that she has hurt you!
- Let her know how your feelings of inadequacy get triggered when she criticizes or judges you.

- Notice how she responds to any of these vulnerabilities from you. Does she freak out? Does she go-off by criticizing or judging you? Does she react in the way your worst fear would predict? Or does she listen and accept what you say, even if she disagrees? Does she comfort you and offer her emotional support?
- Give her the opportunity to hear and learn what you feel by actually expressing it! It isn't her job to read your mind and figure out how you feel. It is your job to tell her.

Get Out of Jail

Despite how women, people of color, and LGBT's have spoken up for the last 50 years against the persecution and contempt imposed upon them from a culture of white male privilege, men have yet to speak up en masse and do their part to redefine patriarchal masculinity. Our inaction lends tacit support to the institutionalized misogyny, sexism, racism, and homophobia that torments and discriminates against anyone who is not aligned with that oppressive ideology.

Taking action requires us initially to acknowledge whatever leftover tendencies of these traits are floating around in our own personalities. How could we as men not have residue of these traits inside us at some level given the fact that we are the recipients of thousands of years of patriarchal evolution? Until we admit that we have all, at times, *been capable* of being misogynistic, sexist, racist, and/or homophobic, it will: 1) continue to be a blind spot in our awareness that unfairly leaks out onto others, and 2) be difficult, if not impossible, to eradicate those tendencies from our psyches, our culture, and our planet.

Another ongoing challenge for men will continue to be the lack of role models for how to *dis-identify* from the overbearing nature of traditional masculinity. Women, people of color, and LGBT's were more consciously able to separate themselves culturally because they were on the receiving end of the ruthless behavior of those who maintained male power and privilege. It was easier for them to wake up and organize themselves to stand up against a status quo that did not include them nor care about what they wanted and needed. They were also able to take advantage of the *zeitgeist* that evolved after World War II, which finally tested the American values of equality, individualism, and freedom of speech. The double standard of judging the value of people by their station in life is hypocritical and inhumane.

The confounding piece for men has been the denial that has kept them ignorant of their own pain and suffering at the hand of patriarchy themselves. While these hardships have not been as clearly egregious as the ones suffered by other groups, men are not immune to subtler forms of exploitation and mistreatment. As I stated earlier in this book – patriarchy being the equal opportunity oppressor that it is – the personal price men have paid has been to become desensitized to the act of controlling and abusing other human beings. On the low end of the spectrum, this sacrifice of self-respect and personal dignity for "masculinity" may seem unexceptional. The other end of the spectrum, however, is devastating and incomprehensible, like the men and boys in villages in underdeveloped countries that are fighting extremist factions are separated from the women and girls, lined up and executed, while the women are forced into being trafficked and sold as sex slaves.

By drinking the patriarchal Kool-Aid over the millennia, men have "made a deal with the devil," in terms of compartmentalizing their compassion for humanity by colluding with a system that *seeks to gain power over others in order to serve the masculine ego.* The toll this takes on a man's self-worth is deplorable. This pain is self-inflicted, of course, and men quite often blame others for it. This is the jail cell men are imprisoned within, and it keeps them disconnected from their True Hearts. Those who choose to hold on to their survival-based self-definition for no reason other than its familiarity will only weigh down the progress needed to help change this tragedy at a global level.

I have come to realize, both professionally and personally, that learning to explore and articulate my emotional experiences has become a way for me to answer the question "Who am I?" out loud. As this has become an expression of my true manly self, this has also helped me to "normalize" my feelings against the brainwashing from my boyhood that my emotional world had no value other than to make me "too feminine." I now have my own understanding of how Erikson's developmental model makes sense, especially the stages from adolescence through young, middle, and mature adulthood. I can clearly see how my lack of emotional maturity – especially from my adolescence to young adulthood and into my middle-age years – set me up to be astonishingly ignorant about loving and honest relationships with women. It makes sense to me now that as I consult my True Heart for my authenticity, that it also gives me access to my soul, which helps me connect with a higher purpose in my life. I am also very grateful for all of the humbling Life lessons I have experienced throughout my life, because each one of them has helped me forge my identity as a man that finally feels real and authentic. This has become my new definition of what feels masculine.

Until we understand and accept that the same patriarchal cultural influences that have oppressed others for centuries also oppresses men, we will forever remain prisoners of that paradox. While I understand how men have benefited in many ways materially from exerting their power and authority over others, the emotional and psychological blowback has been too costly. It has created a "hole" in our ability as men to be truly happy.

Living a Life That Is "PONO"

There is a simple word in the Hawaiian language that I have always thought captures the essence of what I value most about my life. I have yet to find a similar word in the English language. That Hawaiian word is *pono*. Living a *pono life* means living with integrity. It means making a conscious decision to do the right thing regarding how I treat myself, how I treat others, and how I treat the environment I live in. It means having a respectful relationship with the people I love and work with. *Being pono* means putting discord back into balance, resolving inner and outer conflict, and restoring harmony in a way that all parties are *pono* with each other again.

The whole point of this book is to give any guy who reads it a concrete understanding and strategy for coming back into balance with himself. Men have been misinformed and misled about the importance of their emotional world. It would be the same as if someone told us we would be better off to live our lives avoiding the use of our intellect. It certainly might be possible to do that, but how could we ever survive and thrive by neglecting such a useful and amazing tool as our intellect? The same goes for the True Heart of a Man. It is the container of the unrepeatable experiences of each of our unique personalities. It maintains the specific timeline of our lives in a way that our brains cannot.

It is my hope that any man reading this can use the framework of this book as a point of reference along his journey toward the emotional awareness that will grow him into his mature and healthy masculine self.

Chapter 8

---

7 Steps to HEALTHY MASCULINITY

*"You must give up the life you planned in order
to have the life that is waiting for you."*

-Joseph Campbell

Like any adventure, Healthy Masculinity requires us to take risks that are a reflection of our courage to grow. Waking up to the need for second-order change will start men on a path toward their True Heart that, while unfamiliar at first, will ultimately introduce them to a deeper experience of authenticity, personal integrity, and self-respect. Though the adventure is fraught with challenges, there really is no bigger or better act of self-love than to seek out and embrace the Truth of who you are and why you are here. Healthy Masculinity is the reward for living life from your True Heart. This level of personal responsibility will enable you to contribute positively and unconditionally to your family, your community, and to the world at large. Despite whatever fears make us question our resolve to start on this journey, it must be our longing for personal freedom that inspires us to press on.

I offer the seven steps below as a "Roadmap to Being Real" for you to follow toward an experience of Healthy Masculinity that is relevant to our 21st century world. Before you begin, prepare to take these steps by first acknowledging the two essential mindsets from which to approach this excursion into your True Heart:

MINDSET #1:

Bring a "beginner's mind" attitude of openness and lack of preconceptions to this process.

The following steps are but one way of identifying and working on your blind spots. Chances are high that you have tried everything you already know to figure out the piece of your personality that keeps you unhappy in your life. Remember: the Wake-Up Call that got you here was the beginning of a new chapter of your life. There is always more for you to learn about life and about yourself. Keep an open mind!

(Read *"SIGNS You Are Getting a WAKE-UP CALL"*, p. 37)

MINDSET #2:

The goal is to courageously explore and become the Mature Man you are here to be – *whether or not anyone else approves or agrees with it.*

This is not an exercise in trying to please others or get their approval. In fact, this is an opportunity to finally give yourself permission to live your life from the inside out in a way that only you know how to be. The best reason to change and grow *is for yourself* – NOT for anyone else. Anyone that truly loves you will appreciate this approach. Discovering the Mature Man that defines your authentic self beneath the mask that you wear is the goal that all humans strive for. Along the way, you must deal with the demons in your head that keep you hidden behind that false mask. Challenge the Mature Man inside you to guide you through this process. He is eager to help set you free from your immaturity. Check your mindset in each of the following steps to make sure you approach the needed Second-Order Change in a sincere way.

(Read *"First-Order Change, Second-Order Change"*, pp. 125-126)

WARNING BEFORE YOU BEGIN

This is NOT a quick fix.

You must give yourself time to change in an authentic way. You have been wired the way you currently are for many years. It will require weeks and months to re-wire your belief system about yourself and the world. Take each step one at a time and give yourself permission to let each step take effect before you move on to the next one. Your patience with yourself will be tested, but that is always part of the growth process. Set aside a couple of hours each week to address each step. Think about each exercise of each step throughout the week in order to integrate it into your awareness.

DO NOT RUSH THROUGH THESE EXERCISES!

STEP 1

Survival vs. Masculinity

Get an *objective perspective* about the events in your
early life that taught you how to SURVIVE and how to
BE A MAN – and the differences between the two.

THE PROBLEM:

Until you are able to "see yourself" from a more objective
viewpoint, it will be difficult for you to understand the "big
picture" of how and why you react and make choices the way
you do in your life. Whether you are aware of them or not, your
emotions inform many of your choices and behaviors. Without
some kind of *objective perspective about yourself,* this puts
you at risk of making shortsighted, irresponsible decisions
about your life. Ignorance of your emotional world limits your
objective perspective of yourself and creates "blind spots" that
can keep you feeling insecure, inadequate, and prone to feeling
victimized.

Two foundational pieces of a man's identity are his *survival
instinct* and his sense of *masculinity.* A common blind spot for men
is how these two personality traits often overlap to the point of being
essentially synonymous. If this is the case, your ability to be *openhearted* with the woman you love will be severely limited because
your survival instinct will override and shut down any attempt
you make toward being emotionally vulnerable. Remember: any
kind of vulnerability – either physical or emotional – will activate

your survival instinct. This lack of vulnerability also props up our public persona of masculinity as a way to avoid being perceived as being unmanly and weak. This is what happens to us as men when someone asks us to share a feeling. The resulting lack of vulnerability prevents us from identifying whatever emotional experience we are in the middle of, much less be willing and able to express it out loud to a loved one. This immature version of masculinity not only keeps us out of integrity with ourselves and others, it is also destructive to our self-worth and destroys trust in our relationships. Lastly, it is what is at the root of the patriarchal misogyny, sexism, racism, and homophobia throughout the world. It is crucial for us as men to construct an identity of masculinity that defines us beyond our survival instincts and toward a more courageous and emotionally mature way of living our lives.

(Read "SIGNS You Are in SURVIVAL MODE", p. 89)

THE SOLUTION - DO THIS!

1) Imagine that you are the only person sitting in the audience at a movie theater, and the film showing on the movie screen is *the movie screen is the story about the first 18 years of your life,* with you as the main character. "Watching" the movie, try and remember the events of your young life that shaped your personality and character, but from an *objective perspective,* as if you were watching someone else's life pass before your eyes.

Ask yourself these questions about *"the-guy-in-the-movie":*

- As you watch this "movie" about your life that goes as far back as you can remember, what were the key moments/events in your early life that shaped and influenced your personality?

- Given the environment *the-guy-in-the-movie* grew up around – parents, siblings, living conditions, neighborhood, school, church, and culture – what did he learn about being able to trust or rely on others? Did he feel loved and valued, or did he feel judged and criticized? What did he learn about his own moral compass and personal values?

- Can you as *"the-guy-in-the-audience"* recognize the moments that caused *the-guy-in-the-movie* fear, pain, anger, sadness, and shame, even if he wasn't aware of those feelings at the time? What insecurities and "blind spots" did he develop as a result? Did he learn to believe in his own abilities? Did he learn to just do what he was told? Did he learn to be accountable for his mistakes, or did he blame others for his own shortcomings?

- Has he/you lived life from a position of showing people who he/you REALLY are and what his genuine values have been as a male? Or has he always lived his life from behind a mask/persona?

2) Ask trusted family and friends who were around you as you were growing up to give you feedback about what kind of kid you were. Ask questions gleaned from your growing *objective perspective* about yourself to fill in any holes of information that you cannot remember

yourself about your childhood. Ask that the feedback from them to be compassionate and respectful rather than judgmental and criticizing.

3) Take a sheet of paper, turn it on it's side, and label the top of the page **"STEP 1"**. Right underneath that, write **"TIMELINE OF MY LIFE"**. Now, half way down the page, draw a horizontal line from left to right. At the left endpoint of the horizontal line, put a hash mark on the line and label it "birth." At the right endpoint, put a hash mark on it and label it "today." As you remember the events of your life and "watch" the journey of *the-guy-in-the-movie* meet his life challenges, make hash marks on the line that represent the age at which these challenging moments occurred. These hash marks represent the major moments of your life that have shaped your personality and self-concept. Label each hash mark with your age and a word or two about that event.

4) Turn this sheet of paper over and draw a vertical line down the middle of the sheet. Label the top of the left column **"MY SURVIVAL"** and top of the right column **"MY MASCULINITY"**. Based on your observations of *"the-guy-in-the-movie,"* list the qualities or traits you learned or were taught as a boy to believe about how to survive. Put them into the left column. In the right column list the qualities or traits you learned or were taught to believe about masculinity or what it took to "be a man". Compare both columns and make a note of any similarities between your survival traits and masculinity traits. This is important information for

you to know about yourself that we will discuss in the next step.

THE BENEFITS:

Gain an objective awareness of how: a) all of the important moments/events of your life have contributed to your personal identity and created your belief system about yourself and the world; b) an understanding of where your character flaws and "blind spots" were created as a result of your lack of emotional awareness; c) a frame of reference for the unhealthy patterns of behavior and choice-making that challenge you to this day.

Identifying a connection between your sense of masculinity and your instinct to survive will give you an indication of the difficulty you may have with being emotionally vulnerable. Until you can distinguish and separate what feels masculine from your instinct to survive, *you will always instinctively avoid emotional vulnerability* because your limited vision of masculinity and survival will feel like the same thing. Until you can see them as different, you will be incapable of creating emotional vulnerability for yourself in a relationship.

YOU ARE READY TO GO TO STEP 2 WHEN...

...you have more of an ***objective perspective*** of yourself and a deeper understanding of the emotional impact of the important life events that have shaped your identity.

...you can start to see a pattern of how these events influenced your identity as a man.

...you understand at least intellectually – if not, emotionally – any unconscious similarity between your sense of survival and your sense of masculinity.

...you recognize at least intellectually – if not, emotionally – how a survival mentality prevents any vulnerable expression of your emotional world.

...you see at least intellectually – if not, emotionally – how crucial it is to develop and expand your masculine identity beyond a survival perspective.

STEP 2

Your Dark Side

Use your *objective perspective* to examine and
embrace the unexplored fear, pain, anger, sadness,
and shame that is your DARK SIDE and that keeps
you *emotionally immature* and living your life in
"survival mode".

THE PROBLEM:

Because we have been trained our whole lives to believe
that "real men" avoid showing their feelings, we remain
emotionally immature Little Boys in grownup bodies. *This
lack of emotional maturity has sadly become a trademark of traditional
masculinity.*

This emotional ignorance and immaturity has many
negative effects on a man's life: 1) Despite his chronological age,
it keeps him stuck running his adult life from the perspective
of being a wounded Little Boy; 2) It prevents him from gaining
an *objective perspective* about the life experiences that have
shaped his identity and personality; 3) this immature approach
to his life keeps his survival instinct consistently activated –
and vice versa; 4) It renders him incapable of being authentic
and honest with others.

The biggest blind spot to recognize and overcome is how
much you run your adult life from a survival-minded, wounded
Little Boy perspective. As long as you are unfamiliar with your
feelings of fear, pain, anger, sadness, and shame, you will be

prone to a high level of emotional reactivity. This is a sign of immaturity. This is a sign that you are in survival mode. This is a sign that the Little Boy in you is in charge of your adult life.

(Read *"SIGNS You Avoid Being EMOTIONALLY VULNERABLE"*, p. 152)

THE SOLUTION - DO THIS!

1) On a sheet of paper, label it at the top of the page as **"STEP 2"**. At the top write **"MY FPASS LIST"**. (FPASS is an acronym for your feelings of Fear, Pain, Anger, Sadness, and Shame.) Down the left hand side of the page, write down each of these feelings in a column: *fear, pain, anger, sadness, and shame.* Give yourself room to write about each of these feelings separately. Use your *objective perspective* to correlate how each of the events on your timeline from STEP 1 more than likely had a lasting emotional effect that connects to one or more of these feelings. Write about the resulting emotional residue that each event created in you as well as how each event has shaped your personality and belief system about yourself. On your TIMELINE, write next to the hash mark of each event the feeling elicited from that moment. Did *"the-guy-in-the-movie"* deal with any of those feelings directly, or did he retreat into denial about them? Has he ever shared the toughest of these experiences with anyone? Are you able to see the personal price you have paid by allowing your avoidance of these feelings to keep you from being fully open and present with others? Based on the events

you listed on your TIMELINE, identify the triggers in your life today that activate each of these feelings. Write these triggers under each feeling in your FPASS LIST.

2) Turn this page over. At the top of the page write **"MY LITTLE BOY"**. It is crucial for you to know both the immature and mature aspects of your personality, which we call the LITTLE BOY and the MATURE MAN. Becoming aware of the differences between these two parts of yourself give you the ability to choose "who" is making the decisions of your adult life at any given moment. We will define the MATURE MAN in STEP 6.

The LITTLE BOY is the part of a man's personality *today* that is emotionally immature, unaware, and still highly sensitive to the feelings that you identified on the other side of this page. Below is a list of immature traits and behaviors. Check *AT LEAST FOUR TRAITS* from the list below that describe you when you are feeling stressed, upset, or under pressure about something. Write down all of these traits on the page under MY LITTLE BOY. This will hopefully start to paint a picture of this immature part of you and how "he" walks and talks in your everyday life.

Here is the list.

My Little Boy:

- ☐ is not emotionally aware
- ☐ feels entitled to special treatment
- ☐ can be self-centered and arrogant
- ☐ unable to be emotionally vulnerable

- ☐ avoids having important conversations
- ☐ can be quick to judge and criticize others
- ☐ expects perfection from himself and others
- ☐ speaks more from his head than from his heart
- ☐ cannot be trusted to follow through on agreements
- ☐ is afraid to hurt, piss off, or disappoint other people
- ☐ doesn't believe he deserves to be happy and healthy
- ☐ has fear of conflict, so walks on eggshells around others
- ☐ has difficulty seeing the effect his behavior has on others
- ☐ looks down on others as a way to feel good about himself
- ☐ struggles at times to feel empathy or compassion for others
- ☐ can be highly defensive and reactive to feedback from others
- ☐ is insecure enough to demand others prove their worth to him
- ☐ is insecure enough to feel the need to prove his worth to others
- ☐ manages his anxiety by controlling others and his environment
- ☐ reluctant to take responsibility and be accountable for his choices
- ☐ is not willing to live up to the same standard he holds everyone else to
- ☐ thinks and functions more like a "me" than like a "we" in relationships
- ☐ blames others for his own unhappiness and can have a victim mentality
- ☐ makes decisions from an approach that is short-term gain, long-term pain
- ☐ gets disappointed in others due to having unrealistic expectations of them
- ☐ treats others in a way that is disrespectful, aggressive, passive, or shaming

☐ has a confused and immature way of expressing anything that is non-logical

THE BENEFITS:

As you learn to see yourself more objectively, you will notice how challenging it is to stay in contact with your feelings whenever your fight-or-flight anxiety is triggered, which in turn prevents you from being emotionally open and honest with others. STEP 2 asks you to look deeper into this part of your emotional world in order to understand and appreciate without judgment the experiences of your life that have created your personality.

Becoming more and more aware of the immature aspect of your personality called the *Little Boy* gives you an objective viewpoint of the amount of power this emotionally under-developed part of you has over your adult life. This step is crucial for you to "see" how immaturely reactive you are in your life, which has become your excuse for not being courageously honest and real with others. Despite his wounds, the Little Boy is also the playful, innocent part of you that is crucial for you to keep in your life for his humor, exuberance, and sense of fun. But it is the Mature Man who will create emotional intimacy with the woman you love – NOT the Little Boy.

YOU ARE READY TO GO TO STEP 3 WHEN...

...you are able to recognize how much the Little Boy in you is in charge of your adult life decisions.

...you are able to recognize the *high personal price* you pay whenever the Little Boy is in charge of your adult life decision-making.

...you are able to start to see the patterns of immature behavior that have run your decision-making.

...you are able to get more and more of a sense of the Mature Man in you.

STEP 3

Your "Inadequacy Myth"

**Use your *objective perspective* to write out the story
of the INADEQUACY MYTH playing in your head
that perpetuates the lie that you are somehow NOT
"lovable enough" or "good enough" or "man enough".**

THE PROBLEM:

Your survival instinct directed you to show others your light side in order to get their approval and love. This was a way to protect yourself from the story rattling in your head of your inadequacy and insecurity. Not only did you come to believe in your inadequacy, but you also came to believe that this part of you was not good enough to be loved. This became your dark side and is now the part of you that you hide from the view of others by wearing a mask or persona. Your worst fear is that -- if you showed this real part of yourself to someone you truly cared about -- that person would judge you to be inferior and thus, reject you in the same way that you felt rejected or judged as a boy.

**(Read *"SIGNS of Your Own TOXIC
MASCULINITY"*, pp. 118-119)**

THE SOLUTION - DO THIS!

1) On another sheet of paper write at the top of the page **"STEP 3"**. Under that write **"MY INADEQUACY MYTH"**. There

is a critical voice in your head that repeats a lifelong story on an endless loop to remind you how imperfect, insecure, and inadequate you are as a person. As long as this story continues to "rent space in your head", it will have the power to sabotage your happiness. Write out the story of your "Inadequacy Myth" that the critical voice in your head beats you up with whenever you make a boneheaded decision or you are on the receiving end of someone else's judgment. Start the story off with the words, *"What I learned to believe about myself as a Little Boy based on the feedback other people gave me was..."*

HELPFUL HINTS TO WRITE THIS STORY
(Read *"The INADEQUACY MYTH"*, p. 5)

a) Use your OBJECTIVE PERSPECTIVE and TIMELINE from STEP 1 to identify and write out the Who, What, When, Where, and Why circumstances (wounds) of your childhood that contributed to your insecurity, self-doubt, and low self-esteem.

b) Use your FPASS LIST from STEP 2 to identify and write about the fear, pain, anger, sadness, or shame that came about as a result of these circumstances. These previously unexplored feelings make up your dark side and get triggered today when similar events happen to you. Your deeper awareness of these feelings will help you to deconstruct the story of your insecurity.

c) Continue writing the story of your INADEQUACY MYTH by using your SURVIVAL/MASCULINITY comparison from STEP 1 to identify and tie in how you were "trained" by these two aspects of your personality to avoid feeling the pain of inadequacy that those circumstances created.

2) Turn this sheet of paper over and write at the top of the page **"MY LIFE TODAY"**. Identify and write about the circumstances that occur in your life today that trigger your INADEQUACY MYTH to get loud in your head. Reference the emotional wounds of your childhood and how those old feelings currently get activated, which then activate your survival mode. Identify and write down whatever things you need to remember to say to yourself to get out of survival mode. Write about the ways you know you still hide out from others for fear of their rejection or judgment. Write about whatever ways you still struggle with being vulnerable and showing your true feelings by "wearing a mask" – especially if you think it will hurt or disappoint others. Identify and write about the mask/persona you wear today. Who is "the guy" you show to others? Is he funny, competent, laid-back, confident, self-effacing? How much is this persona a reflection of the real you? How much is this persona a cover-up to your INADEQUACY MYTH?

THE BENEFITS:

Being the imperfect human beings that we all are, our flaws create insecurity in our minds about whether or not we are worthy of being loved and admired. *No person escapes this challenge.* We all must deal with the critical voice in our heads that reminds us of the story of this INADEQUACY MYTH. The good news is that it keeps us humble. The bad news is how we draw the erroneous conclusion that, because we have these flaws and imperfections, it must mean we are not worthy of love and admiration. The lie or mythology of our story is NOT that we are imperfect. Our imperfection is our reality. The myth we are burdened by is that we are *somehow not lovable because we are imperfect.*

It is important to find a way to stay humble while at the same time not drink the kool-aid that is the lie of our Inadequacy Myth. The best way to do this is to "lean in" to the story and reality check the fact that no human being has a free pass out of his or her own imperfections. Many people use their egos to convince themselves and others that they may not have flaws, but that is just another part of their Inadequacy Myth that helps them stay in denial about their disappointment in themselves. Becoming emotionally mature requires a deeper understanding of how our very human feelings of fear, pain, anger, sadness, and shame have had an effect on our self-concept. Knowledge is power. Embracing our dark side allows us to reality check the Inadequacy Myth, accept our humanity, and have compassion for ourselves. This is what sets us free from the Paradoxical Prison we occupy.

YOU ARE READY TO GO TO STEP 4 WHEN...

...you have a better understanding of how your fear, pain, anger, sadness, and shame have shaped your personality.

...you are able to also appreciate the valuable lessons you have learned in your life as a result of exploring the experiences that have led you to those feelings.

...you can finally articulate the Inadequacy Myth that runs through your head and that you beat yourself up with unnecessarily, so that you can finally accept your flaws and find compassion for the person you have become as a result of the emotional life you have led.

STEP 4

Compassion & Forgiveness

Have *compassion* for your dark side -- rather than
judgment -- so that you can: a) *forgive yourself* for
believing the lie of your Inadequacy Myth, and b)
forgive others for how they've done the same thing to
themselves at your expense.

THE PROBLEM:

As you start to understand how your authentic self has
both a light side (strengths, talents, abilities) and a dark side
(insecurities, self-doubt, low self-esteem), *you must embrace
both sides as an honest expression of your unique personality.* By
"embrace" I mean to carefully and painstakingly know both
sides. To fully allow someone else's love into your heart, you
must first feel wholehearted love for yourself. You must heal
the insecure, wounded, anxious part of you that is burdened
by the story (Inadequacy Myth) you learned about yourself as
a boy from the people that raised you.

The immature aspect of your personality that we are
calling your Little Boy represents your childhood experiences
of how your young personality was shaped by your early
environment. If you grew up surrounded by unconditional
love and nurturing, you grew up believing that your *real self*
was worthy of love. If, however, you got love and approval
based on how you adjusted your personality to the likes and
dislikes of those around you, your Little Boy probably grew

up believing that his real self was "not good enough" and, therefore, not worthy of love.

This trained you as a child to "wear a mask" to hide your dark side in order to please others and get their approval and love. If you succeeded at getting this positive feedback, your Little Boy learned that the version of yourself that wore a mask was more valuable and acceptable than the real version that was flawed. Until you can accept and have COMPASSION for being the imperfect, insecure, flawed human child that you were, this immature Little Boy part of you will continue to control your adult decision-making and interactions with others to gain their approval and praise -- even if it means selling out your authenticity, personal integrity, and self-respect. *You do not want your Little Boy running your adult life!* Left to his own devices, the Little Boy makes decisions from this wound that leads to narcissism, depression, anxiety, addiction, violence toward self and others, powerlessness, and isolation.

Being able to accept and have compassion for yourself and others is what leads to the FORGIVENESS that is necessary to heal any emotional wound. To forgive any misdeed that we committed or was committed against us is the only way that we can genuinely "move on" with our lives. Forgiving yourself can only come from having compassion for the young and innocent Little Boy part of you who believed the lie that your authentic self was not worthy of love and therefore did not deserve success or happiness.

(Read "SIGNS You LACK COMPASSION for Yourself and Others", p. 109)

THE SOLUTION - DO THIS!

1) On a separate sheet of paper, label the top of the page **"STEP 4"**. Underneath that write **"FORGIVE MYSELF"**. Gather and utilize all of your solutions from STEPS 1, 2, and 3, i.e., your OBJECTIVE PERSPECTIVE, your TIMELINE, your SURVIVAL/ MASCULINITY comparison, your FPASS LIST, your LITTLE BOY description, and your INADEQUACY MYTH.

Try to pinpoint and understand where the story of your Inadequacy Myth comes from, how it has served an important "purpose" in your life, and why it continues to sabotage your self-worth and overall happiness. Imagine if you had a 7-year-old son and he approached you feeling embarrassed after losing a soccer game or getting a bad grade in school. If he verbalized his belief that his poor performance was due to the fact that he was somehow deficient in his character as a person, what would you say to him? Could you put yourself into this Little Boy's shoes and imagine what he really needs to hear in that moment? Would you try and comfort him? Or would you jump on the bandwagon along with the critic in his head and nitpick him into loser-ville? What do you remember your father and mother saying to you when you were a boy being plagued by self-doubt? What words would you have appreciated hearing from someone who knew you back when you were that Little Boy that could have helped you believe in yourself?

It is crucial that you feel *compassion* for the way you grew up believing that you somehow were not good enough or lovable enough to those around you. You know that Little Boy inside you better than anyone else. You know best what he needed to hear about being the beautiful, imperfect human being that he was, and how his flaws were far outweighed by the amazing quality of his character. Write down the words that you deserved to hear about yourself that no one else was capable of saying to you. This is the comfort the Little Boy must get from you in order to *forgive himself* for ever believing the lie of his Inadequacy Myth.

The following phrases may or may not be applicable to your upbringing. Choose any one or more of them that fit your own story. If none of these fit, then write your own to describe what it is exactly that you needed to hear as a Little Boy in order to forgive yourself for believing the lie of your Inadequacy Myth. Start with:

"As I think of what I learned about myself as a Little Boy, I can now feel compassion for..."

- how no one ever told me that my mistakes, insecurities, and embarrassments were a part of every human being's imperfect life.
- how difficult it was for me when I felt judged by others for being this flawed, imperfect Little Boy to the point where I even judged and felt critical of myself.
- how I believed I had to hide this authentic part of myself by "wearing a mask" to please others in order to get love and approval. This became my survival strategy to ward off the fear and pain I would feel of not being loved. Consequently, by hiding this insecure part of myself, I also locked-in the story of my "Inadequacy Myth" into my self-concept.
- how much of a good person I was as a kid – despite there being times when I felt insecure, misunderstood,

unappreciated, awkward, defiant, uncoordinated, painfully shy, scared, hurt, angry, sad, or ashamed.

- how every part of my insecure and imperfect personality *deserved then and deserves now to be loved* – whether or not I truly get that love from another person.
- how I was only doing what I knew how to do in order to survive my circumstances, and that I can now *forgive myself for not accepting myself for being the flawed, loving, imperfect, decent human being that I have always been.*

Complete this statement of compassion with the following phrase of forgiveness:

> *"By understanding now how my personality was shaped by certain emotional events in my life, I can appreciate the amazing survivor I became. I can also accept the fact that my dark side is equally as important a part of my authentic self as my light side, and that it helps define my humanity. I can now forgive myself for ever believing the lie that my imperfections somehow made me unworthy or undeserving of being loved."*

Integrate this compassionate self-talk into the "personal profile" you already have of yourself, so that you can remember the Truth of **who you are** whenever your Inadequacy Myth starts to crawl through your head.

2) Turn the page over and label it: **"FORGIVE OTHERS"**. Using your OBJECTIVE PERSPECTIVE, your TIMELINE from STEP 1, and your FPASS LIST from STEP 2, make a list of all the people you can remember who have scared, hurt, angered, abandoned, or shamed you in some way, shape, or form over the course of your life – including from your family-of-origin. Write their names down, then write what you remember feeling as a result of how they treated you. Just as you learned in STEP 4 to have compassion for your own insecurities and limitations as an imperfect human being, you must also have compassion for and forgive others who are equally as limited and imperfect as you are.

Whether or not you contact them in person is not as important as how you forgive them in your heart, knowing they more than likely did the best they could at the time that they mistreated you as a result of their own lack of self-respect and self-worth. Take a look at whatever ways your INADEQUACY MYTH intensified as a result of how they treated you. Forgive these people – NOT as a way to "let them off the hook". Forgive them to FREE YOURSELF from carrying around the pain of their flawed choices that you never deserved in the first place.

THE BENEFITS:

By forgiving yourself for having ever believed that you are not lovable or good enough or man enough, you free yourself to live your life as the imperfect, flawed, but lovable, valuable human being that you are. You also detach from any need to hide out, and you empower the Mature Man in you to sustain the emotional maturity necessary to live an authentic life.

YOU ARE READY TO GO TO STEP 5 WHEN...

...you begin to have compassion for yourself and can understand the life circumstances that taught you to sacrifice your personal integrity and truth.

...you no longer live your Life through the filter of your Inadequacy Myth.

...you forgive yourself for being the limited, mistake-prone, imperfect human being that you are.

STEP 5

Emotional Maturity

Hold yourself accountable to a healthier standard
of masculinity that relies on *emotional maturity* as
both a strength and a healthy skill set – as well as a
pathway to living an *authentic life*.

THE PROBLEM:

Because traditional masculinity has never placed a value
on emotional maturity, men may grow up physically and
intellectually, but not emotionally. Emotional growth comes
from the desire to know *"Who Am I?"* Emotional immaturity
shuts that process down and wreaks havoc on a man in three
ways:

1) By ignoring the FPASS emotions of his dark side, a man
   empowers his wounded ego to run his life. This in turn
   shuts down his authenticity, personal integrity, and
   self-respect.

2) This lack of realness also hinders his ability to create
   emotional intimacy with the woman he loves.

3) He placates and appeases others in order to receive love,
   as opposed to being courageously honest and real, even
   in the face of disapproval and rejection.

**(Read *"SIGNS You Are OUT OF
INTEGRITY With Yourself"*, p. 158)**

THE SOLUTION - DO THIS!

1) Find a photo of yourself as a Little Boy. It's best if you can remember a challenging age in your early life and find a photo from that time period. Put the photo on your bathroom mirror or in a frame that you look at frequently. Remember the events you marked on the TIMELINE from Step 1 and how each of those moments affected who "he" was and how he felt about himself. In your own mind, "talk" to the Little Boy in the photo as if he was your own biological son. Talk to him as if you were actually having a conversation with this younger version of yourself. What would you say to him that you wished someone had said to you at that age? *Remind him* of all the things you have written down in these FIRST FOUR STEPS. *Remind him* how amazing he was and still is, despite how others treated him or thought of him. *Remind him* that the way he was taught to "be a man" also taught him to feel weak and inadequate if he tried to live up to that image of manliness by not showing emotion. *Remind him* how he learned to *wear a mask* to get the approval and love of others – *even though he was already lovable the way he was and still is.* As you talk to that Little Boy, become aware of the Mature Man in you who is talking to him. *This is the part of you who needs to be making the adult decisions of your life.*

2) Take a sheet of paper and at the top of the page write **"STEP 5"**. Underneath that write **"MY MATURE MAN"**. Copy the seven statements below onto the page. Use these statements as goals for you to aspire to,

given the fact that you have done the work of the first four STEPS. It is important that you take each statement separately and challenge yourself to consider each one having value for the personal growth you have committed yourself to. Each of them is a result of the journey outlined in the previous steps that hopefully you can relate to. If these statements are perplexing, then use each of them as a launching point for doing your own personal work with a therapist or coach.

The 7 Signs of an EMOTIONALLY MATURE MAN

1) I no longer worry about pleasing my parents or living up to their expectations of me. I have an adult-to-adult relationship with them now and am able to have empathy and compassion for them because I see the very human flaws that have created each of their own Inadequacy Myths.

2) *I now understand that the version of masculinity taught to me by my father was synonymous with his survival instinct. Therefore, by inheriting his "legacy of masculinity", I have limited my own experience of being a whole person by negating and ignoring what lives in my own True Heart. I did this as a boy because I could not prevent my need-to-survive from defining me as a male the same way that my father's need-to-survive defined him.*

3) My authenticity, personal integrity, and self-respect have become more important to me than maintaining any

kind of "mask of masculinity" to get another person's approval or love.

4) *I accept that my emotional world is the doorway to my authenticity, personal integrity, and self-respect, which requires my courage to both explore and express.*

5) I have learned that my willingness to be emotionally vulnerable – challenging as it may be to sustain – helps me create closeness and trust in my relationships.

6) *I accept that knowing and sharing my emotional world not only takes care of my relationships, but it is also one of the best ways for me to take care of myself.*

7) I understand that the one thing I need the most – *which is to believe that I am worthy of someone else's love even if no one else loves me* – is also the one thing I learned to avoid because I've been too afraid to risk being rejected if I show someone the "real me" that lives in my True Heart. Because of this, I have relied heavily on my survivor mentality to just "get by", but have also consistently kept true intimacy and love away from me in order to avoid feeling that potential, devastating pain of rejection. Because this is my absolute worst fear, the most courageous thing I can do is to make a choice to live my life beyond my fight-or-flight prison by risking to let someone see my True Heart in order to feel truly seen and loved – flaws and all – by that other person.

THE BENEFITS:

Becoming more and more aware of the Mature Man in you gives you the opportunity to live a more courageous life of authenticity, personal integrity, and self-respect. Living life from this mature and honest perspective is the best form of *self-care* possible. Becoming aware of when you are in Little Boy mode and becoming adept at switching into Mature Man mode will keep your life in balance and your relationships healthy. Learning to embrace the humanness of your dark side will keep you out of denial and accountable to the choices you make in your life. This will teach you compassion toward yourself and others.

Talking to that photo of the Little Boy also gives you a way to become aware of *the Mature Man part of you that needs to grow up, show up, and run your adult life.* Recognize how knowledge of both the light side and the dark side of your emotional world empowers the Mature Man in you to make responsible, mature decisions in your adult life.

YOU ARE READY TO GO TO STEP 6 WHEN...

...you no longer fear that you will appear somehow weak or "unmanly" when you share your honest feelings.

...you no longer fear that you will appear somehow weak or "unmanly" when you share your honest feelings.

...you are making the *effort* and have the *willingness* to see yourself through this new lens of authenticity, personal integrity, and self-respect.

...you are able to identify more clearly when you are in Little Boy mode versus when you are in Mature Man mode in your decision making.

...you feel the Mature Man in you to be more and more in charge of your adult life.

STEP 6

Emotional Intimacy

Challenge the MATURE MAN in you to bring
this authentic and real version of yourself to your
intimate relationships.

THE PROBLEM:

Your avoidance of emotional vulnerability has kept you out of integrity with yourself and with the people you love. Trust between two people cannot be built without sharing courageous and sincere truth with each other. This emotional vulnerability is crucial if you are to be the "real you" in your life. The challenge for a man is that emotional open-ness also triggers the survival instinct of fight-or-flight as a way to defend against that very vulnerability. Because this exact same defense against vulnerability also happens to be a very consistent trait of traditional masculine identity, vulnerability does not come easy.

This is the reason men often walk on eggshells around women out of the fear of revealing something she may not like. Any display of emotional vulnerability triggers a man's shame response regarding his potential appearance as weak and unmanly, and therefore, an unsuitable potential partner with which to procreate.

But a healthy intimate relationship is impossible to create when either party brings a lack of personal integrity into it in the form of infidelity, deceit, control, physical/emotional/sexual abuse or violence, walking on eggshells, lack of accountability, uncontrolled emotional reactivity, or unrealistic expectations – just to name a few.

(Read *"SIGNS of Your BLIND SPOTS in a Relationship"*, pp. 199-200)

THE SOLUTION - DO THIS!

1) Get another sheet of paper and at the top of the page write "STEP 6" and underneath that write "MY ACCOUNTABILITY". Make a list of all the people in your life that you can remember either betraying, hurting, pissing off, abandoning, or shaming – including members of your family-of-origin. Write down their names, and write down what you remember "doing" to them that you never were accountable for. Because you have already forgiven yourself for your human-ness in STEP 4, you are now able to not only forgive others, but to also be more accountable to others for your own flawed actions. If at all possible, find the people on this list – even if by letter or email – and apologize to them. Here is the most important piece of this exercise: *have ZERO EXPECTATIONS that they will either forgive you or accept your apology.* You must NOT hope or expect them to understand and/ or forgive you. This exercise is a way to lighten your own accumulated-burden-of-a-lifetime that has become part of your INADEQUACY MYTH. It is their choice to handle whatever they can handle emotionally for

themselves, but you no longer have to put any part of your life on hold waiting for their approval or love. Because you have already forgiven yourself and others, *you get to see the fact that you have always been good enough, man enough, and lovable enough.*

2) Take the sheet you filled out as The Solution to STEP 2. Read the front page of MY FPASS LIST as well as the MY LITTLE BOY on the back of the STEP 2 page to your intimate partner. Ask your partner *how it feels for her* to hear this information. Ask her if she has any questions about what you have read to her. Ask her if she can relate to anything you shared with her.

3) Wait a few days before you do this next suggestion. Take the sheet you filled out as The Solution to STEP 3 and read both sides of this page to your intimate partner. These are MY INADEQUACY MYTH and MY LIFE TODAY. Again, ask your partner *how it feels for her* to hear this information. Ask her if she has any questions about what you have read to her. Ask her if she can relate to anything you shared with her.

4) Wait a few more days before you get to this next piece, which I'm sure you can predict already! Take the sheet you filled out as The Solution to STEP 4 on COMPASSION and FORGIVENESS, and read this to your intimate partner. It is up to you whether or not you share the photo of yourself as a Little Boy. That piece is a very private one that is not necessarily part of the connection with your partner. Once again, ask your partner *how it feels for her* to hear this information. Ask her if she has any questions about what you have

read to her. Ask her if she can relate to anything you shared with her.

5) DO NOT share (just yet) the *"7 Signs of an Emotionally Mature Man"* from STEP 5 with your partner. I challenge you to hold off letting anybody know this piece of your journey until you feel you have authentically integrated whatever pieces of it you relate to into your self-concept. If and when you DO share this with your partner, please DO NOT share it as a way of impressing her or trying to get her approval or love. ***Work with a therapist or coach to make sure you relate to and integrate this into whatever experience you have of your authentic self at a deeper level.*** This list is FOR YOU as a destination on this "Roadmap to Being Real". Achieving this means that you have freed yourself from the Paradoxical Prison that we as men have been imprisoned by.

YOUR ONGOING RELATIONSHIP CHALLENGES

a) Follow through on your commitment to your relationship with the woman you love by first having a *commitment to yourself* to live a life of authenticity, personal integrity, and self-respect.

(Read *"The Need for Authenticity, Personal Integrity, and Self-Respect"*, p. 153)

b) Tell the woman you love specifically *what it is* YOU NEED to be happy in a committed, healthy, intimate relationship with her. Then ask her *what*

SHE NEEDS to help you create a healthy, intimate relationship. Put those two sets of needs together, and come up with a picture of the type of intimacy and connection that makes sense to the both of you.

(Read *"What Men Need -- Without Being Needy"*, p. 136)

c) Practice empathy by trying to relate to what your partner may be experiencing emotionally at any given moment. Put your own opinions/feelings to the side for a minute, and wonder what it is that she may be feeling.

d) Build trust with your partner by being totally accountable for every choice you make in your life – despite how humbling it may be to admit your mistakes. If you need to apologize, do so in a way that commits to learning a lesson from your mistake in order to avoid repeating it.

e) Think and act more like a "we" than a "me" in your relationship. Get out of your self-centered world and show interest in who your partner is, what she needs, and how she looks at you and her own life. Be interested in her world view.

(Read *"Accountability and Empathy"*, p. 197)

f) Make mutual agreements with your partner about all aspects of your relationship rather than immaturely assume or expect you know what you both want and need.

(Read *"Parent-Child vs. Adult-Adult Relationships"*, p. 201)

THE BENEFITS:

Learning to hold your partner's wants and needs in your heart actually challenges you to love yourself in a powerful and unique way. It requires a level of emotional maturity that is a reflection of the Mature Man in you and puts "him" in charge of your adult intimate relationships. Being a healthy, compassionate, mature partner is a sign that you love yourself. It is a sign that you are now acting in your life in ways that feed your heart and soul – not your ego. By making mutual agreements with your partner, you learn how to build trust with another person, and in the process, you learn how to trust that what you know comes from your True Heart.

(Read *"Ten Things Men Can Do to Become Better Emotional Partners in Their Relationships"*, p. 206)

YOU ARE READY TO GO TO STEP 7 WHEN...

...you become more and more familiar with how to access the courage needed to be authentic and real – even in the face of disagreement or judgment from others.

...you hold your personal integrity to be a sacred part of who you are as a man, which means that you hold yourself to this high standard of conduct whether it is apparent to anyone else or not.

...you begin to trust that the best way for you to take care of yourself is to make sure the Mature Man in you is running your life.

...you no longer seek to avoid confrontation or conflict or disagreement, but instead seize the opportunities to express your unique, personal truth in a respectful way and come to mutual agreements that avoid misunderstandings and unspoken resentments.

STEP 7

Masculinity 2.0

Challenge yourself to create a life that has *meaning,*
passion, and *purpose* by doing something to make the
world a better place in which to live.

THE PROBLEM:

For the middle-aged man, it is a lifelong lack of self-knowledge that is at the core of feeling stagnant and disappointed about his life. Having a successful career and raising children successfully are great ways of feeling fulfilled. Yet, there can come a time when a man's self-interest wanes, and he looks back at his life, wondering if he has made positive changes that benefit other people. If a man cannot see how his life has somehow made a contribution to the planet, he may have a classic "mid-life crisis."

It might feel natural for him to look at his marriage as another experience of opportunities missed or mistakes made. What might also feel natural is to look outside of himself for the answers to his dilemma in the form of a change in job, change in location, or change in life partner. The consistent message from all six of the previous steps offered here is that the information needed to feed a man's heart and soul comes from the authentic and real experience he has of himself – both the light side and the dark side. If a man courageously explores his True Heart, his life will gain more and more meaning. If he stays attached to his ego, he will remain ignorant and out of touch with his True Heart, and his middle and older adulthood years will feel stagnant and unsatisfactory – not because he needs to change his job or his spouse, but because he has never become acquainted with his authentic self.

(Read *"SIGNS Your Life Feels Stagnant from LACK OF SELF-KNOWLEDGE"*, p. 214)

THE SOLUTION - DO THIS!

1) Use your AWARENESS of your True Heart now to guide whatever intuition you have about yourself, and begin to wonder how you can make some amount of difference on the planet – whether anyone else ever knows about it or not. Use your journey through this exercise to identify all the ways you have been trained as a man to live life under the ignorance of unhealed fear, pain, anger, sadness, and shame in order to see how prevalent that model still is on our planet. As you have endeavored to free yourself from the toxic masculinity that has kept your life immature, notice how these same exact principles serve as the basis for many of the world's problems.

2) Turn to page 227 in this book and read *"My Challenge to the Reader"*:
- Pick *one* item from the list on pages 225 and 226 to simply Google and learn more about that particular issue.
- Identify how any of these personal/social conditions may affect the lives of the people around you.

- Become conscious of the degree to which male privilege, power, and influence permeate whatever culture you live in.

- Recognize in your own life how any of these patterns of male privilege and power have shaped your own sense of masculine identity *both positively and negatively.*

- Self-assess your own behavior and prejudice toward women, people of color, or members of the LGBT community, and be willing to educate yourself about the injustices that have kept those groups at a political, social, and economic disadvantage.

- Commit to speaking up against any and all forms of abuse and control over women, people of color, or members of the LGBT community no matter where you encounter them.

- Implement *one* possible course of action, *however small or large,* to help reality-check, dismantle, or extinguish that particular issue at an individual, interpersonal, family, community, tribal, municipal, national, or global level.

3) Use your True Heart now to guide whatever intuition you have about yourself, and begin to wonder how you can make some amount of difference on the planet – whether anyone else ever knows about it or not. Use your journey through this exercise to identify all the ways you have been trained as a man to live life from fear, pain, anger, sadness, and shame in order to see how prevalent that model still is on our planet. As you have endeavored to free yourself from the toxic masculinity that has kept your life immature, notice how these same

exact principles serve as the basis for many of the world's problems. Use your newfound courage to combat the misogyny, sexism, racism, and homophobia that stays in place from patriarchal ideology around the world.

THE BENEFITS:

Finding a sense of higher purpose and meaning for your life not only will ward off depression and anxiety for you personally, but it will also help humanity to evolve toward a global coexistence of collaboration and mutual understanding – a world in which our differences can be celebrated and encouraged.

Bibliography

Addis, M.E., and J.R. Mahalik. (2003). "Men, Masculinity and the Contexts of Help-Seeking." *American Psychologist*, 58(1), 5-14.

Aston, Maxine. (2007) Affective Deprivation Disorder. Available from URL: http://www.maxineaston.co.uk/cassandra/AfDD.shtml. Accessed February 12, 2014.

Berger, J. L., M.E. Addis, J.D. Green, C. Mackowiak, and V. Goldberg. (2012). "Men's Reactions to Mental Health Labels, Forms of Help-Seeking, and Sources of Help-Seeking Advice." *Psychology of Men & Masculinity*. Advance online publication. doi: 10.1037/a0030175

Bergquist, William. (1993). *The Modern Organization: Mastering the Art of Irreversible Change*. San Francisco: Jossey-Bass.

Bradshaw, John. (1994). *Creating Love: The Next Great Stage of Growth*. New York: Bantam Books.

Brown, Brené. (2012). *Daring Greatly: How the Courage to Be Vulnerable Transforms the Way We Live, Love, Parent, and Lead.* New York: Gotham Books.

Campbell, Joseph. ed. (1976). *The Portable Jung.* New York: Penguin Books.

Center for Disease Control (CDC), Suicide Rates, 2007. Available from URL: http:www.cdc.gov/injury/wisqars/index.html. Accessed July 14, 2014.

_____. (2011) "National Data on Intimate Partner Violence, Sexual Violence, and Stalking." *The National Intimate Partner and Sexual Violence Survey: 2010 Summary Report.* Available from URL: http:www.cdc.gov/violenceprevention/pdf/nisvs-fact-sheet-2014.pdf Accessed July 14, 2014.

Cleary, Anne. (2012). "Men, masculinities and suicidal behavior." *Social Science & Medicine* 74 (4): 498–505.

Collins, Sam. "'Choking Girls All Around the World' Seminar Ends In Australia Amid Protests." ThinkProgress. org, November 7, 2014. Available from URL: http://thinkprogress.org/health/2014/11/07/3590366/julien-blanc/ Accessed November 9, 2014.

Cummins, Denise D. (2000). "How the Social Environment Shaped the Evolution Of Mind." *Synthese* 122: 3-28. Kluwer Academic Publishers.

David, Deborah and Robert Brannon. (1976) *The Forty-Nine Percent Majority: The Male Sex Role.* Boston, MA: Addison-Wesley Publishing Co.

Diagnostic and Statistical Manual of Mental Disorders (DSM-V). American Psychiatric Publishing, 5th edition (May 27, 2013)

Eblen, R.A. and W. Eblen. (1994). "Think Globally, Act Locally." *The Encyclopedia of the Environment.* Boston: Houghton-Mifflin Company.

Ellis, Ralph and Sara Sidner, CNN News. (May 27, 2014) "Deadly California Rampage: Chilling Video, But No Match for Reality." Available from URL: http://www.cnn.com/search/?query=deadly+california+rampage&x=-1043&y=-89&primaryType=mixed&sortBy=relevance&intl=false. Accessed May 28, 2014.

Erikson, Erik H. (1950). *Childhood and Society.* Madison, CT: International Universities Press.

_____. (1959). *Identity and the Life Cycle.* Madison, CT: International Universities Press.

_____. (1968). *Identity: Youth and Crisis.* New York: W.W. Norton.

Fitzgerald, Michael and Mark Bellgrove. (2006). "The Overlap Between Alexithymia and Asperger's Syndrome." *Journal of Autism and Developmental Disorders,* May 2006, 36(4): 573-576.

Freud, Sigmund. (1933). *New Introductory Lectures on Psycho-Analysis.* New York: W.W. Norton.

Goleman, Daniel. (1995). *Emotional Intelligence: Why It Can Matter More Than IQ.* New York: Bantam Books.

Goodman, J. (1995). "Change Without Difference: School Restructuring in Historical Perspective." *Harvard Educational Review,* 2: 1-5.

Harper, J.M. and M.H. Hoopes. (1990) *Uncovering Shame: An Approach Integrating Individuals and Their Family Systems.* New York: W.W. Norton & Co.

Hooks, Bell. (2000). *Feminist Theory: From Margin to Center.* Cambridge, MA: South End Press.

_____. (2004). *The Will to Change: Men, Masculinity, and Love.* New York: Atria Books.

Johnson, Allan A. (2005) *The Gender Knot: Unraveling Our Patriarchal Legacy.* Philadelphia: Temple University Press.

Johnson, Robert A. (1993). *Transformation: Understanding the Three Levels of Masculine Consciousness.* San Francisco: Harper Collins.

Jung, Carl G. (1959). *The Archetypes and the Collective Unconscious.* New York: Bollingen Foundation, Inc.

_____. (1989). *The Psychology of Shame: Theory and Treatment of Shame-Based Syndromes.* New York: Springer Publishing.

Kiselica, M. and M. Englar-Carlson. (2010). "Identifying, affirming, and building upon male strengths: the positive psychology/positive masculinity model of psychotherapy with boys and men." *Psychotherapy Theory, Research, Practice, Training,* 47(3): 276–287.

Lerner, Gerda. (1986). *The Creation of Patriarchy.* New York: Oxford University Press.

Malti-Douglas, Fedwa. (2007). *Encyclopedia of Sex and Gender.* Detroit: Macmillan Reference.

Mayo Clinic Report, "Male depression: Understanding the Issues." Available from URL: www.mayoclinic.com/health/male-depression/MC00041. Accessed May 15, 2014.

Meth, R.L. and R.S. Pasick. (1990) *Men in Therapy: The Challenge of Change.* New York: Guildford Publishing.

National Coalition Against Domestic Violence. (2014). "Domestic Violence Facts." Available from URL: www.ncadv.org/files/Domestic%20Violence%20Stylized–GS%20edits.pdf Accessed September 29,2014.

National Institute of Mental Health (NIMH). (2012). "Men and Depression." Available from URL: http://www.nimh.nih.gov/health/publications/men-and-depression/index.shtml. Accessed October 20, 2014.

National Network to End Domestic Violence. (2013) "2013 Domestic Violence Counts, National Summary." Available from URL: www.nnedv.org/downloads/Census/DVCounts2013/DVCounts13 Natl Summary.pdf. Accessed October 4, 2014.

Newell, Peter. (2005). "Race, Class and the Global Politics of Environmental Inequality." *Global Environmental Politics*, Massachusetts Institute of Technology, 5(3): 70-94.

Nichols, Michael P. (1991). *No Place to Hide: Facing Shame So We Can Find Self-Respect.* New York: Simon & Shuster.

Oudekerk, Barbara A., Joseph P. Allen, Elenda T. Hessel and Lauren E. Molloy. "The Cascading Development of Autonomy and Relatedness From Adolescence to Adulthood", *Child Development*, Article first published online : 23 OCT 2014, DOI: 10.1111/cdev.12313

Panetta, Leon. *Statement on Women in Service.* As Delivered by Secretary of Defense Leon E. Panetta, Pentagon Press Briefing Room, United States Department of Defense Website. January 24, 2013

Player, M.J., Proudfoot, J., Fogarty, A., Whittle, E., Spurrier, M., Shand, F., et al. (2015). *What Interrupts Suicide Attempts in Men: A Qualitative Study.* PLoS ONE 10(6): e0128180. doi:10.1371/journal.pone.018180.

Real, Terrence. (1997). *I Don't Want to Talk About It: Overcoming the Secret Legacy of Male Depression.* New York: Simon & Shuster.

Robinson, Marcus, Delyte Frost, Joan Buccigrossi, Charles Pfeffer. (2003). *Gender: Power and Privilege*, Rochester, NY: wetWare, Inc.

Salovey, Peter, and John Mayer. (1990). "Emotional Intelligence." *Imagination, Cognition, and Personality*, 9(3): 185-211. Amityville, NY: Baywood Publishing Co.

Silverstein, L.B. (1996). "Fathering Is a Feminist Issue." *Psychology of Women Quarterly*. 20 (1), 3-38. http://pwq.sagepub.com/content/20/1/3.abstract

Sterba, Richard. (1934). "The Fate of the Ego in Analytic Therapy." *Journal of the American Psychoanalytic Association*, 1994; 42(3): 863-873.

Taylor, G.J. and H.S. Taylor. (1997). "Alexithymia." In M. McCallum & W.E. Piper (Eds.) *Psychological Mindedness: A Contemporary Understanding*. Munich: Lawrence Erlbaum Associates, 28–31.

Taylor, S. E., Klein, L. C., Lewis, B. P., Gruenewald, T. L., Gurung, R. A. R., & Updegraff, J. A. (2000). Biobehavioral responses to stress in females: Tend-and-befriend, not fight-or-flight. *Psychological Review, 107*, 441-429.

Thrane, Gary (1979). "Shame and the Construction of the Self." *Annual of Psychoanalysis*, 7: 321–341.

Twenge, Jean M. and W. Keith Campbell. (2009). *The Narcissism Epidemic: Living in the Age of Entitlement*. New York: Simon & Schuster.

Vaknin, Sam. (2013). *Malignant Self-Love: Narcissism Revisited*. Skopje, MK: Narcissus Publications.

Vierra, Hanalei. (1994). *The Effects of Childhood Experiences of Shame on the Development of Adult Masculine Identity.* Unpublished doctoral dissertation, University for Humanistic Studies, Del Mar, CA.

Waters, J., R. Marzano, and B. McNulty. (2004). "Leadership That Sparks Learning." *Educational Leadership,* 61(7). Alexandria, VA: Association for Supervision and Curriculum Development.

Watzlawick, Paul, John Weakland, and Richard Fisch. (1974). *Change: Principles of Problem Formation and Resolution.* New York: W. W. Norton.

Webster's Encyclopaedic Unabridged Dictionary of the English Language. Thunder Bay Press (CA); Indexed edition (August 1, 2001)

Yeh, Jennifer. (2002)."Dominance Hierarchy." *Animal Sciences.* 2002. Retrieved November 01, 2014 from Encyclopedia. com. Available from URL: http://www.encyclopedia. com/doc/1G2-3400500111.html

CPSIA information can be obtained
at www.ICGtesting.com
Printed in the USA
FSHW012144200819
61238FS